THE MUSSAR
TORAH COMMENTARY

*A Spiritual Path to Living
a Meaningful and Ethical Life*

THE MUSSAR TORAH COMMENTARY
ADVISORY COMMITTEE

Rabbi Joshua L. Bennett

Rabbi Mari Chernow

Rabbi Jennifer A. Gubitz

Rabbi Andy Kahn

Rabbi Jonathan Kraus

Rabbi Pamela Wax

The Mussar Torah Commentary

*A Spiritual Path to Living
a Meaningful and Ethical Life*

Rabbi Barry H. Block, Editor

with a foreword by
Alan Morinis, DPhil

and an introductory essay by
Rabbi Lisa L. Goldstein

CENTRAL CONFERENCE OF AMERICAN RABBIS
5780 New York 2020

RJP, a division of CCAR Press
355 Lexington Avenue, New York, NY, 10017
(212) 972-3636
ccarpress@ccarnet.org
www.ccarpress.org

ISBN: 978-0-88123-354-4 (paperback)
978-0-88123-355-1 (ebook)
LC record available at https://lccn.loc.gov/2019952213

Text designed and composed by
Scott-Martin Kosofsky
at The Philidor Company
Rhinebeck, New York

Printed in the U.S.A.
10 9 8 7 6 5 4 3 2 1 0

Contents

LEVITICUS

NUMBERS

DEUTERONOMY

Middah Chart

Middah	Translation of the *middah* focus on this	Commentary through the lens of this *middah*	Suggestions for further study
Acharayut	Responsibility	*Acharei Mot, Matot*	*B'midbar, Ki Teitzei, Ki Tavo, Nitzavim, Vayeilech*
Anavah	Humility	*B'reishit, Va-eira, T'tzaveh, B'haalot'cha, Nitzavim, Haazinu*	*Vayeishev, B'shalach, Vayak'heil, Tzav, Sh'mini, K'doshim, B'chukotai, Pinchas, Mas'ei, D'varim, Eikev, Shof'tim*
Bitachon	Trust	*Vayigash, B'shalach, B'har, Vayeilech*	*Yitro, Ki Tisa, Sh'mini Matot, Va-et'chanan, Haazinu, V'zot Hab'rachah*

Boshet Panim	Stubbornness		*Balak*
Bushah	Shame	*M'tzora*	
Chesed	Compassion		*B'reishit,* *Noach,* *Vayeira,* *M'tzora*
Chutzpah	Audacity	*Chukat*	
Emet	Truth	*Tol'dot,* *Va-y'chi,* *Yitro*	*Chayei Sarah,* *Vayeitzei,* *T'rumah*
Emunah	Faith	*Mikeitz* *P'kudei,* *Va-et'chanan,* *V'zot Hab'rachah*	*Noach,* *Lech L'cha,* *Va-eira,* *B'shalach,* *Chukat,* *Haazinu*
G'vurah	Strength	*D'varim*	*Vayigash,* *B'har,* *B'midbar,* *Sh'lach L'cha,* *Matot,* *Haazinu*
Hakarat hatov	Gratitude	*K'doshim,* *Eikev,* *Ki Tavo*	*Toldot,* *Vayishlach,* *Bo,* *Mishpatim*
Histapkut	Simplicity	*B'chukotai*	
Hitlamdut	Apprenticing		*Sh'mot*
Kaas	Anger	*Ki Tisa,* *Balak,* *Pinchas*	*B'haalot'cha,* *Chukat*

Kavod	Honor	*Bo* *R'eih*	*Va-y'chi,* *Yitro,* *Tzav,* *Acharei Mot,* *K'doshim,* *Mas'ei*
Kinah	Jealousy		*Korach*
Lev Patuach	Open-Heartedness		*R'eih*
M'chilah	Forgiveness		*Mikeitz*
M'nuchat hanefesh	Equanimity	*Chayei Sarah,* *Mishpatim*	
N'divut	Generosity	*T'rumah,* *Vayikra,* *Naso,* *Eikev*	*Va-y'chi* *P'kudei* *M'tzora* *R'eih*
Ometz lev	Courage	*Sh'mot*	*B'shalach,* *T'tzaveh*
Pachad	Fear		*Sh'mot*
Rachamim	Mercy	*Vayeishev,* *Tazria,* *Ki Teitzei*	*Vayigash,* *Sh'mot,* *Ki Tisa,* *Sh'mini,* *Mas'ei,* *Ki Tavo*
Savlanut	Patience	*Vayeitzei,* *Sh'lach L'cha*	*Tazria,* *B'har,* *Eikev*
Seder	Order	*Tzav,* *B'midbar*	*Noach,* *Vayikra,* *Acharei Mot,* *Emor,* *Pinchas*

Sh'tikah	Silence	*Sh'mini*	*Korach*
Shvil Hazahav	Moderation	*Emor*	
T'shuvah	Forgiveness		*Naso*
Tzedek	Justice	*Noach, Mas'ei, Shof'tim, Ki Teitzei, Haazinu*	
Yirah	Awe	*Lech L'cha, Vayishlach*	*Balak, Va-et'chanan*
Yoshrah	Integrity		*Chukat*
Z'rizut	Alacrity	*Vayeira, Vayak'heil, Naso, Korach*	

Foreword

ALAN MORINIS, DPhil

THE MUSSAR TEACHERS through the centuries have sought deep, accurate, and useful insights into human life. They drew on the Torah and their own experience to stake out the ideal path along which we, who are living our own lives, can set our feet. The notion that life is a path along which we guide ourselves shows up in many of the titles of their books that have come down to us. To identify what is ideal, they have always looked to the Torah. Mussar then becomes the pathway to embodying the ideals for human life that the Torah outlines.

This book falls squarely into that tradition. It looks to the Torah as the source of fundamental guidance for human living, and each of the authors draws out relevant and practical lessons from the Torah that are applicable to the lives that you and I are living.

True to the Mussar perspective, the authors focus their lessons on specific *middot*, the Hebrew term for "inner traits." It is a Mussar axiom to say that every human being is endowed with every single one of the traits—there is no one who is entirely without anger, or generosity, or kindness, or worry, or any other inner attribute. What makes us unique individuals, and what carves out a specific path for each of us, is the fact that those traits reside within each of us in different measures. Indeed, the word *middah* also means "measure."

When I first encountered the teachings of Mussar, I was impressed by the fact that its teachings focus on the reality that each of is a unique soul following a unique life path. That focus contrasted sharply with what I had experienced growing up in the Jewish world of the late twentieth century, where everything I encountered seemed to focus on the collective, and the inner life of the discrete individual was nowhere to be found on any Jewish agenda. But I speculated that the Jewish community could not have endured for thirty-five hundred years on responsive reading alone, and I knew that I could not be the only one feeling that my life was a unique creation, gift, and challenge, and so I sought out a perspective within the Jewish world that addressed the reality that we are individuals. I knew I had found just that when I came upon the teachings of Mussar.

Later, when I had already been teaching Mussar for several years, the importance of a focus on the individual became even clearer to me when Shayna Lester, a chaplain in the California prison system, invited me to give a talk to the women who were part of the Mussar group she led in the California Institute for Women, a euphemism for a medium-security women's prison.

As the date for my visit approached, I found myself wondering whom I would see when I met these imprisoned Jewish women. Because I had no experience of prisons, I could not imagine whether I would be meeting tough characters who fulfilled the images of hardened outlaws I had absorbed from TV police shows, or white-collar criminals who just happened to have made an unfortunate decision in their accounting or legal practice, or someone else altogether.

When the date for my visit arrived and I finally stood before the group and looked out at their many faces, I saw what I should have realized much earlier: I saw a diverse group of women who fit no single stereotype. I said to myself, "They are just *n'shamahs* ("souls") in unique circumstances." As soon as I had given voice to that realization, I slapped myself on the forehead and exclaimed, "We're ALL *n'shamahs* in unique circumstances."

That description captures the basic reality of human life. We are all *n'shamahs* who find ourselves living in unique circumstances, and those of us sharing that experience right now are very fortunate to have wise ancestors who accumulated insights into human life over the past eleven hundred years in the name of Mussar. Although our lives are different from theirs in so many ways, human nature itself has not changed whatsoever, and we can learn valuable lessons from their observations.

The contributions in this book are situated within that tradition and are true to that tradition, because the chapters reflect contemporary insights into perennial sources and issues. Since about 1840, when Rabbi Yosef Zundel was a primary link in the chain of Mussar transmission, every generation of Mussar teachers has articulated Mussar perspectives in ways that are suited to the differing needs and temperament of their generation, which meant that they continued to revise and innovate to address the life of their times.

When Rabbi Eliyahu Dessler began teaching Mussar in Israel in 1948, other teachers of his time criticized that what he was teaching was "not Mussar," despite the fact that he had studied in the primary Mussar yeshivah of Kelm, Lithuania, for eighteen years. "What am I to do?" he responded. "If I teach this generation as I learned in Kelm, they will run away from me."

The same notion applies today, and the result is that the contributors to this book are much more diverse than was conceivable in previous generations—but to have it be otherwise would be inconceivable in our generation.

Yet the differences from one generation to the next in how Mussar is conveyed do not obscure the reality that the lessons themselves are perennial. What we learn from a sixteenth-century text about anger or an eighteenth-century source about humility might need to be expressed with different examples or illustrations in order to be meaningful to a twenty-first-century audience. However, the essence of the lessons will be the same, because the anger or humility or envy or worry we experience today is the very same inner trait our wise ancestors were writing about in previous centuries.

The ultimate source of those teachings about our inner lives is the Torah itself. The chapters in this book build on eleven hundred years of Mussar commentary, to help us understand how the Torah's lessons about specific *middot*—Cain's envy, Moses's anger, Abraham's loving-kindness, Joseph's trust, and so on—are relevant and useful to us today within the reality of being unique *n'shamahs*, each in our special circumstances. However, the importance of the Torah's lessons about living a human life extends beyond what we can learn about the specific *middot* from its many stories and directives. The Torah provides guidance on the path that leads to the ideal for each of the human inner traits. It also highlights the goal for which improving the inner attributes (*tikkun middot*, "soul-trait repair") is the necessary means.

That ultimate goal of life, as clearly stated in the Torah, provides the rationale for *why* we should bother to foster awareness and to undertake the effort required to bring about inner change. In various places and in various ways, the Torah tells us that the highest goal toward which we should orient our lives is "holiness" (*k'dushah*). In its most famous articulation, the Torah tells us: *K'doshim tih'yu*, "You shall be holy" (Leviticus 19:2). Despite its general terseness and concision, the Torah repeats the injunction to sanctify ourselves many times over. Clearly, we are supposed to grasp that the pursuit of holiness is our ultimate purpose and the highest goal to which a human being can—and should—aspire.

Many disciplines offer lessons and tools to deal with the challenges our inner traits create for us. Many of them may be effective at bringing about change and improving our lives. What sets Mussar teachings apart is their embrace of the Torah's injunction to be holy, which provides the rationale for working on personal transformation. The point is not to improve your life or be a better person; the point is to become spiritually elevated. Self-improvement is the path, not the end goal. As one of the primary leaders of the nineteenth-century Mussar movement, Rabbi Nosson Tzvi Finkel, is reported to have said, "Don't be better; be higher."

And yet the trick is that you cannot get spiritually higher without taking steps to become more emotionally adept and ethically refined. In Mussar terms, becoming whole (*shaleim*) is not the goal but rather the ladder by which to climb toward holiness (*k'dushah*), which is the goal. And so, as a Mussar student, you seek to master your anger not for the purpose of reducing conflict in relationships, for example, but because that trait is a rung on your ladder to holiness. Similarly, grappling with arrogance could be a rung on my ladder to holiness. For someone else, surmounting their envy, or their tendency to lie, or a weakness or exaggeration in another quality will be a rung on their ladder to holiness. Learning to be patient may well improve relationships and even provide more inner peace, just as mastering your anger is very likely to reduce conflict in your relationships. However, those are mere side effects to the primary goal, which is to be holy.

As you read through the chapters in this book, you will gain valuable insight into the Torah's teachings on specific inner traits as refracted through the different consciousnesses and experiences of the diverse group of authors whom Rabbi Barry H. Block has assembled. He has done a great service by making available to us insightful teachings that highlight both the ideals and the pitfalls of those traits. Studying the Torah's lessons on the *middot* provides you with a mirror in which you will see reflected the realities, challenges, and potentials of your own human life—and the path on which you personally are traveling. This book offers you a clear, reflective glass for deepening your self-awareness.

Ultimately, though, what you hold in your hand is a guidebook to becoming holy. Grasping and keeping in mind that lofty goal—even as you work through the various specific lessons about character traits—encapsulates the spiritual path of Mussar: We all have traits that could use some improvement. Recognizing that the work we do on ourselves is how we ascend the holy mountain provides a meaningful rationale for doing the work, as well as powerful motivation.

May your journey take you higher.

Introduction

Rabbi Barry H. Block

STUDYING *PARASHAT HASHAVUA*, the weekly Torah portion, lies at
the heart of Jewish learning. Whenever Jews gather—not only when
we come together for study, but often even when we have assembled
for other reasons—we make reference to the place at which we find
ourselves in the annual cycle of Torah readings, whether we cite the
parashah as a jumping-off point or craft our entire message around
the weekly selection.

Mussar study and practice, by contrast, is not based on any particular cycle, annual or otherwise. I translate "Mussar" as "(Jewish)
ethical discipline"—though, as my teacher Alan Morinis points out,
it is often translated as "correction, discipline, ethics, and instruction" or even "rebuke or reproach."[1] As Morinis writes, "The Mussar masters began . . . by charting the inner life. Based on biblical
sources but also on observation, they concluded that the essential
aspect of a human being is their soul-nature."[2] We are taught to
refine our behavior via focusing on *middot*, literally "measures," but
more helpfully translated as "soul-traits"—qualities such as *anavah*
(עֲנָוָה, "humility"), *savlanut* (סַבְלָנוּת, "patience"), and *kavod* (כָּבוֹד,
"honor")—and so forth. Morinis offers the words of Rabbi Eliyahu
Lopian to describe the purpose of Mussar as "making the heart feel
what the mind knows."[3]

How do we train our "heart" to behave as we already know we
should? The faithful practitioner focuses on each *middah* for a week
or two at a time. We may be engaged in an externally designed curriculum, designating *anavah* (עֲנָוָה, "humility"), for example, for the
first two weeks, followed by *histapkut* (הִסְתַּפְּקוּת, "simplicity") or perhaps *z'rizut* (זְרִיזוּת, "alacrity"), and so forth. We may, on the other
hand, design our own curriculum, based on an assessment of the

areas in which we need work. I'll use myself as an example. As contributors to this volume, my own children, and leaders of the congregations I have served may attest, I do well to concentrate on *savlanut*, "patience," striving to behave more patiently in the hope of resetting my internal patience meter over time.

While focusing on a particular *middah*, we study Mussar texts "dated to the writings of Saadyah Gaon in the tenth century, and books that have been added to the tradition right up to the present."[4] Morinis describes the critical modern transformation of Mussar: "Until the nineteenth century, Mussar was solely an introspective practice undertaken by an individual seeker. In the mid-1800s, however, Rabbi Yisrael Salanter perceived that Mussar could be an answer to the diverse social tensions that were tearing at the Jewish community and its members in Europe at that time."[5] Disciples of Rabbi Salanter in the Slabodka Yeshiva focused on behavior, "asking [their] students to internalize and then conduct themselves with the deportment of people who really believe that we are made in the image of God."[6]

Mussar study does often include references to the Torah. No study of *anavah*, for example, is complete without citation and often exegesis of the verse that proclaims Moses to be *anav m'od mikol haadam asher al p'nei haadamah* (עָנָיו מְאֹד מִכֹּל הָאָדָם אֲשֶׁר עַל־פְּנֵי הָאֲדָמָה), "a very humble man, more so than any other human being on earth" (Numbers 12:3). However, Mussar programs do not typically include reference specifically to *parashat hashavua*, nor are Mussar principles often utilized as the lens through which we examine our Torah readings.

My own Mussar journey began in 2011. A congregant[7] asked whether our congregation offered Mussar study. The word was barely in my vocabulary. He told me about a seminar he had recently attended with Dr. Alan Morinis, and he shared a recording of one of Morinis's lectures. I was immediately taken, and I contacted Dr. Morinis to ask him to speak in the congregation.

I was determined to "get the most bang for the buck," that is, Morinis's speaking fee. I asked if he could suggest some texts that I might teach in adult education prior to his visit. I envisioned a Friday night pulpit lecture for all comers, then a *Shabbaton* for those who had studied with me in advance of the visit. Morinis explained to me that, in order to do what I proposed, I would need to begin with the Mussar Institute's online course, "Everyday Holiness," based on his book by the same title. Then, I would have to take *manchim* ("discussion leader, moderator, advisor") training to become certified to teach a Mussar Institute course.

I was taken aback. I thought to myself, "I'm a rabbi. Give me a text, and I'll teach it!" To this day, I cannot locate the source of *anavah* I had to summon to agree to the plan that Morinis laid out for me. Indeed, no sooner did I begin "Everyday Holiness" than I became consciously aware that I needed significant work on that particular *middah*, "humility," with "patience" being a close second. When *z'rizut*, "alacrity," was next in that curriculum, my *chevruta* partner exclaimed, "Barry won't need any work on that one!" However, as we examined the texts, I quickly became aware that, in some matters— above all, ritual observance—my more laid-back *chavruta* partner was and remains far more punctilious than I am.

Mussar has served me well, personally and as a rabbi. When I lost my job, a traumatic event after more than two decades at one congregation, my behavior was tempered by *bitachon* (בִּטָּחוֹן, "trust") that somehow, even with a far less than desired outcome, my family and I would be okay. As a rabbi, I was able to bring scores of souls in two different communities to the work of *tikkun middot* ("soul-trait repair"), and I'm delighted that one of them has become a Mussar teacher in this volume.

In November 2015, I was invited as scholar-in-residence to Congregation Beth Israel in Houston. I'm no Mussar scholar—and, in fact, my principal role during the Houston visit was to ready that congregation for a forthcoming visit by Morinis. David Scott, the congregation's executive director and director of lifelong learning, asked if I would teach Shabbat morning's Torah study from a Mussar perspective, which I had never previously considered.

The portion that Shabbat was *Vayeitzei*. Torah study participants and I evaluated Jacob's actions in terms of a variety of *middot*. We considered the patriarch's *bitachon*, "trust," setting forth from home and hearth to an uncertain future. We discussed his *emunah*, "faith," in the moment he realizes *Achein yeish Adonai bamakom hazeh v'anochi lo yadati* (אָכֵן יֵשׁ יְהֹוָה בַּמָּקוֹם הַזֶּה וְאָנֹכִי לֹא יָדָעְתִּי), "Truly, the Eternal is in this place, and I did not know it" (Genesis 28:16). We evaluated Jacob's *kavod*, "honor," as we examined traditional commentators' perspectives on the moment he realizes that he has been married to Leah rather than Rachel.

That morning's Torah study was invigorating. I returned to Congregation B'nai Israel in Little Rock, where I was facilitating two Mussar *vaadim* ("groups") at the time, eager to continue studying *parashat hashavua* through the lens of the *middot*.

At the same time, I wondered if the idea was a new one. I contacted Morinis and asked him about books that approach *parashat hashavua* from a Mussar perspective. He suggested several, and I have used all of them in my teaching: *Shabbos Shiurim*, by Rabbi Mordechai Miller;[8] *Mussar HaTorah: Pinnacle of Creation; Torah Insights into Human Nature*, adapted from the talks of Rabbi A. Henach Leibowitz on the *parashah*;[9] *Sichos Mussar: Reb Chaim's Discourses; The Shmuessen of the Mirrer Rosh Yeshiva Rabbi Chaim Shmulevitz, zt"l*;[10] and, for Genesis and Exodus, *Strive for Truth!* by Rabbi Eliyahu E. Dessler.[11] Each of these works provides tremendous insight into the *parashiyot* through the lens of *middot*. However, none is written in a way contemporary liberal Jews are likely to find accessible or relatable. Moreover, these sources are not diverse, all emanating from the Orthodox world and written exclusively by and at least primarily for men.

Alan Morinis and I enjoy telling a story that we recounted in a previous CCAR Press publication: "A workshop at the 2013 Biennial of the Union for Reform Judaism reported on the transformative role of Mussar in a variety of Reform congregations. Attendees were energized by lay and rabbinical presenters. As the question period began, one woman asked, 'Has Mussar had any impact beyond Reform Judaism?'"[12] That experience is emblematic of the extraordinary learning that Morinis and the Mussar Institute have facilitated, bringing Mussar out of the yeshiva and into every corner of the Jewish world—so much so, in fact, that our questioner incorrectly imagined Mussar to have its primary home in Reform Judaism.

Rabbi Ira Stone and the Institute of Jewish Spirituality, the latter of which brings a Chasidic approach to *tikkun middot*, have been additional sources of teaching and inspiration across broad swaths of North American Jewry. Credit is also due to the faculty at the Hebrew Union College–Jewish Institute of Religion, where Mussar, a word I barely heard when I was in rabbinical school (1985–1991), is now integral to the vernacular of more recently ordained Reform rabbis.

Blessedly, therefore, I am able to place before the reader a magnificent smorgasbord of Mussar-based commentaries on the *parashiyot*, most of them penned by members of the Central Conference of American Rabbis but also by rabbis of other Jewish streams, cantors, and a notable legal mind.

The approach here is different from the one I took in Shabbat morning Torah study, where we examine each *parashah* through the lens of multiple *middot*. Here, I asked each author to choose one *middah* as the primary lens through which to view the *parashah*. Since this is not a book about Mussar, but rather a Torah commentary based on Mussar, I asked contributors to resist the temptation to write discourses on the *middot*, which is done better elsewhere. Instead, they have crafted Torah commentaries grounded firmly in the *parashah*, teaching Torah while teaching Mussar.

While all of the authors included here are Jewish, and most are Reform rabbis, the reader will find diverse perspectives—beginning, importantly, with those of both women and men. This volume may be the first in Jewish history to present Mussar teachings by more women than men, and not by happenstance. Early in the process of organizing this book, a member of our Editorial Advisory Board, Rabbi Pamela Wax, made me aware of particular struggles that many women face when they come to traditional Mussar texts. I already knew that even women who are accomplished teachers of Mussar, including Rabbi Wax, are often sidelined in the Mussar world in favor of men—often, but not always, Orthodox.

Rabbi Wax also enriched this book by suggesting several authors who come to *tikkun middot* from a Chasidic perspective, a point that was driven home to me by Rabbi Lisa Goldstein's initial response to my invitation to participate. Rabbi Goldstein's question—whether I would welcome a commentary that does not take a traditional Mussar approach—not only elicited an affirmative response, but eventually led to my asking her to write an introductory essay to this volume.

The Central Conference of American Rabbis aims to lift up the diversity of rabbinic experience in all of its endeavors. Practicing the *middah* of *emet* (אֱמֶת, "truth") forces me to acknowledge that we historically privileged older, male, straight, cisgender, and—above all—congregational rabbis. A significant intention of this book is to enable the reader to learn from teachers of diverse ages and experiences—plenty of congregational rabbis, yes, but not all in senior or solo positions; rabbis who work as chaplains and in a wide array of rabbinic roles in educational and organizational Jewish life; recently ordained rabbis; as well as others who are retired and/or disabled. The result is a collection of commentaries that are informed by divergent life experiences but held together by a commitment not only to *tikkun middot*, but also to *parshanut haTorah* ("Torah commentary").

The Torah commentaries invite readers to participate in the discussion, particularly by means of the appendices at the end of each of them. Questions for discussion encourage conversations that may grow from the author's reflection on the *parashah* and *middah* at hand. Suggested Mussar practices enable Mussar practitioners to apply what they have just read to their own lives. Other *middot* for consideration invite the reader to reflect on the same *parashah* through the lens of an alternative *middah*.

Individuals, pairs learning in *chavruta*, and Torah study groups may utilize this volume to study the weekly *parashah*. In the process, over the course of a year, readers may utilize each *parashah* as an opportunity to work on their own *middot*, based on whichever *middah* is presented in the commentary. Mussar practitioners may choose to organize their use of this book differently, studying the commentaries that focus on a specific *middah* rather than on each *parashah* at its season.

When I shared my initial proposal for *The Mussar Torah Commentary* with Alan Morinis, he was characteristically supportive and enthusiastic. He offered only one critique, focusing on the proposed book's title. Morinis suggested changing the word "the" to "a," since other Mussar Torah commentaries precede it. He was too kind to ask me what the title might say about my own curriculum with respect to the *middah* of *anavah* ("humility"). But "The" it is—partly a marketing decision made by my publisher, and partly an acknowledgment that for the CCAR, it is indeed *The Mussar Torah Commentary*, in the mix of other Reform Torah commentaries. My personal hope is that this book will come to be known as "The 2019 CCAR Mussar Torah Commentary," because it will have spawned others like it, leaping from individual, *chavruta*, and group study, and from questions and suggestions proposed at the end of each of the commentaries.

Notes

1. Alan Morinis and Barry H. Block, "Mussar and the Development of Spiritual Practices," in *A Life of Meaning: Embracing Reform Judaism's Sacred Path*, ed. Dana Evan Kaplan (New York: CCAR Press, 2018), 494.
2. Ibid., 495.
3. Eliyahu Lopian, *Lev Eliyahu: A Collection of Talks* (Jerusalem: Goldberg Press, 1975), 1. Citation provided by Dr. Alan Morinis, email to the author, May 9, 2019.
4. Morinis and Block, "Mussar and the Development of Spiritual Practices," 494.
5. Alan Morinis, *Everyday Holiness: The Jewish Spiritual Path of Mussar* (Boston: Trumpeter, 2007), 8.
6. Ibid., 9.
7. Dr. Barry Menick, referred to me at the time by Steven A. Rubin, then president of Temple Beth-El in San Antonio, Texas.
8. Mordechai Miller, *Shabbos Shiurim* (Jerusalem: Feldheim, 2015). From the copyright page: "This edition is a revised collection of the essays published in *Sabbath Shiurim* (Vol. 1, 1969; Vol. 2, 1979) and *The Sabbath Shiur* (2004)."
9. A. Henach Leibowitz, *Mussar HaTorah: Pinnacle of Creation; Torah Insights*

into Human Nature, Adapted from the Talks of Rabbi A. Henach Leibowitz on the Parashah by Rabbi Aryeh Striks and Rabbi Shimon Zehnwirth (Brooklyn: Mesorah Publications, 2007).

10. Samson R. Weiss with Bezalel Rappaport, eds., *Sichos Mussar: Reb Chaim's Discourses; The Shmuessen of the Mirrer Rosh Yeshiva Rabbi Chaim Shmulevitz, zt"l*, trans. Eliyahu Meir Klugman and A. Scheinman (Brooklyn: Mesorah, 1989).

11. *Michtav Me'Eliyahu, Strive for Truth! Selected Writings of Rabbi E. E. Dessler Rendered into English and Annotated by Aryeh Carmell* (Jerusalem: Feldheim, 1999).

12. Morinis and Block, "Mussar and the Development of Spiritual Practices," 493.

13. See in particular Morinis, *Everyday Holiness*.

Fine-Tuning Our Middot as a Spiritual Practice

Rabbi Lisa L. Goldstein

WHY WOULD A PERSON want to engage in a serious practice of fine-tuning their *middot* (*middah*, plur. *middot*; מִדָּה, מִדּוֹת)?[1] Every person doing *middah* work might have their own answer for this question. For some, the focus is primarily on the self; it is a kind of "Jewish self-help," a way to more fully actualize the way they want to be in the world. For others, the focus is on their relationship to others; it is a method of cultivating a greater ethical commitment to the wholeness and well-being of all. And for still others, working with *middot* is foremost a spiritual practice that helps connect them with God.

This last possibility—working with *middot* as a spiritual practice—requires some clarification. It is not immediately obvious why working on strengthening one's capacity for compassion, generosity, truth-telling, or patience should be a path of connection to God. Some might see this work as making us better people, more worthy of divine approval, but that is different from experiencing an actual connection to the Holy One. How can refining our *middot* help us open our awareness to the presence of the Blessed Holy One in our lives?

The question of the exact nature of closeness and connection to God has been pondered for centuries. The Talmud[2] itself raises the issue: Rabbi Chama bar Rabbi Chanina wondered about the meaning of the biblical verse, "It is the Eternal your God alone whom you should follow" (Deuteronomy 13:5). What could this possibly mean? How closely can one actually follow God? Is there not another verse in Deuteronomy—"For the Eternal your God is a consuming fire"

(Deuteronomy 4:24)—that seems to indicate that closeness to God might be dangerous, even deadly?! God is not some easy-to-understand "person" whose footsteps are easily followed. On a certain level, God is absolutely unapproachable. We attempt to come close at our own risk.

"Following God," concludes Rabbi Chama bar Rabbi Chanina, must mean that we should take on the attributes (*middot*) of the Blessed Holy One. Just as God made clothes for Adam and Eve, we should clothe the naked. Just as God visited Abraham when he was healing from his circumcision, we should visit the sick. Just as God comforted Isaac after Abraham's death, we should comfort the mourners. Just as God brought Moses to his grave, we should bury the dead.[3]

However, there will always be a distance between humans and God. The Torah itself says that Moses was the only human who was privileged to know God "face to face" (Deuteronomy 34:10). The rest of us must make do with acting like God in deeds of kindness toward the people around us. We shouldn't worry about getting too close.

Still, there have always been Jews hungry for spiritual connection for whom this instruction was not enough. Yes, acting like God is one way to come close; but how exactly does God act? What are the qualities that God brings to these actions? How does acting like God help us feel connected to God?

Over the centuries, the Sages investigated which *middot* are inherent to Divinity. They turned to Exodus 34:6–7, where God answers Moses's plea for greater understanding of God's nature. Moses had begged for insight into God's essence as the only thing that would make it possible for him to continue to lead the rebellious Israelites. The Sages formulated this response into the Thirteen *Middot* ("Thirteen Attributes") characterized by God's loving-kindness, patience, and forgiveness.[4] Our liturgy evokes these words on the Festivals and, most poignantly, on Yom Kippur, always in front of the open ark. These are the days when we feel vulnerable and open, facing our great fallibility and our own mortality. These are the days when we seek those godly qualities of patience, love, and forgiveness.

But are God's qualities only love and patience? Surely not. From early Rabbinic interpretation, the Sages understood the two primary names of God in the *Tanach* as pointing to two different qualities: *YHVH*—the Tetragrammaton, often translated as "the Eternal" or "Lord"—representing "loving-kindness" and "mercy"; and *Elohim*, "God," representing "justice."[5] Yes, we humans are in particular need of God's compassion, but this world also depends on law and morality; actions do and should have consequences. Much of Rabbinic theology is an exploration of the dynamic between God's two contradictory *middot*: "loving-kindness" and "justice."

Along came the medieval mystics, who elaborated on this paradox. The medieval mystics said there is not one divine quality or two, but rather ten. They developed a schematic map of the *s'firot* (סְפִירוֹת), or ten *middot*, of God—a dynamic map that explores the relationship, for example, between pouring out love (*chesed*, חֶסֶד) and setting clear boundaries (*g'vurah*, גְּבוּרָה), moving out energetically into the world (*netzach*, נֵצַח) and opening to receive what is (*hod*, הוֹד), all as God's manifestations. The *s'firot* provide a dualistic lens that greatly expands the divine qualities: male and female, facing outward and turning inward, the heavenly and the earthly realm. This map was also a detailed investigation into our question: What are those qualities of God that we might imitate, and how do we use our work of imitation to connect to God?

To make God's qualities even more concrete, the mystics mapped these *s'firot* directly onto the (biologically male) human body. *Chesed* ("loving-kindness, generosity") is located in the right arm; *g'vurah* ("restraint, patience, judgment") in the left; *tiferet* (תִּפְאֶרֶת, beauty, honor") in the heart; *netzach* ("action, alacrity") and *hod* ("receptivity, gratitude") in the legs; and *y'sod* (יְסוֹד, foundation, connection") in the phallus. This correspondence to the body is important. If we set the mystics' map alongside the Genesis teaching that human beings are created in the divine image (Genesis 1:27), it becomes obvious that the mystics envisioned the divine *middot* as already embedded into our bodies. They are not foreign to us. They are already here, as part of our spiritual DNA.

This insight merits a pause. What are we doing when we cultivate desirable *middot*? As Rabbi Chama bar Rabbi Chanina suggested, we are indeed trying to manifest divine qualities in ourselves. But, perhaps counterintuitively, we are not trying to be inherently better than we already are. The *s'firot* map of the human body reminds us that we are created with these *middot* already fully present. Why, then, is it not easier for us to act in wise, loving, and just ways all the time? Too often, we act out of confusion, distraction, or hurt, which blocks the divine qualities from properly manifesting. When we work on our *middot*, we are clearing away the blockages that prevent us from radiating the inner divinity that is our human birthright.

Let's take it one step further: Despite all the distinctions and component parts, the mystical tradition reminds us over and over again that the Divinity is essentially and finally One. It goes without saying that the various divine attributes are not separate but interconnected. It means that on a very deep level, even the paradoxical *middot*, like justice and loving-kindness, are not actually different from each other because they are both vessels that garb the same animating force. The Baal Shem Tov, the founder of the Chasidic movement, taught that the prophet's words "The whole world is filled with God's presence" (Isaiah 6:3) actually mean there is nothing in this world that is not God.[6] Every thing, every action, every being is a vessel for God's presence. All is one: mercy, judgment, male, female, inward, outward, heavenly, earthly, even good and bad. It is all God.

That should raise some eyebrows. Why should we aspire "to be good" if everything is God? Why should we make effort to behave morally? I noted at the beginning that fine-tuning our *middot* is, among other things, an ethical endeavor. If the spiritual understanding of *middot* work is about letting God shine through our actions, and if God is present in all things, where does moral behavior come in? Why should we work on subduing the *yetzer hara*, the "selfish impulse"?

The Chasidic masters taught that we humans do have mean, base, and unwholesome tendencies that block our ability to let the divine *middot* manifest in their proper form. Instead of simply subduing those tendencies, pushing them away, or shoving them under the carpet, the Chasidic masters invite us to have a closer look at them. For example, Rabbi Dov Baer, the Magid of Mezritch, offered an astute teaching to students who struggled to concentrate during prayer and Torah learning: "When you are consumed by lust, know that this is a fallen form of love. When you are too anxious, know that this is a fallen form of awe. When you feel prideful and arrogant, know that this is a fallen manifestation of the beauty of the divine image in which you were created."[7] The goal is not to avoid feeling lust, anxiety, or pride. These, too, are human experiences. Instead, the goal is to "sweeten the root," to see the "little bit of good,"[8] even in the shameful thought or act. Interestingly, mindfulness work asks us to do the same thing. There, too, we observe difficult or painful thoughts and emotions without trying to push them away or judging ourselves. Instead, we simply pay attention to them, which in the end can allow the thought or emotion to release its grip on us.

When we can realign the fallen form of a *middah* with its higher, purer form, we fully actualize who we were intended to be in this world. We contribute to the wholeness and well-being of others. We make space for the divine attributes to emerge in our lives, thereby bringing more divinity into the world. Just like the many *middot* of God, the different motivations for engaging in *middot* work are actually not separate. They are all one.

NOTES

1. This approach to *middot* work has been developed by Rabbis Sam Feinsmith, Nancy Flam, Marc Margolius, Jonathan Slater, and myself at the Institute for Jewish Spirituality.
2. *Babylonian Talmud, Sotah* 14a.
3. Ibid.
4. *Sifrei D'varim* 49.
5. See, e.g., *B'reishit Rabbah* on Genesis 12:15.
6. See, e.g., Arthur Green and Barry Holtz, *Your Word Is Fire: The Hasidic Masters on Contemplative Prayer* (Nashville: Jewish Lights, 2017), 7.
7. Dov Baer, the Magid of Mezritch, *Likutei Amarim* (or *Magid D'varav L'yaakov* #53; Schatz-Uffenheimer #29).
8. Nachman of Bratzlav, *Likutei Moharan*, 282.

Acknowledgments

THE WORK OF GOD, which some would call serendipity, brought together forces that make this book possible.

I have been blessed by a friendship with Rabbi Hara Person—now chief executive of the Central Conference of American Rabbis, but for the purpose of this book, publisher of CCAR Press—since our first days as undergraduates in 1981. We regale listeners with stories about those days—the boy from Texas from a long line of southern Reform Jews, a self-professed liberal from a conservative environment, who had no idea what hit him when he met the young woman from Brooklyn, a newly Reform family, and an infinitely more progressive milieu. Our professional and personal partnership has enriched my work ever since, certainly including this book, germinated under her guidance.

Providence also brought me to Mussar at a time when I did not know I needed it. My Mussar journey to the point of editing this book is chronicled in the introduction, but let me add words of gratitude here to congregants at Congregation B'nai Israel in Little Rock—and before that, at Temple Beth-El in San Antonio—who have learned and practiced Mussar with me. I am thankful, too, to the folks at Houston's Congregation Beth Israel—where I, like my parents before me, was raised and where a "scholar"-in-residence weekend offered the initial impetus to explore weekly Torah portions through the lens of Mussar. I owe a deep debt of gratitude to my teacher Dr. Alan Morinis, for his friendship and attention to my own Mussar journey and those of many of this book's contributors. His scholarship and extraordinary ability to translate teachings of a bygone era to contemporary society are in evidence throughout this volume.

Lay leaders and staff colleagues at Congregation B'nai Israel in Little Rock—led by President Carol Parham and Eileen Hamilton, our director of Education, Administration and Youth Engagement—have not merely been patient, but have been enthusiastically supportive of my work on this book and the time I devote to CCAR leadership and CCAR Press publications.

As Hara moved into her new position, I worked most closely with CCAR Press's fabulous editor, Rabbi Sonja Pilz, PhD, who partnered with me in facilitating CCAR Press's work on this book with extraordinary skill and sensitivity. Sonja was supported at the outset by Sasha Smith, then CCAR Press's editorial assistant, and later by Hebrew Union College–Jewish Institute of Religion's cantorial intern Gabriel Snyder and Leta Cunningham, the new CCAR Press publishing assistant. CCAR Press operations manager, Debbie Smilow, worked her magic as the book neared completion, as she has on each CCAR Press publication for so long that many of us think she must have joined CCAR Press before her bat mitzvah.

Contributors to this book include dear personal friends and colleagues whom I haven't yet met in person. Each one has added a uniquely valuable voice to this volume. I can be something of a taskmaster. Our contributors are volunteers. Nevertheless, they delivered excellent work in a timely fashion and repeatedly responded to requests and inquiries that enabled us to bring this book to press several months earlier than originally planned.

Members of the Editorial Advisory Committee, most of whom are also contributors, made creative suggestions at a critical stage, deepening this book immeasurably.

My sister Alison and I were raised in an extraordinarily nurturing environment that few people experience. All four of our grandparents—Sabina and Shelton Block, Bertha Alyce and Irvin Shlenker, all of blessed memory—lived in town and were consistently present and influential throughout our childhood and beyond. I grew up knowing my grandparents' friends and my friends' grandparents, many of them the same people, in a community that nurtured and valued Congregation Beth Israel, Reform Judaism, and one another.

I was raised, too, at URJ Greene Family Camp and in TOFTY (now NFTY's Texas-Oklahoma Region), which inspired me toward the rabbinate through unparalleled opportunities to lead and teach in the Jewish community.

Through the eyes of my mother, Gay Block, I came to experience a broader array of Jewish life—even Yiddishkeit, a concept that was foreign to my youth. My father, Gus Block, like his mother before him, has been an exemplar of unconditional love, making family a priority greater even than his successful, rigorous career. My mother's wife, Billie Parker, is a welcome addition to our family, as are Alison's husband, Stephane Gerson, and their children—Julian, Owen, z"l, and Elliot. My stepmother of twenty-nine years—Dorathy Dreeben Block, z"l—left an indelible mark of grace and etiquette, not merely rules to be followed, but kindness and gratitude to bestow on the people in our lives.

I am grateful to Toni Dollinger, my children's mother, who has been the perfect parenting partner, both when we were married and now that we are friends rather than a married couple. I continue to value Toni and her family, which I'm grateful to call my own.

Robert Loewenberg Dollinger Block and Daniel Dollinger Block are the loves of my life. In the twilight of their teens, they are emerging into happy, creative, dedicated young Jewish adults. I am grateful for the role that our congregation in Little Rock and URJ youth programs continue to pay in their lives. I dedicate this book to their own journeys—through the Torah deep into their souls, for lifetimes to come.

—*Rabbi Barry H. Block*
Little Rock, Arkansas
Erev Shabbat Shuvah 5780/October 4, 2019

GENESIS

B'REISHIT—GENESIS 1:1–6:8

Anavah—Humility:
Shabbat as a Return to Our
Authentic Selves

RABBI MICHELLE PEARLMAN and RABBI SHARON MARS

> "On the seventh day, God had completed the work that had
> been done, ceasing then on the seventh day from all the work
> that [God] had done. Then God blessed the seventh day and
> made it holy, and ceased from all the creative work that God
> [had chosen] to do."   —*Genesis 2:2–3*

AN ONLINE BLOGGER writes the following about her struggle to
find her authentic space in the world: "My outsides and my insides
don't always match. They don't match for the online world, they
don't match for people I see every day. . . . Because sometimes putting on a brave face when you're hurting is part of being an adult.
And a mother. And a friend. And a business owner . . . [but] if I'm
being perfectly honest, I miss me."[1]

The feeling captured in the blogger's writing is one of disconnection and feeling fragmented in this world. In *Parashat B'reishit*, we
learn that each of us is created in the image of God (Genesis 1:27).
Just as God breathed life, *nishmat chayim* (נִשְׁמַת חַיִּים, "breath of
life"), into Adam (Genesis 2:7), each one of us has a *n'shamah* (נְשָׁמָה),
a "soul" that is an essential gift of the Divine. In Mussar, we are
taught that this soul is the shining light and essence of our entire
being. And, as we read in our morning liturgy, *Elohai n'shamah she-
natata bi t'horah hi* (אֱלֹהַי נְשָׁמָה שֶׁנָּתַתָּ בִּי טְהוֹרָה הִיא), "My God, the soul
You have given me shines pure." However, when we strive and fight

every day, the light of our soul can feel obscured. Like the blogger, we may feel pressured to fill the expansive roles of "best parent," "most loving friend," "most successful business owner," and the like. This inflated, exhausting striving may require us to put on a brave but false face. Though the light of our *n'shamah* shines from within, it may appear obscured or dimmed on the outside. Like the blogger, we may begin to feel disconnected from ourselves, feeling fragmented and inauthentic. We, created in the image of God, may find ourselves distanced from the essence of the most personal of God's creation, our true selves. However, focusing on the *middah* of *anavah* (עֲנָוָה, "humility") and the practice of observing Shabbat, both illuminated in *Parashat B'reishit*, can help us to reconnect with our essential selves.

Just as the Torah begins with *Parashat B'reishit*, Mussar practice begins with the *middah* of *anavah*. All other *middot* are accessed through this core character trait. The *middah* of *anavah* is essential for living with integrity. When we think of humility, we may imagine someone who is the picture of modesty and meekness. However, in Mussar, humility is not defined as being so humble that you disappear; rather, it is about having all of your character traits in balance so that the inner light of the soul shines pure and clear as originally intended. As Mussar teacher Alan Morinis puts it, "Being humble doesn't mean being nobody: it just means being no more of a somebody than you ought to be."[2]

Imagine a continuum between self-deprecation on the one hand and arrogance on the other. We know that it is unhealthy to live at either pole. According to Mussar teaching, a person who has mastered the *middah* of humility would be centered on that continuum, being neither a meek shadow nor an overblown narcissist, but rather perfectly balanced. Rav Kook further elaborates that *anavah* is associated with a strong connection with one's essential self. He writes, "Humility is associated with spiritual perfection. . . . When humility effects depression it is defective. When it is genuine it inspires joy, courage and inner dignity."[3] Morinis defines humility in a Jewish context as "limiting oneself to an appropriate amount of space while leaving room for others."[4]

Lurianic Kabbalah teaches that the world was actually created through *anavah*. In a creation myth called the "Shattering of the Vessels," or *sh'virat hakeilim* (שְׁבִירַת הַכֵּלִים), attributed to the sixteenth-century mystic Isaac Luria, before the world was created God's presence filled up every bit of space in the universe. Then, through the process of *tzimtzum* (צִמְצוּם, "contraction"), God pulled inward, contracting in order to make space for Creation. Through that *tzimtzum*, God's light was honed to contain God's very essence. Only then was the divine light sent forth to create the universe.

That *tzimzum* continued. With great humility, God withdrew from the work of Creation on the seventh day and embraced the *middah* of *anavah* by resting—that is, God set a limit to Godself. On Shabbat, we are commanded to do the same. Six days of the week, we are consumed with the outside work of the world: we try to expand ourselves and our lives; but on the seventh day, we draw ourselves inward. We, too, make space for the essence of Creation, returning with loving attention to the selves we are supposed to be.

Just as God cultivates *anavah* as an essential element of Creation, we, too, must nurture the *middah* of humility in order for our own creative, spiritual, emotional, and physical selves to flourish. If we fail to do so, we do at our own peril. Our insides cannot possibly match our outsides under these circumstances; the negative consequences for our bodies, minds, and souls are unavoidable.

The opening chapters of the Book of Genesis contain two narratives that can be read as cautionary tales. These tales warn us of the consequences of losing ourselves.

The first story to consider is the exile from *Gan Eden*. God had forbidden the first man and woman to ingest the fruit from the Tree of Knowledge. When they eat it in spite of the prohibition, they are struck with an ultimate awareness of who they are in the world: naked and vulnerable. Ultimately, God expels the humans from God's Garden.

Why does Adam and Eve's overstepping of divine boundaries cause exile? The human relationship to the Divine does not change because the humans went against God's prohibition. Rather, it changes because of Adam's answer to God's question, *Ayekah?* (אַיֶּכָּה), "Where are you?" (Genesis 3:9). However, with this question, God is not only asking "Where are you?" but also "Who are you? Are you ready for your mission?" Adam's reply—*Et kolcha shamati bagan va-ira ki-ei-rom anochi va-eichavei* (אֶת־קֹלְךָ שָׁמַעְתִּי בַּגָּן וָאִירָא כִּי־עֵירֹם אָנֹכִי וָאֵחָבֵא), "I heard the sound of You in the Garden; I was afraid because I was naked, so I hid myself" (Genesis 3:10)—makes clear that Adam is not ready; he is hiding his truth. The Holy One has caught him deceiving his Creator. The human being tries to hide and disguise his core essence and therefore cannot stay in God's Garden of Truth.

In our own lives, we hide our authentic selves from the truth of our lives. When we live out of balance, despite the fact that we may be falling apart on the inside or on the outside, we betray our lives. We take up either too much or too little space; either we take away space from others, or we abandon them when they need us. Our sacred connection to anything important—our families, our communities, our work—all suffer when we neglect to live life with *anavah* in balance. Celebrated with intention, Shabbat provides the time, space, and opportunity to reconnect to our core essence, reacquire a sense of proportion, and connect anew with the people and projects in our lives with both humility and presence. *Anavah*, approaching our lives with humility, means not taking up too much space in the Garden, not trying to fool others with some disguise of our true selves; but to honestly offer our truest selves to the people and work we encounter in our lives.

The second cautionary tale from Genesis is the story of the world's first two brothers, Cain and Abel. When Abel's offering is preferred over his brother's, Cain responds by vengefully killing his own sibling. Then, God asks Cain, *Ei hevel achicha?* (אֵי הֶבֶל אָחִיךָ), "Where is your brother Abel?" (Genesis 4:9). With Cain's reply, *Hashomeir achi anochi?* (הֲשֹׁמֵר אָחִי אָנֹכִי), "Am I my brother's keeper?" (Genesis 4:9)—again, a disguise of the truth that he just killed him—Cain is doomed to wander the earth, cursed, alone, and marked for life.

Cain could use a good dose of *anavah*. Blinded by his sense of deserving God's reward, an abundance of arrogance, Cain resorts to violence. Rather than taking a step back, Cain chooses an irreversible course. Rather than humbly stepping into his proper space and making room for his brother, he does the radical opposite. Tragically, he forgets the words that God spoke to him just two verses prior to the murder: "If you do not do well—sin is a demon at the door; you are the one it craves, and yet you can govern it" (Genesis 4:7).

In both Cain's and Adam's cases, an attempt to hide the core essence of a person causes a greater distance in the human-Divine relationship. Insecurity need not necessarily become negatively manifested if we take care of these emotions by becoming more skilled at thoughtfully evaluating and strategically expressing them. When we leave pain unexpressed, jealousy can turn to anger, and as a result, we might become dangerous to others. When we are faced with challenging circumstances, we ought to ask ourselves, "Where are you? Where are the others?" Cultivating the *middah* of *anavah* might support us in finding our soul's rightful place. Shabbat provides us both with a weekly liturgical and narrative reminder of *anavah* and with the time and space to practice it. Shabbat calls us back to God's Garden of Truth; Shabbat calls us to get a sense of proportion for the space we are taking up. Shabbat calls us to live our lives with integrity.

The Talmud teaches, "Any Torah scholar whose insides do not match that person's outsides is not a true Torah scholar."[5] Torah scholars, bloggers, and other all human beings can learn to live lives of authenticity. Taking stock of our lives, we can make sure that our own inner light shines unobscured by incongruent outer actions. The *tikkun* (תִּקּוּן, "repair") prescribed by the study of Mussar and the practice of taking time out to rest on Shabbat may help us to reconnect with our *n'shamah*, our essential self, gift of God's Creation.

Questions to Ask

Set aside some time to ask yourself this coming Shabbat:

> Where am I in my most important relationships? How much space do I take up?
>
> How might I tend to my most sacred relationships on Shabbat?
>
> Which relationships have I been paying too much attention to? And for whom have I not been present?
>
> How might I make time to feel and deal with my emotions before Shabbat arrives or on Shabbat itself?
>
> How can *anavah* help me understand the place of emotion in my life?
>
> How much space do I give myself to feel strong emotions?

Practices for the *Middah* of *Anavah*

The major practice of *anavah* is to find some way to experience Shabbat rest that feels meaningful to you. Give your devices a rest, sign off of social media, put an away message on your e-mail. It is liberating to know that you can pull back from work and other entanglements and restore your energy and creativity. It is also possible to find the rest of Shabbat in small ways in other parts of your week. Consider taking ten minutes at the end of an hour of work for meditation or a yoga stretches.

Another *Middah* to Consider

The Genesis story is a depiction of God creating the world through great *chesed* (חֶסֶד, kindness). Out of the void, we are gifted a world filled with light and darkness, where creatures of all kinds, including human beings, abound. And God says that it is good.

But how can we be good? By nature, we strive against one another, competing for things, status, and territory.

Genesis 1:27 brings the great equalizer. Created as we are *b'tzelem Elohim* (בְּצֶלֶם אֱלֹהִים, "in God's image"), we are not to treat one another poorly. In the Talmud, we learn that the Torah begins and ends with *chesed*.[6] The gift of this world is a gift of kindness. In creating Adam and Eve, God clothed them in garments of skin (Genesis 3:21), and at the end of the Torah, God models *chesed* by burying Moses (Deuteronomy 34:6). The Talmud also reminds us that we are to do kindness in following the example of our Creator.[7] Just as God clothed the naked (Genesis 3:21), so we should clothe the naked. Just as God visited the sick (Genesis 18:1), we should visit the sick. Just as God comforted those in mourning (Genesis 25:11), we should comfort those in mourning. Just as God buried the dead (Deuteronomy 34:6), we too should bury the dead.[8] Forged from *chesed*, we follow the Divine's example here on earth, creating our own relationships and new worlds with acts of kindness.

NOTES

1. Danielle Smith, "A Beautiful Mess: When Your Insides and Outsides Don't Match," *Pretty Extraordinary* (blog), accessed July 21, 2019, https://www.prettyextraordinary.com/a-beautiful-mess-when-your-insides-and-outsides-dont-match/.
2. Alan Morinis, in "Reading for Humility," from the course *A Season of Mussar* (copyright 2008), http://media.Mussarinstitute.org/SoM/week1/Humility.pdf.
3. Abraham Isaac Kook, *The Lights of Penitence, Lights of Holiness, The Moral Principles: Essays, Letters and Poems*, trans. Ben Zion Bokser (Mahwah, NJ: Paulist Press, 1978), 176.
4. Morinis, in "Reading for Humility."
5. *Babylonian Talmud, Yoma* 72b.
6. *Babylonian Talmud, Sotah* 14a.
7. Ibid.
8. Ibid.

NOACH—GENESIS 6:9–11:32

Tzedek—Justice:
Noah as Tzaddik

RABBI ANDY KAHN

AT THE BEGINNING of the story of Noah, we are told: *Noach ish tzadik tamim hayah b'dorotav* (נֹחַ אִישׁ צַדִּיק תָּמִים הָיָה בְּדֹרֹתָיו), "Noah was a righteous (*tzadik*) man in his generation" (Genesis 6:9)—that is, Noah's *middah* of *tzedek* (צֶדֶק) was the most complete of his entire generation. The Torah does not define this term, *tzadik* or *tzedek*, for us, though. We are left to guess, along with many generations of Jews before us, as to what *tzedek* entails, which in turn makes it difficult for us to define the *middah* of *tzedek*. Sometimes it is translated as "righteousness," sometimes as "justice."

A *sugya* in the Talmud attempts to elucidate the specifics of what *tzedek* might mean:

> It has been taught: *Tzedek, tzedek tirdof* (צֶדֶק צֶדֶק תִּרְדֹּף, "Justice, justice you shall pursue," Deuteronomy 16:20). The first [use of the word *tzedek*, "justice"] refers to a decision based on strict law; the second, to a compromise. How so? . . . If two camels met each other while on the ascent to Beth-Horon; if they both ascend [at the same time] both may tumble down [into the valley]; but if [they ascend] after each other, both can go up [safely]. How then should they act [when ascending]? If one is laden and the other unladen, the latter should give way to the former. If one is nearer [to its destination] than the other, the former should give way to the latter. If both are [equally] near or far [from their destination,] make a compromise between them, the one [which is to go forward] compensating the other [which has to give way].[1]

Not only does *tzedek* mean to discern the law but it is also about being able to distinguish the nuanced and compassionate way of applying that law. Further, *tzedek* requires follow-through. Not only must one do the work to discover the truest application of law, one must then do the work to carry it out, while compromising along the way. *Tzedek* means working toward clarity of what is most right in any situation and having the *chutzpah* (חֻצְפָּה) to stand up for that clear rectitude without fear of the outcome.

From another angle, we learn from Shimon the Tzadik, "Do not be as servants who are serving the master in order to receive a reward, rather be as servants who are serving the master not in order to receive a reward; and may the fear of heaven be upon you."[2] A true *tzadik*, such as Shimon was, does not act with *tzedek* in pursuance of any reward other than enacting *tzedek* in the world.

If we accept these two pieces of Rabbinic wisdom as a baseline definition of *tzedek*, the story of Noah glows with new light. Noah, according to the midrash, brought order to the world with his very birth. His presence in the world changed the ways of nature from a chaotic hodgepodge of planted seeds sprouting randomly as other grains,[3] animals of all species mating with each other,[4] and tides fluctuating wildly,[5] to the laws of nature we see today. This change reflects a line well cited throughout Jewish literature: *Tzadik y'sod olam* (צַדִּיק יְסוֹד עוֹלָם), "The *tzadik* is the foundation of the universe" (Proverbs 10:25). These midrashim point to *tzedek* as an inherent quality of Noah's very existence. By his mere birth, the natural order became clearer—*tzedek* was established throughout the fabric of Creation. Further, his birth righted the power relationships between humans and farm animals, which had rebelled,[6] and brought about the invention of farming tools.[7]

The agricultural metaphors in these midrashim guide us to a deeper understanding of the relationship between Noah, *tzedek*, and the universe. The reordering of crops and farm animals gives us a sense of the power of *tzedek*. Without it, the regularity and stability we require for our subsistence is undermined, leading to the destabilization of the very foundation of our civilization. Noah's connection to the tools of farming also shows the effects of *tzedek*. Not only does *tzedek* order the disordered, but it provides the tools to harvest this order.

These impacts of Noah's birth display the underlying character of *tzedek*, but his lived experience of preparing for the destruction of the world are even more instructive as to the role *tzedek* plays in our human interactions. The Torah itself has little to say about Noah's process in creating the ark, but one midrash elaborates upon the story:

> Rav Huna said in the name of Rabbi Yosei: For one hundred and twenty years, the Holy One kept warning the generation of the flood in the hope that they would resolve to repent. When they did not repent, God said to Noah, "Make thee an ark of cedarwood." Noah proceeded to plant cedars. When asked, "Why these cedars?" he would reply, "The Holy One is about to bring a flood upon the world, and God told me to make an ark, that I and my family might escape." They mocked and ridiculed him. In the meantime, he watered the cedars, which kept growing.[8]

We may compare the generation of the Flood to the rest of the world prior to Noah's birth. Just as there was no order to agriculture, the humans of that world were depraved. Just as there were no agricultural tools, the humans of that world were impeded in accomplishing right action. In short, the people of the generation of the flood were unable to behave justly and act upon the information they were granted. When confronted with a person with clear purpose who is working toward a specific end in the name of a divine command, their only response is ridicule.

The midrash continues:

> Finally [Noah] cut the cedars down, and as he sawed them into planks, he was again asked, "What are you doing?" He replied, "What I said I would do," even as he continued to warn the generation of the flood. When they did not repent even then, the Holy One brought the flood upon them. At last, when they realized that they were about to perish, they tried to overturn the ark.[9]

In the face of ridicule, Noah stuck to his mission and continued to do the work he knew was necessary. He used his tools to sharpen and refine his task, while those around him continued to try to undermine his confidence and his work—and, finally, once his task had been accomplished and they realized they had been mistaken, his mockers attempted to destroy him.

In short, Noah exemplifies the often misattributed words of the great Jewish labor and union activist Nicholas Klein: "First they ignore you. Then they ridicule you. Then they attack you and want to burn you. And then they build monuments to you."[10]

Unbending confidence like Noah's can be quite dangerous when taken in the wrong direction. A key element of *tzedek* is discernment, based on a foundational sense of justice, as well as a willingness to compromise toward the ultimate goal, as described in the Talmud *sugya* above.

Further, as Rabbi Kaufmann Kohler wrote, "The Jewish principle of justice [by which Kohler clearly meant *tzedek*], moreover, includes love and mercy. . . . It claims the surplus of the rich for the poor, the help of the strong for the feeble, of the fortunate for the unfortunate, not as a mere gift of condescending charity or befriending sympathy, but as a command and a condition of a divine readjustment."[11]

The *middah* of *tzedek*, then, requires discernment from a place of compassion. We see this kind of discernment displayed in Noah's continual willingness to ask his fellow human beings to repent and to prepare for the flood. Embodying justice, then, is not meant to be harsh or to lack empathy, but instead to move with confidence in the direction of our highest moral truths, while maintaining compassion for others.

Tzedek can then be summarized as the quality of being able both to discern one's place in the world and to act skillfully and compassionately, regardless of the popularity of one's discernment. *Tzedek* is a confident sense of directed moral mission.

To readdress the proverb *Tzadik y'sod olam* (see above), *tzedek* is the ability to bring into being our individual foundational truths; to manifest our individual, unique Torah in the world. Noah's mastery of *tzedek* led him to be the true foundation of the world—to be the new Adam, germinating the human race once again. We, too, must cultivate our inner *tzedek* in order to bring our Torah into the world and to continue the mission of Israel toward a world united in the messianic dream of equality, safety, and freedom for all.

Questions to Ask

When have you backed down from something you had determined to be right? What led you to back down? How can you prepare yourself to be more steadfast in the future?

When have you pushed too hard without compromise? How can you prepare yourself to be open to compromise without fully giving up on your belief?

In what small way can you begin to implement something you know is necessary and right today? What single steps can you take over the next days, weeks, or months to begin the process?

Practices for the *Middah* of *Tzedek*

Key phrase: Recite *Tzadik y'sod olam* throughout the day. Use this phrase to question what kind of truth lies at your foundation and how you can express this truth compassionately in the world today.

Journaling: Every evening, record the ways in which you took strides toward expressing both your core truths and your moments of criticism, fear, or lack of confidence in which you were unable to do so.

Kabbalah: Each morning, decide upon one way in which you will, regardless of its conventionality or normalcy, enact your inner *tzedek* in the world around you.

Other *Middot* to Consider

Seder (סֵדֶר, "order"): Noah's role in the story is to be the one who bears *seder*, "order," forward in a world turned to

chaos, both by humanity's behavior and then by the flood.
How can we use Noah as an example to embody *seder*
when our worlds feel like chaos?

Chesed (חֶסֶד, "loving-kindness"): In the midrash above, Noah
continues to warn his fellow human beings about the
incoming disaster, regardless of their mocking him. How
can we maintain this type of *chesed* in the face of those who
show none themselves?

Emunah (אֱמוּנָה, "faith"): The resilience Noah displays, even
as he watches the world destroyed before his very eyes, is
powered by *emunah*, his faith in God. How can we learn to
charge our own *emunah* based on Noah's powerful ability
to remain resilient amidst harrowing challenge?

NOTES

1. *Babylonian Talmud, Sanhedrin* 32b.
2. *Mishnah, Pirkei Avot* 1:3.
3. *Tanchuma B'reishit* 11, in *The Book of Legends*, ed. Hayyim Nahman Bialik and Yehoshua Hana Ravnitzky, trans. William G. Braude (New York: Schocken Books, 1992), 25.
4. *B'reishit Rabbah* 28:8, in *The Book of Legends*, 26.
5. *B'reishit Rabbah* 25:2, in *The Book of Legends*, 25.
6. Ibid.
7. *Tanchuma B'reishit* 11, in *The Book of Legends*, 25.
8. *Tanchuma B'reishit* 5, in *The Book of Legends*, 27.
9. Ibid.
10. *Proceedings of the Biennial Convention of the Amalgamated Clothing Workers of America* (1919), 53, https://books.google.com/ books?id=QrcpAAAAYAAJ&pg=PA53.
11. Kaufmann Kohler, "Three Discourses on Jewish Ethics," in *Studies, Addresses and Personal Papers* (New York: Alumni Association of the Hebrew Union College, 1931), 244–45.

LECH L'CHA—GENESIS 12:1–17:27

Yirah—Awe:
Accompanying an Awe-Filled Journey

RABBI RICHARD M. C. KELLNER

BLUE SKIES SPREAD over the horizon as crisp air chilled the morning in Kanab, Utah. Driving southward toward the North Rim of the Grand Canyon, I was captivated by the beautiful forest with patches of snow polka-dotting the fields between the road and the tree line.

With hours of driving ahead, I planned to spend only a short amount of time at the North Rim—ten minutes would suffice, I thought. As I approached the edge of the Grand Canyon and beheld the incredible sight, I was captivated by the splendor. The majestic colors and the rock formations that pierced the air took my breath away. Was this what Moses felt like when he beheld the Burning Bush? Was this what Abraham felt like when God called to him, saying Lech l'cha (לֶךְ־לְךָ), "Go forth" (Genesis 12:1)? I then sat on a bench looking out at this wondrous landscape. Five minutes quickly turned into ninety. I was in awe; I had no words, silenced by the picture of grandeur before my eyes.

Each of us has experienced a moment when we were captivated by the divine paintbrush—gazing upon the night sky, watching a child being born, looking upon the Grand Canyon, or welcoming Shabbat as the sun sets over the Mediterranean. Grandeur, Heschel writes, fills us with yirah (יִרְאָה, "awe").[1] The potential to feel that awe, however, must be nurtured within us. We are easily distracted by our own thoughts, daily worries, or concerns, and we miss the moment.

Parashat Lech L'cha invites us to accompany Abram on his journey as we watch him cultivate awe within his soul. Walking alongside

Abram, we witness his response to both grand and mundane moments. "Awe," writes Alan Morinis, "is a natural human response to an overwhelming profound experience. . . . But only an inner instrument that has been polished and honed will find just as much awe in less dramatic situations. . . . Cultivate the capacity to feel awe and the whole world becomes awesome."[2] In what ways does Abram polish his inner instrument?

"The Eternal said to Abram, '*Lech l'cha*—Go forth from your land, your birthplace, your father's house, to the land that I will show you. I will make of you a great nation, and I will bless you; I will make your name great, and it shall be a blessing'" (Genesis 12:1–2). Completely awed by the moment, Abram responds with silence, contemplating the outcome, hoping that the encounter with the divine voice and the sacred word would endure far beyond the spoken moment. Heschel writes, "When we stand in awe, our lips do not demand speech, knowing that if we spoke, we would deprave ourselves. In such moments talk is an abomination. All we want is to pause, to be still, that the moment may last. . . . The meaning of the things we revere is overwhelming and beyond the grasp of our understanding."[3] Abram's silence demonstrates the awe within him being perfectly in balance. We would expect Abram to respond by reaching out to his beloved Sarai or his nephew Lot to share with them the grandeur he just experienced and the awe he felt. Abram's silence, an expression of awe, permits him to recognize God's presence in his life, whereas the spoken word would have minimized that awe-inspiring moment of hearing God's voice.

When Abram finally does speak, after his journey, he addresses Sarai. "Look, now—I know what a beautiful woman you are! So when the Egyptians see you, and say: 'This is his wife,' they may kill me; but you they shall keep alive. Please say then that you are my sister, so that on your account it may go well for me, and that my life may be spared because of you" (Genesis 12:11–13). Abram's *yirah* is no longer in balance. God had already reassured him that his descendants would possess the land. How quickly Abram has forgotten this promise! His *yirah* is misdirected toward Pharaoh's power rather than toward God's. Had Abram been able to direct his awe properly in this less dramatic situation, he might have behaved differently.

Abraham's journey to cultivating awe continues in *Parashat Vayeira*. The psychological, intellectual, and ethical implications of the *Akeidah* are overwhelming. When God asks Abraham to bring his son as an offering, we wonder how he could have willingly acquiesced. Reading this through the lens of awe, perhaps we might wonder if Abraham held too much awe for God and not enough for his son or fellow human beings. His readiness to offer his son as a *korban* ("sacrifice") teaches that his *yirah* motivates him to act mindlessly according to God's will. Only later does Abraham bring his *yirah* back into balance, the angel even mentioning the *middah* when calling to him, telling him not to harm Isaac: "[The angel] then said, 'Do not lay your hand on the lad; do nothing to him; for now I know that you are *y'rei Elohim*—one who fears God, as you did not withhold your son, your only one, from Me" (Genesis 22:12). Abraham restores balance to his *yirah* when he is able to behold both God's presence and the value of his son's life in the same moment.

As human beings, we must learn that God's presence is everywhere—found in the grandeur of the Grand Canyon and reflected back to us when we bear witness to the image of God that is within the vessel of another human soul. Morinis writes, "However it may come to us, a moment of awe gives us a small taste of the cosmic mystery, and an intuitive intimation of the divine. Awe does not protest phenomenal reality; rather, it offers direct affirmation of the eternal that lies within the worldly."[4] When we nurture awe, we deepen our connection to God, to the oneness of the universe, which helps us recognize the godliness in all of Creation.

At the conclusion of *Parashat Lech L'cha*, God changes Abram's name to Abraham and Sarai's to Sarah, establishing a covenant with them (Genesis 17:1–8, 17:15). A Chasidic teaching illuminates the addition of the letter *hei* (ה) within Abraham and Sarah's new names as an allusion to Creation. Torah explains the story of the heavens and the earth as *b'hibaram*, "they were created" (Genesis 2:4). Chasidic wisdom interprets this to mean *b'hei b'ra-am* (בְּרָאָם = ברא אותם), "God created everything with the letter *hei*," teaching us that the addition of the *hei* to Abraham and Sarah's names cultivates a sense of awe for the divine presence contained within grandeur of Creation.[5]

Why cultivate awe? According to Heschel, awe of God is the beginning of wisdom and is "an intuition for the creaturely dignity of all things and their preciousness to God."[6] In addition to being in awe of God's presence and God's role in creating the natural wonders of the world, Heschel reminds us that we are to behave in a way that recognizes God's presence in every person's soul. Could this be what God meant when telling Abram, *Veh'yeih brachah* (וְהְיֵה בְּרָכָה), "Be a blessing" (Genesis 12:2)? Being a blessing is the consummate act of *yirah* in balance. When we are a blessing, we are aware of the divine presence contained within the mystery of existence. Awe leads to wisdom, which leads to holy behavior.

How do we cultivate such awe? We place ourselves in moments when we can become captivated and mesmerized. We notice the sunsets, behold the rainbows, and are captivated by the majesty of a leaf budding in the spring or a bee buzzing in a flower. By restraining cognitive analysis, which causes us to consider only parts of the whole, we open awe's pathway. To put it simply, we stop thinking and start feeling. Additionally, we appreciate the divinity within every living soul.

There is a story about Rabbi Nachman Kossover,[7] a great Chasidic preacher who always perceived the divine name before him by seeing the divinity in the faces of those in his synagogue. Times changed and he found himself as a merchant in the marketplace, where he could no longer concentrate on God's presence. He hired a special assistant to remind him of the godliness of every soul. In the midst of the chaos of the marketplace, he would look at the face of his assistant, and then Reb Nachman would remember God's name.

As we walk through nature or the marketplace, let us notice the wonder. As we look upon the face of another, we can behold God's presence. When we can perceive the divine seeds, even the mundane can become magical.

Questions to Ask

In what ways does cognitive analysis get in the way of your being captivated by the grandeur of the moment?

What encounters with people or nature have inspired awe within you?

Think about another human being. What about that person inspires awe within you? How do you see God's presence within that person?

Practice for the *Middah* of *Yirah*

Go on a nature walk (perhaps on Shabbat afternoon). Look around at the beauty; when you see something that gives you a sense of wonder, spend time appreciating what you see. You might say: *Mah gadlu maasecha Adonai*, "How amazing are Your works, Adonai"!

Another *Middah* to Consider

When God shows Abram the heavens and asks him to count the stars, Abram put his faith in God (Genesis 15:5). It must have taken incredible faith (*emunah*, אֱמוּנָה) to listen to God and move his entire existence to an unknown place. Evaluate Abram's faith in light of his hearing God's voice. Then, consider your own faith in response to your encounters with the divine presence.

NOTES

1. Abraham Joshua Heschel, *Man Is Not Alone* (New York: Farrar, Straus and Giroux, 1951), 3.
2. Alan Morinis, *Every Day, Holy Day: 365 Days of Teachings and Practices from the Jewish Tradition of Mussar* (Boston: Trumpeter, 2010), 358.
3. Heschel, *Man Is Not Alone*, 26.
4. Morinis, *Every Day, Holy Day*, 176.
5. *Shaar Emunah V'Yesod HaChasidut*, Rabbi Gershon Hanoch Leiner comment on Genesis 17:5, Sefaria, https://www.sefaria.org/Shaar_HaEmunah_Ve'Yesod_HaChassidut%2C_Introduction_to_Beit_Yaakov.13?lang=bi.
6. Abraham Joshua Heschel, *God in Search of Man* (New York: Farrar, Straus and Giroux, 1955),74–75.
7. Arthur Green, *Seek My Face* (Woodstock, VT: Jewish Lights, 2011), 29.

VAYEIRA—GENESIS 18:1–22:24

Z'rizut—Alacrity:
The Alacrity of Abraham

RABBI ALEXANDRIA R. SHUVAL-WEINER
MEd, RJE, MAJS

"I have hurried and not delayed to keep Your commandments."
—*Psalm 119:60*

THE EIGHTEENTH-CENTURY SCHOLAR Rabbi Moshe Chayim Luzzatto defined the *middah* of *z'rizut* (זְרִיזוּת, "alacrity") as "the immediate engaging in mitzvot and their completion, as the Sages of blessed memory said: 'The zealous are early to perform the mitzvot.'"[1]

The *middah* of *z'rizut* constitutes the core of Abraham's spiritual DNA. As with many of the *middot*, we can see Abraham act with *z'rizut* in both laudable and deplorable ways. We may learn from Abraham's example how to, and how not to, cultivate our own *z'rirut*.

At the opening of the *parashah*, we read, "Looking up, [Abraham] saw: lo—three men standing opposite him! **Seeing** [them], he **ran** (*vayar vayarotz*) from the entrance of the tent to meet them" (Genesis 18:2).

Abraham is shown as rushing to fulfill the mitzvah of *hachnasat orchim*, welcoming guests. Immediately prior to the arrival of these strangers, Abraham is found sitting in the heat of the day, convalescing from his *b'rit milah* [2]—that is, in a weakened and diminished emotional and physical state. When he looks up and sees the approaching strangers, he harnesses all of his energy and rushes out to meet them, caring only for their comfort. It is taught: *G'dolah hachnasat orchim mikabbalat p'nei hash'chinah*, "Greater is hospitality than even welcoming the Divine Presence."[3] Abraham makes the priority of enthusiastically fulfilling this mitzvah of *hachnasat orchim*—audacious hospitality to its completion. Water, food, and shelter from the blistering heat are immediately and generously provided. In return, a message of good news is delivered by the strangers: Abraham and Sarah learn that, after many years of infertility, the promise will come to fruition—Sarah will birth the promised and much anticipated child, Isaac (Genesis 18:10). After the messengers complete their task, they prepare to depart, and Abraham escorts them, to see them safely off.

After this, Abraham learns of the divine plan to destroy the cities of Sodom and Gomorrah. Abraham immediately intercedes on behalf of the community. His sense of moral justice is clear, certain that the righteous merit salvation. Abraham wastes no time in challenging the decree, another example of *z'rizut*. Without hesitating, "Abraham steps up" with great alacrity—*vayigash Avraham*—and protests with full voice: "Will You indeed sweep away the innocent along with the wicked?" (Genesis 18:23). Abraham, speaking truth to power, makes the case that justice must be tempered by *rachamim* (רַחֲמִים, "mercy").[4]

Abraham's natural desire to passionately fulfill the mitzvot of hospitality, mercy, and justice are attributes that become the foil to the derelict character values found in Sodom. As we see in the text, ultimately only Lot and his family are saved from destruction (Genesis 19:29). The actions that prove to seal the fate of Sodom and Gomorrah are due to their moral insensitivities—inhospitable behavior (Genesis 18:4–9). Unlike Abraham, who argues on behalf of an unknown community, in Sodom not a single voice was heard in protest as the mob surged to attack Lot and his guests. The Sodomites thereby violate the following commandment in the Levitical Holiness Code: *Hochei-ach tochiach et amitecha*, "Reprove your kin" (Leviticus 19:17).

As we move further into the *parashah*, Abraham's decision-making seems to become more challenged. Not that he dawdles in anything he does; to the contrary, Abraham continues to be quick to take action and does so with deliberate intensity and promptness.

Following the destruction of Sodom and Gomorrah, Abraham sojourns to Gerar, where he has an encounter with the Canaanite king Abimelech. Repeating a defensive action he had taken years earlier (Genesis 12), Abraham presents Sarah to the king as his sister. Acting with too much *z'rizut*, Abraham quickly thinks to save his own life at the risk of Sarah's being raped (Genesis 20:2). God appears to Abimelech in a dream, commanding him to restore Sarah to Abraham as his wife (Genesis 20:3–7). Upon awaking, Abimelech rebukes Abraham for putting him in a position of potential sin: "What were you thinking of, that you did this?" (Genesis 20:10). In this situation, Abraham's own fear and mistrust of the unknown led him to act impetuously and without faith in the power and promise of God, with whom he has only recently engaged.

Now let us consider one of the most dramatic and difficult narratives in the Book of Genesis, *Akeidat Yitzchak*, the binding of Isaac, in Genesis 22. After being commanded to sacrifice his son, Abraham acts with *z'rizut*: *Vayashkeim Avraham baboker*, "Abraham rose early, saddled his donkey, chopped wood for the burnt-offering, took Isaac his son and his two lads, and set out for the place that God had spoken of to him" (Genesis 22:3). As one studies these verses, the reader psychologically sojourns to Moriah with Abraham. Considering Abraham's earlier heroic, holy *chutzpah* (חֻצְפָּה), challenging God in chapter 18, one questions the direction of that alacrity now.

The Sages need to avoid the moral ambiguity inherent in the act of offering one's child to God as a fire sacrifice and instead assert that Abraham's *z'rizut* is found in the diligence and speed he exhibits when commanded to take Isaac up to Mount Moriah.[5]

It is true that one who works to cultivate *z'rizut* must focus on the task with commitment. There are three aspects to completing a task: the enthusiastic start, the sustaining energy and perseverance to move forward, and finally, moving to successful completion. It's no wonder that the Sages consider Abraham the paradigm of an *ish zariz* ("a man of alacrity") when considering the description of the *Akeidah*.

Still, the direction of Abraham's *z'rizut* in the final chapters of the *parashah* contrast to what we read earlier in the portion, leading us to moral consternation. Is it possible to become so meticulous in one's practice, so infused with *z'rizut*, that we lose sight of the things that are most important? Thankfully, at the very last minute, with the knife poised above Isaac's head, we hear the divine call, "Abraham! Abraham! . . . Do not lay your hand on the lad; do nothing to him" (Genesis 22:11–12). Isaac is spared when an angel of God stops Abraham from going through with the sacrifice.

We also know that God and Abraham never speak again. Nor does Abraham again converse with his wife or with Isaac. Sarah will soon die; and yet, Abraham will conclude his life "old and contented" (Genesis 25:8).[6]

How do we evaluate Abraham's actions as a model for our own moral and spiritual development? Throughout *Parashat Vayeira*, the verbs associated with Abraham's actions are those of exuberance, purpose, urgency, and diligence to the task—all hallmarks of the *middah* of *z'rizut*.

Abraham is indeed an exemplar of *z'rizut*, from the first encounter in *Parashat Lech L'cha*, when he leaves all that he has known and lights out for places unknown to the moment of his final breath in *Parashat Tol'dot*. We may emulate Abraham, striving to engage with our tasks deeply, pursuing our relationships and the world with enthusiasm and veracity, developing the commitment never to give up working for the betterment of all. We can also learn from the times that Abraham's *z'rizut* takes him astray. Most importantly, we must cultivate awareness of when we may be allowing the work to take us away from what is most important in our lives. By committing to live in this way, we become better people, which in turn makes our world more sacred, kinder, and more compassionate.

Questions to Ask

We are taught that if you have started a mitzvah, you should finish it, for "a mitzvah is judged only upon its completion."[7] How much enthusiasm and follow-through do you bring to the tasks to which you commit yourself?

Where in your *avodah*, spiritual and practical work, can you bring more diligence, passion, enthusiasm, and task commitment?

When might you need to step back and focus on self, family, or other important relationships?

Are you bringing the same level of *z'rizut* to those relationships as you are to the external work?

Practice for the *Middah* of *Z'rizut*

Z'rizut is a trait we can cultivate through our own behavior modification. Try this exercise: From the moment you awake in the morning, intentionally meet the day with enthusiasm. Set your intention for the day. Find the spark that will ignite passion and motivation for you, and act upon it. Be actively attuned to discover the sacred moments and miracles all around, and rejoice in them. Seize opportunities to speak out on behalf of truth, righteousness, and justice. Find ways to take note of the successful completion of your particular tasks, even the tiniest, and celebrate them.

Another *Middah* to Consider

Chesed (חֶסֶד, "loving-kindness"): Abraham demonstrates compassion for so many. He is concerned for the comfort of his guests; he worries about others and speaks out on their behalf.

NOTES

1. Moshe Chayim Luzzatto, *M'silat Yesharim (The Path of the Just)*, chap. 6, citing *Babylonian Talmud, P'sachim* 4a.
2. Rashi on Genesis 18:1.
3. *Babylonian Talmud, Shabbat* 27b.
4. See also *Babylonian Talmud, P'sachim* 4a.
5. Rashi on Genesis 22:3.
6. The translation found in Sefaria is used in this case.
7. Rashi on Numbers 31:3.

Chayei Sarah—Genesis 23:1–25:18

M'nuchat HaNefesh—Equanimity: Calming the Soul Amid the Storms of Life

RABBI JENNIFER A. GUBITZ

IT IS ANOTHER BREATHTAKING MOMENT in the Genesis journey as we encounter *Chayei Sarah*, the *parashah* named for Sarah's life that so poignantly begins with her last breath. Nearly the entire portion focuses on the lives of Isaac and Abraham, her son and husband. When Sarah dies, Abraham negotiates with Ephron to purchase the burial site in Machpelah and sends a senior household servant to procure a wife for Isaac. Discovering the beautiful maiden Rebekah, who befits all the qualities of the perfect wife for Isaac, the servant negotiates with Rebekah's family and brings her back to her new home, where she kindles comfort and love in Isaac's life. Abraham lives out his days with his new wife Keturah; and upon his death, Ishmael returns to join Isaac to bury their father. With his parents Sarah and Abraham both deceased, Isaac and his beloved Rebekah settle in Be'er-lachai-ro'i.

This was a place previously known to Isaac, for it was in Be'er-lachai-ro'i, "the well of the living One who sees me," that he settled after the *Akeidah* (the Binding of Isaac). It was the place, too, where Hagar had gone after she and Ishmael were saved by an angel from near-fatal thirst in the wilderness. Be'er-lachai-ro'i twice punctuates the peaks and valleys of Isaac's journey.

In tracing Isaac's life throughout Genesis—from the *Akeidah* to the moment when Rebekah "alights" from her camel, literally "falling" in love with him, until his dying breath at the end of Genesis

35— we wonder: how does Isaac endure a life that vacillates between joy and deep pain, comfort and trauma, loss and love? We might ask if and how he is able to maintain "equanimity" (מְנוּחַת הַנֶּפֶשׁ, *m'nuchat hanefesh*) during his soul-stirring life journey? What can we moderns learn from his life as we face the highs and lows of being human? And what are the ways the Mussar value of equanimity can sustain us, as well?

Mussar scholars describe the *middah* of equanimity with various Hebrew terms: *m'nuchat hanefesh* ("calmness of the soul"), *yishuv hada'at* (יְשׁוּב הַדַּעַת, "a settled mind"), or *shalvah* (שַׁלְוָה, "serenity"). It is a state of being through which a person can face any situation—from turmoil to tranquility—without being moved from the centered self. Like a surfer in the ocean, no matter the destabilizing waves splashing and smashing down around us, one with attuned equanimity is anchored by a stable inner core.

"The Mussar teachers," writes Alan Morinis, "point to anger, jealousy, lust and other strong inner states as the source of the turbulence that destroys the calmness of the soul. They advise us that the way to respond to these internal storms is to develop the capacity for inner distancing."[1] In this way, as Rabbi Menachem Mendel Leffin offers in his book *Cheshbon HaNefesh*, a person can rise above the good and the bad.[2] Reb Eliyahu Lopian writes of the ways one pursues tranquility through prayer. A disciplined prayer and Torah study practice pursued with intention and tranquility helps one to achieve a calmness of soul.[3]

When we encounter Isaac returning from Be'er-lachai-ro'i, the midrash suggests that there he re-encounters his mother's handmaid, Hagar.[4]

As modern midrashists, we can imagine this meeting: When Hagar notices a man approaching her tent, she sees that he is thin, with a modest set of shoulders that hunch a bit but exude strength. She recognizes that soft jawline and kind face. It had been so long. So much has transpired. Could it really be the son of Abraham? Not her own son Ishmael. Could this man be Isaac? When Hagar and Isaac finally stand face-to-face in conversation, "How are you, my boy?" Hagar asks, even though he is now a man.

One of the last times Hagar saw Isaac, he was but a small boy playing with Ishmael. But Sarah, as she often did, found fault in Ishmael. "You're not playing," she accused. "You're teasing him, you're roughing him up."[5] So when Abraham, at Sarah's bidding, sent Hagar and Ishmael off into the wilderness with only a skin of water, Hagar looked back only once. Isaac was curled up in Sarah's lap crying. Tears pouring down that soft jawline, a kind face like that she could never forget. After all those things, Hagar never imagined she'd see Isaac again.

"How are you, my boy?" she asks, even though he is now a man. "How are you . . . after all those things?" The words and stories that pour out of Isaac are as if a well overflowing with emotion, drenched in memory, and coursing with questions. "Didn't Ishmael tell you, Hagar?" he asks. "We buried our father, Abraham, together in Machpelah.[6] I told him everything there. Everything that happened on Mount Moriah. How my father had me carry the wood myself, how our One God told him to bind me on an altar and how he did. It was a ram in the thicket that saved me. Abraham went home after that. But I had to get away."

"Isaac," Hagar asks, "where have you been? How did you do it? After all those things you faced in your life, how did your soul become whole again?"

"I studied. I prayed," Isaac answers. "I spent time outside. I spent time alone. I wondered and I wandered. And I searched."

Rabbinic Sages teach that after the trauma of the *Akeidah* and then his mother Sarah's death, Isaac took a long leave of absence from his family. In the Torah text, we hear about him, but we barely hear a word from him.

Some commentators actually suggest this silence was a permanent and final departure—that the trauma was so painful that he died of fear.[7] Others imagine he was blinded.[8] Other commentaries envision that it was neither death nor illness, but rather that Isaac's departure was a multifaceted journey of resilience and recovery. *B'reishit Rabbah* teaches that after the *Akeidah*, Isaac went to study in a *beit midrash*, a "house of learning."[9] Drowning his sorrows and his past in the books and traditions of our people, he immersed in a community of learners and seekers.

At another point on his journey of resilience and recovery, Genesis describes: *Vayeitzei Yitzchak lasuach basadeh lifnot arev* (וַיֵּצֵא יִצְחָק לָשׂוּחַ בַּשָּׂדֶה לִפְנוֹת עָרֶב), "[Isaac was] going out toward evening to stroll in the field" (Genesis 24:63).

The eleventh-century commentator Rashi teaches that this was not just an ordinary walk in the fields.[10] Rather, Isaac had gone to the fields to meditate and pray. Thirteenth-century Rabbeinu Bachya teaches that Isaac's walk was a stroll in the fields to enjoy nature and its restorative powers.[11] Fifteenth-century Sforno concurs: It wasn't just a nature walk; rather Isaac had detoured from his regular path out into the fields in order to pour out his heart to God in prayer.[12] The Sages go as far as to suggest that Isaac invented the afternoon prayer service.[13]

The first steps in Isaac's journey of resilience followed a pathway of study, learning, and seeking, developing a spiritual practice of being in communion with nature, finding moments of meditation and breath, discovering words of prayer—be they gratitude or anger—and seeking out connection to a presence greater than himself.

In this generous read of Isaac's life and recovery, establishing a Mussar practice is not to be equated with medicine. Rather, as we trace Isaac's story, we see the ways in which his *m'nuchat hanefesh* grows and develops through a resilient practice of meditation, Torah study, prayer, devotion to God—and even relationship! Isaac changes through his relationship with Rebekah, and the change is never completed or finalized. Ultimately, Mussar practice is a process; like Isaac, one never reaches completion or mastery of any trait. It may be appealing to live a life without the contrasts of highs and lows, love and loss. However, Alan Morinis reminds us that "praiseworthy calmness is not an unperturbed steady inner state, and we are deluded if our aim is to smooth out our inner experience in the hope of making it safe and unruffled."[14] Rabbi Joshua Loth Liebman's *Peace of Mind* teaches that "no normal person can face life without experiencing countless fears and worries. They are part of the fee we pay for citizenship in an unpredictable universe." He anchors inner stability, too, on equanimity, quoting Bertrand Russell's *A Free Man's Worship*, that "man's greatest triumph . . . is to achieve stability and inner repose in a world of shifting threats and terrifying change."[15]

Morinis also directs us to Rabbi Adin Steinsaltz's book *The Thirteen Petalled Rose*, which echoes this idea: "The Jewish approach to life considers the person who has stopped going—one who has a feeling of completion, of peace, of a great light from above that has brought him to rest—to be someone who has lost his way. Only one whom the light continues to beckon, for whom the light is as distant as ever, only that one can be considered to have received some sort of response."[16]

Isaac's development of equanimity does not smooth over his past experiences or lead him to a future without pain, trial, or suffering. Rather, it is the practice of the *middah* of equanimity as a constant journey and spiritual exercise that brings understanding and even peace. For Isaac, his return again and again to Be'er-lachai-ro'i may be imagined not just as a pilgrimage to a place where God can see him, but a journey to where he can see himself. In that place, he develops clarity as an inner witness to his life experience. When we explore the life of Isaac through the spiritual practices imagined by the Rabbis and enhanced by our own hearts, we see his spiritual growth from silence to prayer, from loss to love. Elie Wiesel might as well have been talking about Isaac when he spoke of his own journey of resilience: "On the verge of despair, [Isaac] does not give up. On the contrary, he strives to find a place among the living."[17] Through study, prayer, relationship, and reflection, *m'nuchat hanefesh* is the balm for Isaac's soul.

Questions to Ask

Consider the unsung female heroes—Hagar, Sarah, and Rebekah—in this *parashah*'s exploration of Isaac's life. How
do they embody equanimity (*m'nuchat hanefesh*)? What
other *middot* do they embody that support Isaac's growth?
What Mussar values does Abraham exhibit as he negotiates
a burial site for Sarah and ensures a wife for Isaac?

Practice for the *Middah* of *M'nuchat HaNefesh*

Notice a situation in your life that arouses an extreme emotion
within you. Imagine yourself still and balanced, riding the waves
as they come crashing down around you. Decide to experience the
joy or anger, but try to protect yourself from feeling crushed, overwhelmed, excessively proud, or knocked off your center.

Another *Middah* to Consider

Another *middah* to consider is *emet* (אֱמֶת, "truth"). Isaac endures tremendous struggle in his life but rarely speaks of it, choosing the quiet
path to healing. Imagine facing a trying situation in life and speaking
truthfully about the experience. How might this Genesis story have
evolved differently if Isaac, Abraham, Sarah, or Hagar had spoken
out?

NOTES

1. Mussar Institute, Everyday Holiness curriculum, lesson 6, element 3.
2. Menachem Mendel Leffin, *Cheshbon HaNefesh* (New York: Feldheim, 1995),
   109-117.
3. Eliyahu Lopian, *Lev Eliyahu* (Jerusalem: Eliezer Fisher, 1989), accessed
   from Mussar Institute, Everyday Holiness curriculum, "Equanimity."
4. *B'reishit Rabbah* 60:14.
5. Rashi, Kimchi, and Sforno on Genesis 21:9.
6. See Genesis 25:9.
7. *Pirkei D'Rabbi Eliezer* 31.
8. *B'reishit Rabbah* 65:10.
9. *B'reishit Rabbah* 56:11; Targum Pseudo-Jonathan on Genesis 22:19.
10. Rashi on Genesis 24:63, including *B'reishit Rabbah* 60:14.

11. Rabbeinu Bachya, *Chovot HaLevavot* (Duties of the Heart), quoting Ibn Ezra and David Kimchi on Genesis 24:63.

12. Sforno on Genesis 24:63.

13. *Babylonian Talmud, B'rachot* 26b and *Avodah Zarah* 7b.

14. Alan Morinis, "Through a Mussar Lens: Calmness Leads to Elevation," Mussar Institute, November 2016, https://mussarinstitute.org/Yashar/2016-11/mussar_lens.php.

15. Joshua Loth Liebman, *Peace of Mind* (New York: Simon and Schuster, 1964), 81.

16. Adin Steinsaltz, *The Thirteen Petalled Rose: A Discourse On The Essence Of Jewish Existence And Belief* (New York: Basic Books, 1980).

17. Elie Wiesel, "Hope, Memory, and Despair" (Nobel Lecture), December 11, 1986.

TOL'DOT—GENESIS 25:19–28:9

Emet—Truth,
Hidden and Revealed

RABBI LISA L. GOLDSTEIN

TOL'DOT IS A TROUBLING PORTION for those who are seeking guidance on how to live an upright, ethical life; indeed, it seems more attuned to those with a Machiavellian orientation toward getting what they want. Upon first reading, *Tol'dot* is an account of falsehood upon falsehood, deceit upon deceit, as the members of Isaac and Rebekah's family each act for their own personal gain.

Trickery characterizes everything we read about Esau and Jacob. In the first interaction we witness between them, Jacob takes advantage of Esau's exhaustion after a day of hunting and coerces Esau into selling his birthright to Jacob (Genesis 25:29–34). Later, Rebekah instructs her favorite son, Jacob, to disguise himself as his brother in order to receive the blessing Isaac intends to give Esau. Despite some initial trepidation (Genesis 27:11–12), Jacob complies, identifying himself boldly—and falsely—to his blind father as *anochi Eisav b'chorecha* (אָנֹכִי עֵשָׂו בְּכֹרֶךָ), "I am Esau your firstborn" (Genesis 27:19), and therefore receives the blessing. Even Isaac plays the role of deceiver. Faced with famine, he takes refuge with Abimelech, king of the Philistines, and pretends that Rebekah is his sister because he fears that Abimelech would kill him and take his beautiful wife (Genesis 26:7).

The Rabbinic tradition largely sets about to destabilize the truth even further. Rashi, for example, tell us that it was not Jacob who was the great trickster between the two brothers, but rather Esau. By describing Esau as one who "understands hunting," Rashi comments that the text suggests that Esau was skilled at entrapping and deceiving his father with his mouth.[1] Rashi also interprets Jacob's declaration of identity quite differently than one might expect. Instead of understanding *anochi Eisav b'chorecha* as "I am Esau, your firstborn," the plain meaning of the words, he reads Jacob's words as "It is I! Esau is your firstborn," transforming the lie into a technical truth.[2]

What is going on here? How are we to understand the actions of our mythic ancestors and their apparent complete disregard for the "truth" (*emet*, אֱמֶת)?

The truth about truth is that it is not always so simple. We get a glimpse of this uncomfortable reality in a midrash about the creation of the first human being. Rabbi Shimon taught that when the Blessed Holy One decided to create the first human, the ministering angels divided into opposing blocs, some of whom said that humans should not be created, while others said that humans should indeed be created. The Angel of Loving-Kindness and the Angel of Justice argued in favor of the creation of humans, who would strive to do acts of loving-kindness and justice. But the Angel of Truth and the Angel of Peace disagreed. The Angel of Peace argued that humans would be entirely made up of conflict, and the Angel of Truth argued that humans would be entirely made up of lies. In response, the Blessed Holy One flung the Angel of Truth to the earth, whereupon all the other ministering angels gathered around and said, "But Master of all the worlds, is not Truth Your own seal? Raise Truth back up from the earth!"[3]

The Angel of Truth, of course, speaks the truth: we humans are indeed "entirely made up of lies." Look no further than our Torah portion and then at our own experiences. We, like Rebekah, Jacob, and Isaac, are profoundly limited in our perspective, in our awareness, in our understanding of our own desires. We make assumptions about others' motives all the time. How can we even begin to speak about truth?

It is not our fault that we cannot recognize the whole truth. According to the midrash, our inability to recognize the full truth is essential to the way we were created. Still, truth matters. The midrash suggests that truth is so important, so connected to the essence of divinity, that it—more than all the other qualities—is the divine seal, while at the same time proposing that perhaps it would have been better for humanity not to have been created given our inability to tell the truth.[4]

Fortunately, the Chasidic master Rebbe Gedalya of Linitz (d. 1803–1804) offers us a path forward with his insight about the nature of truth:

> It should be obvious to anyone who pays attention that the quality of truth is the vital force sustaining all Creation. . . . Truth is contained even in the husks [k'lipot], and it is its force that sustains them as well. This is the mystery . . . the teaching of the Sages, "Any falsehood that does not also have some truth in it will not in the end be sustained" (Babylonian Talmud, Sotah 35a).[5]

Rebbe Gedalya is offering a very helpful teaching. When he speaks about "the vital life force," the chiyut, he is describing a fundamental Chasidic way of understanding God. In this understanding, God is not ultimately a character in the Tanach, but rather "the vital life force" that unfolds through time and space, supporting and renewing Creation moment to moment. When we say that truth is God's seal, it is another way of saying that truth is the essence of the life force itself, that there is a truth at the core of everything that exists. However, sometimes the truth is hidden. Just as, according to the Lurianic Creation story,[6] there are husks or shells that hide sparks of divine light, so, too, husks can hide the truth. However, that does not mean truth is not there. In fact, without truth, lies cannot exist.

We see an example of this phenomenon as we return to our parashah. At the very beginning, Rebekah, greatly suffering during her pregnancy, demands an explanation from God and receives the following insight:

> Two peoples are in your belly;
> two nations shall branch off from each other [as they emerge]
> from your womb.
> One people shall prevail over the other;
> the elder shall serve the younger. (Genesis 25:22–23)

In other words, Rebekah on some level already knows the truth hiding under the lies. Instructing Jacob to disguise himself as Esau and to take his blessing by stealth, Rebekah may unconsciously believe she is acting according to God's will: Jacob is the son destined to lead. Of course, deception comes with consequences. Esau's great and bitter cry (Genesis 27:34) and the subsequent enmity between the two brothers hold echoes to this day.[7]

On a mystical level, the more lies are spread, the more husks exist, and the less divine essence reaches the world. In our own lives, the less we are able to discern the truth, the more we bring suffering to ourselves and to those around us.

So what do we do? We bring greater attention to our habits of truth-telling and lying. When is it easy for us to tell the truth? When do we take refuge in a lie? When we find ourselves not telling the truth, we can, like Rebekah, look deeper inside ourselves and search for an explanation from our inner knowing: What is in fact the truth? Is there some truth contained within this falsehood? How might things be different if we could acknowledge that hidden truth?

We humans may be "entirely made up of lies," but we are also made in the divine image. By bringing more truth into the world, we can bring more divinity into the world and lessen suffering for us all.

Questions to Ask

Rebbe Gedalya of Linitz understands truth to be the defining characteristic of the life force of the universe. What does that mean to you? If you would suggest a different characterization, what would it be?

Find an example in your experience in which a lie contained a truth at its core. What kept that truth from emerging?

Practice for the *Middah* of *Emet*

Set an intention to notice each time your instinct is to distort the truth in some way. When you notice that instinct arising, take a moment to ask yourself if there is an element of hidden truth that is yearning to be noticed.

Another *Middah* to Consider

Isaac digs two wells, but the water rights are disputed. He digs a third well, which is not disputed, and names it Rehoboth, or "spacious" (Genesis 26:18–22). Explore how naming something helps amplify *hakarat hatov* (הַכָּרַת הַטּוֹב, "gratitude").

NOTES

1. Rashi on Genesis 25:27.
2. Rashi on Genesis 27:19.
3. *B'reishit Rabbah* 8:5.
4. An ironic note about this midrash: The Rabbis bring a proof text for this battle between the ministering angels from Psalms and then read the verse in a most subversive way. The surface meaning of the verse is that loving-kindness and truth met (*nifgashu*) and justice and peace kissed (*nashaku*). The Rabbis deliberately misread the verbs not in a loving way, but in a violent way, suggesting that "met" means "fought" and that "kissed" means "clashed." This echoes their reading of Jacob and Esau's eventual reunion, in which Esau's kiss is understood to be an aggressive, violent act.
5. Rebbe Gedalya of Linitz, commentary on *Re'eh*, in *T'shuot Chein*, translated by Rabbi Jonathan Slater.
6. See, e.g., Daniel C. Matt, *God and the Big Bang* (Woodstock, VT: Jewish Lights, 2016), 80–82.
7. "Esau" became a symbol in Rabbinic literature for Rome, for Christian Europe, and by extension, the anti-Semitism found in today's white supremacy.

Vayeitzei—Genesis 28:10–32:3
Savlanut—Patience:
Jacob and the Attribute of Savlanut

Rabbi Daniel S. Alexander, DMin, DD

What is *SAVLANUT* (סַבְלָנוּת, "patience")?

According to the contemporary Mussar master Rabbi Shlomo Wolbe, "The patient person is exactly like someone who is carrying a heavy package. Even though it weighs upon him, he continues to go on his way, and doesn't take a break from carrying it."[1] Thus, not only does patience enlist a capacity to wait, to put off gratification, to refrain from impulsivity and reactivity, and to react calmly and without anger, but patience can also be burdensome. In this regard, one notes that the Hebrew *savlanut* contains root letters that can also form the words *sivlot*, "burdens," and *sablan*, a "porter," one who literally bears burdens.

How might one cultivate this *middah*, this attribute of character? According to Rabbi Yechiel Yitzchok Peer, "You can train yourself to be patient. You can train yourself to open the space between the match and the fuse."[2] Like all *middot*, *savlanut* exists on a continuum. At one end of the continuum, one finds non-reactivity or apathy. At the other end, one finds the jittery, knee-jerk reactivity often associated with the emotions of anger, fear, or anxiety. In practicing this *middah*, then, one strives to find an appropriate place of balance for the circumstance while avoiding both extremes.

As *Parashat Vayeitzei* opens, we encounter Jacob leaving his home in Beersheba, fearful that his stronger brother Esau intends to kill him in vengeance. One recalls that Jacob has made off with both the blessing and the birthright purportedly intended for Esau (Genesis 27:41–45).

In the first verse of *Vayeitzei*, we encounter the verb *vayeilech*, which can mean the specific modality of walking (as opposed to running or riding on an animal).[3] One could argue that the Torah invites the reader to imagine Jacob leaving Beersheba on foot, by walking, the slowest mode of travel available to him.

In *Walking: One Step at a Time*, Erling Kagge poses this question: "What is the point of moving slowly from place to place?"[4] He replies, "Everything moves slowly when I walk, the world seems softer, and for a short while, I am not doing household chores, having a meeting or reading manuscripts. A free . . . [person] possesses time. . . . [Ironically,] time moves more quickly when I increase the speed of travel. . . . When I am in a rush, I hardly pay attention to anything at all."[5] To Kagge, walking is not only a slow way to travel, but it has a quality of *savlanut*. I, too, have experienced the way time thickens only when I slow my pace. On a walk in the woods or in the neighborhood, an expansive sense of time opens me up to the possibility of surprise, creativity, and to noticing that which, in a more frenetic frame of mind, might pass me by.

Jacob, in opting to walk, has readied his interior self for a transformative spiritual experience at Beth El. Along the way, Jacob stops to nap. He dreams his famous dream in which angels ascend and descend on a ladder stretching from earth to heaven (Genesis 28:12). When Jacob awakens, he proclaims the dream a spiritual event, saying, "Truly, the Eternal is in this place, and I did not know it!" Trembling, he adds, "How awe-inspiring is this place! This is none other than the house of God, and this is the gate of heaven!'" (Genesis 28:16–17).

By this proclamation, Jacob describes an acute awareness of divine presence. The preeminent theologian Rabbi Abraham Joshua Heschel describes such awareness of divinity in mundane events and in similar experiences of wonder as "radical amazement." In offering pragmatic advice on how to cultivate a sense of wonder, Heschel advises us to pause, not to rush, to refrain from impatience, and to stand still! To Heschel, *savlanut*, in the sense of "slowing down" or "standing still," is the prerequisite for paying attention; and paying attention is the prerequisite for experiencing wonder, for sensing the presence of divinity in a moment.

Although Jacob seems profoundly affected by the dream experience at Beth El, it does not alter the course of his goal of proceeding toward Haran. Having reaped a spiritual reward for his posture of patience, Jacob now continues on his way. The patient person waits or pauses enough, but not endlessly.

Jacob's journey has a twofold purpose. One is to escape the wrath of his brother. The second is to find a wife from among his kin back in the home country of Haran.

Jacob eventually arrives at the well where he meets some shepherds: "Jacob said to them: 'My brothers, where are you from?' 'We are from Haran,' they said" (Genesis 29:4). Rabbi Naftali Tzvi Yehudah Berlin takes note of Jacob's greeting of the unfamiliar shepherds as "my brothers." He interprets it as an example of Jacob's practice of speaking in a polite and friendly fashion to everyone.[6] We might expect that in an encounter with strangers, anxiety, even fear, would run high. In anxiety-infused moments, our speech would likely be characterized by nervousness or constriction. However, a posture of patiently bearing the emotional burden permits us to create distance between match and fuse, to notice our anxiety and to choose the more constructive modality of friendliness.

"He [Jacob] said to them [the shepherds], 'Do you know Laban son of Nahor?' And they said, 'We do know [him].' 'Is he well?' said he to them" (Genesis 29:5–6). Zelig Pliskin credits Sforno for the idea that in asking after the well-being of Lavan, Jacob exhibits sensitivity. "One should not greet a host in the same manner when the host is joyous as when he is unhappy."[7] In addition, learning about someone's well-being in advance could prevent one from saying or doing something that would embarrass the host.[8] That is, a patient disposition in his conversation with the shepherds allows Jacob to achieve a nuanced preparation for encountering Laban with sensitivity.

Eventually, Jacob meets his beloved Rachel; goes to work for her father, Laban; is tricked into first marrying the older sister, Leah; and is forced to work for Laban for a total of twenty years, coming away with two wives, two handmaids, and a sizable quantity of goats and sheep.

Anyone would feel highly burdened by seven years of labor to earn the hand of one's beloved in marriage. We can only imagine Jacob's sense of burden at learning that yet another seven would be required—and then, after that, another six for wages. Jacob's attribute of patience takes the form of persistence and resilience. By bearing the burdens associated with twenty years of labor and delaying his gratification, he comes to thrive as a married shepherd. We might compare the time frame and the patience required of Jacob to the decades of hard work required in our day to become a neurosurgeon, a parent of well-adjusted adult children, a five-star general, a financially secure retiree after a life of labor in farm or factory, or a CEO of a large corporation. However, Jacob's extended period of labor for Laban also raises the question: When does the time arrive to cease exhibiting patience? When does forbearance constitute a kind of abuse? When ought one stop and say, "Enough"?

Parashat Vayeitzei offers us opportunities to consider *savlanut* in action and also in absence. After Jacob marries both Leah and Rachel, a competition ensues between the sisters for Jacob's affection. At the outset, Jacob loves Rachel more than Leah (Genesis 29:30). In its sense of forbearance, Leah lacks patience as she retains a jealous disposition toward her sister. However, Leah initially bears children, while Rachel remains barren.

Leah gives birth to four sons in quick succession (Genesis 29:31–35). Instead of rejoicing at each birth of a nephew, Rachel envies her sister's fertility and cries in anguish to Jacob, "Let me have children; otherwise I am a dead woman!" (Genesis 30:1). The Torah provides Jacob's reaction: "Jacob grew angry with Rachel and said, 'Am I in place of God who has withheld from you the fruit of the womb?'" (Genesis 30:2).

In reacting angrily and without sympathy for his beloved but distraught Rachel, Jacob fails to act with *savlanut*. For each of these moments of heightened family tension, the Torah provides a clear picture about how anger, jealousy, or envy—all enemies of patience—can rise up and control behavior. We can only imagine how a cultivated capacity to lengthen the distance between match and fuse might have engendered a measure of sympathy and how sympathy, in turn, could have strengthened the relational bonds within this complicated, blended family.

A final vignette from a midrash offers an alternative perspective on the way patience plays a role in the relationship of the two sisters. According to the midrash, Rachel suspects her father of intending to switch the sisters on the wedding night. In order to outwit Laban, she arranges signs by which Jacob can recognize her. However, as the wedding night approaches, Rachel comes to the realization that, if she outwits Laban, Leah will suffer severe embarrassment.[9] Rachel, as imagined in the midrash, acts in a patient and considerate manner, without anger or envy, at being upstaged by her sister. In sharing the signs with her sister, Rachel endures the pain of seeing Leah marry in her stead. Some might well regard the degree of patience evinced by midrashic Rachel as an example of patience gone awry. Others might deem it an admirable prioritizing of sisterly love. Either way, the midrash brings the question into focus.

Parashat Vayeitzei provides us with multiple opportunities to contemplate the attribute of *savlanut*, patience, in several of its dimensions. It invites us to reflect on the power of this quality to deepen our experience of a moment and to enrich our relationships with friends, family, and strangers. And while awakening us to contemplate the virtue of patience, it also stirs us to consider the limits within which we best exhibit this virtue.

Questions to Ask

When has walking, or some other means of slowing down, expanded time for you? How might you slow down as a routine of personal practice?

In what circumstances are you challenged to avoid unhealthy reactivity, intemperate speech, or other forms of impatience? What factors contribute to your impatience? With these factors in mind, how might you cultivate the virtue of patience?

Practice for the *Middah* of *Savlanut*

For one week, set an intention to notice the moments during each day when you feel challenged to exhibit patience. Pay attention to the quality of your feelings (irritation, anger, anxiety, boredom, or something else) at these moments. At the end of each day, record your observations in a journal. What learning emerges about the nature of your relationship with this *middah*? In what ways does the mere act of noticing these moments and then reflecting upon them affect your capacity to practice *savlanut*?

Another *Middah* to Consider

Laban deceives Jacob by substituting his older daughter, Leah, for the promised, younger daughter, Rachel. Earlier, Jacob has deceived his father, Isaac, in receiving a blessing intended for Esau. Subsequently, Jacob's sons will deceive Jacob in the matter of Joseph's purported death. And years later in Egypt, Joseph will deceive his brothers about his identity. Consider the implied lessons concerning the virtue of *emet*, "truth," and its absence.

NOTES

1. Quoted in Alan Morinis, *Every Day, Holy Day: 365 Days of Teachings and Practices from the Jewish Tradition of Mussar* (Boston: Trumpeter, 2010), 93.
2. Quoted in ibid., 95.
3. Francis Brown, S. R. Driver, and Charles A. Briggs, *Hebrew and English Lexicon of the Old Testament* (Oxford: Clarendon Press, 1906), 230.

4. Erling Kagge, *Walking: One Step at a Time* (New York: Pantheon, 2019), 8.
5. Ibid., 15.
6. Cited by Zelig Pliskin, *Love Your Neighbor* (Brooklyn: Aish HaTorah, 1977), 99.
7. Ibid.
8. Ibid.
9. *Babylonian Talmud, M'gilah* 13b.

VAYISHLACH—GENESIS 32:4–36:43
Yirah—Awe:
From Fear to Awe

RABBI JUDITH LAZARUS SIEGAL

JACOB GOES THROUGH a major life transformation in *Parashat Vayishlach*, including a wrestling match with God and a change in his name from Jacob to Israel. These changes are reflective of changes in Jacob's character as well, as he goes from a person filled with fear to one who is full of awe and gratitude. His transformation involves resolving old issues and grappling with feelings of guilt over his stealing the blessing and birthright from his brother—and, in the process, lying to their father, Isaac. As Jacob prepares to see his brother Esau in the morning, he lies restless. The Torah tells us of his state of mind: *vayira Yaakov* (וַיִּירָא יַעֲקֹב), "Jacob was terrified" (Genesis 32:8).

Later in the *parashah*, we learn why Jacob is fearful, as he says, "I am afraid of him, lest he advance on me and strike me" (Genesis 32:12), referring to his brother Esau. That night, Jacob takes his family and crosses the Jabbok River, and then he is left alone to wrestle in the night with an unknown man or angel or messenger of God; the Hebrew word used is *ish* (אִישׁ), "man" (Genesis 32:25). Jacob does not let the man go without demanding a blessing. The other says to him, "What is your name?" and he says, "Jacob." "No more shall you be called Jacob, but Israel," says the other, "for you have struggled with God and with human beings, and you have prevailed" (Genesis 32:28–29).

A verse later in the Torah tells us: "Jacob set up a monument in the sacred site where [God] had spoken to him. . . . Jacob named the place where God had spoken to him Beth El [House of God]" (Genesis 35:14–15).

In Jewish thought, "fear" (*yirah*, יִרְאָה) of God is understood to be complementary to "love" or "awe" of God. In fact, the term *yirat HaShem*, or "fear of God," is equal to following the Torah and mitzvot, according to Rabbi Yosef Albo (1380–1444, Spain), author of *Sefer HaIkarim*. In the teachings of Mussar, however, we find a very interesting concept when it comes to the *middah* of "fear/awe." Alan Morinis writes, "Though *yirah* can describe the unified fear/awe experience, the term can also be used for the singular experiences of fear and of awe. . . . *The Duties of the Heart* makes this very point: 'The fear of Heaven has two aspects: the fear of tribulations and Divine retribution, and the awe of His Glory, majesty, and awesome power.'"[1]

In other words, fear and awe can be two separate traits completely, or they can be merged together. Many Mussar teachers encourage us to "orient ourselves toward the side of fear,"[2] especially of divine retribution for our transgressions. The *middah* is clearly about fear in the writings of the Mussar masters, as the words that often accompany this concept involve physical manifestations of fear: people shaking, sweating, quaking, and experiencing some kind of terror. Many people resonate to this idea that we should be fearful of God's retribution for our own wrongdoing and that that fear will keep us on the right path.

However, Jacob is a model of another kind of *yirah*. Jacob is fearful, and rightly so. Not only has he done wrong in the eyes of God, but he has wronged his brother, who may understandably be hurt and angry with him. Jacob moves beyond his fear, symbolized by the wrestling he does with a man (perhaps his conscience?) throughout the night. When we have wronged someone, we, too, must take that fear of what may become of us, either through divine punishment or the anger of the person we have harmed, and turn it into something more productive.

Rabbi Yitzchak Blazer, in his book, *The Gates of Light*, writes that the experience associated with awe is the higher form of *yirah*, saying, "It is clear that the awe of God's majesty is on a more exalted plane than the fear of future accountability."[3] He teaches that awe must stand on a foundation of fear. So, perhaps, to get to awe, we must first go through the fear of punishment, work through it in some way, to get to the other side of it, much like Jacob crossing the River Jabbok, wrestling with a man, and then and only then being able to feel the awe for God that leads him to build a monument.

Rabbi Moshe Chayim Luzzatto teaches us to redirect our fear from retribution to the fear of our own missteps. All human beings have the innate possibility of following the urge to do good, *yetzer tov*, or the inclination to do bad, *yetzer hara*. Luzzatto's teaching is a powerful reminder for us to try to move toward the good and to fear our own capacity to do wrong rather than fearing God.

Mussar teaches us to recognize in ourselves the traits, or *middot*, such as *yirah*, so that we can analyze where on the spectrum we may find ourselves at any given time. Sometimes, we may move toward more fear. At other times, we may move toward awe. Each could be valuable in our lives for different reasons.

Fear can move us away from our base urges. Awe can inspire us to find gratitude and blessing. Rabbi Abraham Joshua Heschel taught about awe as the beginning of wisdom:

> The meaning of awe is to realize that life takes place under wide horizons, horizons that range beyond the span of an individual life or even the life of a nation, a generation, or an era. Awe enables us to perceive in the world intimations of the divine, to sense in small things the beginning of infinite significance, to sense the ultimate in the common and the simple; to feel in the rush of the passing the stillness of the eternal.[4]

When we feel the fear of something that is greater than our humanity and more powerful, we also become aware of our own mortality and limitations. Only then can we move into gratitude for the blessings that we do have.

It is taught that we should say one hundred blessings a day.[5] In order to do so, we must constantly focus on saying a blessing each time we do something. I once challenged a group of students to do this. Then, when we came together again, we reviewed our experiences. It completely changed the way they experienced the world.

Instead of running from one thing to the next, fearful of missing something or that they would not get all of their daily routines done, their experience was transformed into one of gratitude for the myriad blessings around them.

Jacob reminds us that in our own lives we can live looking back over our shoulders, worried about the consequences of our wrongdoing; or we can hold on tight to the present moment, struggle with whatever life gives us, and then try to move ourselves toward the *middah* of awe. We can let the beauty and blessing in our lives inspire us, help us feel grateful, and, like Jacob, feel truly blessed.

Questions to Ask

Has there been a time that you have felt true fear that changed to something else, and if so, how did that change within you happen?

When you think of the *middah* of *yirah*, do you first associate it with fear or with something closer to awe? How are those two qualities linked for you?

Practice for the *Middah* of *Yirah*

Think of a moment of true fear that you have experienced. Trace the source of fear, the change in you physically, and how you were able to overcome that sense of fear.

Another *Middah* to Consider

Consider how Jacob moves from fear to gratitude (הַכָּרַת הַטּוֹב, *hakarat hatov*). The pending confrontation with his estranged brother and the guilt he feels for past wrongdoing first evoke fear in Jacob, as does the encounter with the messenger of God. Yet, after the wrestling in the night, Jacob turns to gratitude, as he is blessed by God during what is an otherwise frightening time.

NOTES

1. Alan Morinis, *Everyday Holiness: The Jewish Spiritual Path of Mussar* (Boston: Trumpeter, 2007), 233.
2. Ibid., 234.
3. Quoted in ibid., 235.
4. Abraham Joshua Heschel, *God in Search of Man: A Philosophy of Judaism* (New York: Farrar, Straus and Giroux, 1955), 75.
5. *Shulchan Aruch, Orach Chayim* 46:3.

Rachamim—Compassion and the Lack Thereof

RABBI BARRY H. BLOCK

RABBI EUGENE BOROWITZ and Francine Weinman Schwartz write, "Compassion for another stems from a gentle stirring of the soul."[1] *Parashat Vayeishev* presents us with stories that exemplify stunning acts of *rachamim* (רַחֲמִים, "compassion") but also glaring failures of kindness.

Joseph lacks *rachamim* when he conveys a negative report about his brothers' behavior to his father at the portion's outset (Genesis 37:2) and when he recounts his grandiose dreams to them (Genesis 37: 6–9). His brothers certainly do not respond with compassion when they conspire to kill him (Genesis 37:19–20) or, later, when they sell him into slavery (Genesis 37:26–28).

We may have an easier time forgiving Reuben than advocating for the other brothers. As the oldest of Jacob's children, Reuben has a reason to resent Joseph. Reuben is the rightful owner of the double portion of inheritance that ultimately flows to Joseph instead. Nevertheless, at a critical moment in our *parashah*, Reuben stands up to his brothers to save Joseph's life. Just as the brothers are about to kill Joseph, Reuben protests, suggesting that they throw him in a pit rather than spilling his blood themselves. The Torah goes on to tell us that Reuben intends to return, retrieve Joseph from the pit, and restore him to Jacob (Genesis 37:22).

What is Reuben's motivation? Rashi suggests that Reuben is no hero and that he merely wishes to escape blame: "He thought, 'I am the firstborn, the oldest of them. This whole mess will be pinned on me.'"[2]

Nachmanides opines that Reuben is demonstrating compassion for his brothers who would be murderers, not for Joseph: "Notice that [Reuben] does not say, 'Do not shed his blood,' which may would convey concern for Joseph. Instead, he tells them not to become 'shedders of blood,' incidentally teaching them that the punishment for causing death indirectly is less than that for shedding blood with one's own hands."[3]

David Kimchi, on the other hand, reads Reuben's words as evidence of Reuben's compassion for Joseph: "'Do not shed blood!' It would be innocent blood. He does not deserve to die. As much as he hurt you with his dreams, you hurt him, too."[4]

If Reuben seeks to save Joseph's life in order to spare himself from culpability (Rashi's interpretation), he is not to be commended for compassion. By contrast, if he is eager to save Joseph's life, even if merely to spare his other brothers the consequences of their evil intent (Nachmanides's interpretation), he is acting compassionately.

We find our answer in the next scene. Reuben returns to the pit, apparently to rescue Joseph and take him home. He finds the pit empty and presumes Joseph to be dead, not knowing that Judah and the others have sold Joseph into slavery. Reuben's palpable distress (Genesis 37:30) testifies to his compassion not for himself or his brothers, but for Joseph.

"Compassion," Alan Morinis writes, "is a deep emotional feeling arising out of identification with the other that seeks a concrete expression. Compassion flows between equals or from the more powerful to the less powerful."[5] Though the tables will later turn, Reuben as the eldest is the most powerful among the brothers at this point in the narrative. Instead of using that power to strike his bothersome little brother, he marshals his position to save Joseph's life.

Later events in our portion offer further opportunities for biblical characters to behave compassionately toward other characters in positions of power or not to do so. Their responses are instructive.

Tamar has a rough life. Widowed twice through no fault of her own (Genesis 38:6–10), her father-in-law Judah nevertheless treats her as if she were a "black widow," responsible for her husbands' deaths.[6] Judah sends Tamar to live in her own father's house, offloading his own responsibility to support his sons' widow. Judah does promise that he will ultimately fulfill his duty by marrying Tamar off to his third son, Shelah, as soon as the boy reaches adulthood (Genesis 38:11).

Time passes. Shelah is grown, but Judah does not send for Tamar (Genesis 38:12–14). Afraid that she might bring about the death of his third son if he permits a marriage between Shelah and Tamar, Judah denies Tamar any semblance of *rachamim*. We may better understand Judah's indifference to Tamar's suffering if we remember that he is wallowing in sorrow after the deaths of his two older sons, whose demise he blithely attributes to Tamar. As Morinis explains, "A habitual ego-bound perspective gives rise to the well-ingrained tendency to look at others with eyes of judgment. What appears before us when we look at another in this way are that person's accumulated deeds and habits as they stand right now, which we judge from our own vantage point."[7]

Judah, in this judging posture, holds power over Tamar. He would be responsible for her financial well-being had he not divested himself of that role. He controls her ability to remarry, which he withholds by insisting that she "settle as a widow" until he marries her to Shelah, which he has no intention of doing.[8] He condemns her to financial dependency at the mercy of her father and brothers, to loneliness, and to childlessness.

Once she realizes that Judah does not intend to make Shelah her third husband, Tamar develops and executes a plan. She disguises herself as a prostitute and stations herself at a place where Judah will encounter her—a place that also happens to be the spot where prostitutes would sit and wait for customers. In return for her sexual favors, Judah promises to send a kid from his flock. Like the clever prostitute she pretends to be, Tamar does not take him at his word, but demands that he leave his seal, cord, and staff as collateral. Eventually, word gets back to Judah, who is enraged when he learns that his daughter-in-law has resorted to prostitution and that she is pregnant. He seeks to have her burned to death, but as he approaches her, she produces the seal, cord, and staff and tells him, "The man to whom these belong made me pregnant" (Genesis 38:14–25).

With this change of events, the power dynamic between Judah and Tamar becomes much more complicated. On the one hand, Judah may insist that Tamar face capital punishment for her alleged prostitution and illicit pregnancy. On the other hand, Tamar now has evidence that would enable her expose Judah's wrongdoing.

Rashi notes, though, that Tamar does not say, "You made me pregnant." Instead, in an act of *rachamim*, kindness that Judah has not earned, she gives him the opportunity to confess his wrongdoing or not. Rashi even suggests that she is willing to suffer the consequences of her morally questionable action rather than embarrassing her father-in-law.[9]

Judah responds with kindness, employing his power to bestow compassion upon Tamar, saying, "She is more in the right than I" (Genesis 38:26). He understands that his own lack of responsibility and blindness to her suffering have forced Tamar to prostitute herself and to trick him into a pregnancy—her entry ticket to a life of safety and dignity.

Both Tamar and Judah overcome the wrong done to them, and their *rachamim* leads to their and our future redemption: the child with whom Tamar is pregnant is Peretz, the very same whom we later come to know as an ancestor of King David—and, we may pray, one day, with God's compassion, also of the messianic redeemer (Ruth 4:18–22).

Sadly, a lack of compassion on the part of those in power dominates the balance of our *parashah*.

Sold into Egyptian bondage, Joseph finds himself enslaved to "Potiphar, one of Pharaoh's officers" (Genesis 39:1). Joseph lives the slave's version of a charmed life, blessed by God and favored by his Egyptian master (Genesis 39:2–6), until Potiphar's unnamed wife seeks to seduce him. Joseph's continued refusal to give in to her sexual demands is particularly commendable, considering that he, as a slave, is subjected to sexual harassment at the hands of a woman who holds power over him (Genesis 39:7–10).[10] Nevertheless, in this instance, the person in power, Potiphar's wife, employs that position of influence to accuse Joseph of attempted rape and consign him to the dungeon (Genesis 39:11–20).

In the dungeon, Joseph again finds himself on the receiving end of divine grace. He achieves an exalted position—while still being, of course, an imprisoned slave in jail (Genesis 39:21–22). There, Joseph meets two of Pharaoh's courtiers who have run afoul of their master and been thrown into prison. One night, the minister of baking and the minister of drinking experience disturbing dreams. Compassionately, Joseph takes note of their distress. They explain, "We each dreamt a dream, but there is no one to interpret it" (Genesis 40:1–8). Joseph then interprets their dreams with startling accuracy (Genesis 40:12–22).

Joseph, the prison slave, has but one request, which he addresses to the minister of drinking when the latter is to be restored to his post at Pharaoh's side: "Only call me to mind when it goes well for you, and keep faith with me: commend me to Pharaoh and get me out of this place!" (Genesis 40:14). However, the courtier, so recently rendered powerless in jail, strives to forget his misfortune and Joseph along with it, as soon as he is restored to power (Genesis 40:23). Joseph continues to languish in prison.[11]

Parashat Vayeisheiv offers us multiple examples of biblical characters in positions of power who offer *rachamim*—compassion that is sometimes earned and sometimes not—to others. We learn that positions of power offer opportunities to do grave harm, but that they also provide occasions for compassion so great that it saves a human life or even the whole world.

Questions to Ask

When has "a habitual ego-bound perspective" (Alan Morinis, as quoted above) gotten in your way of practicing *rachamim*?

In what way have you practiced *rachamim* in encounters in which you were in the more powerful position; and in what way have you practiced *rachamim* in encounters in which you were less powerful?

Practice for the *Middah* of *Rachamim*

Identify a person in your life over whom you exercise power; plan and execute an act of *rachamim* toward that person. Then, identify a person who exercises power over you, and carry out an act of *rachamim* toward that person, too.

Another *Middah* to Consider

When Joseph learns that Pharaoh's courtiers in his custody are troubled by dreams, he says, "Surely interpretations are in God's domain; but go ahead and tell them to me" (Genesis 40:8). Evaluate Joseph's *anavah* (עֲנָוָה—"humility") embedded in these words.

NOTES

1. Eugene B. Borowitz and Frances Weinman Schwartz, *The Jewish Moral Virtues* (Philadelphia: Jewish Publication Society, 1999), 69.
2. Rashi on Genesis 37:21.
3. Nachmanides on Genesis 37:22.
4. Kimchi on Genesis 37:22.
5. Alan Morinis, *Everyday Holiness: The Jewish Spiritual Path of Mussar* (Boston: Trumpeter, 2007), 82.
6. Rashi on Genesis 38:11.
7. Morinis, *Everyday Holiness*, 83.
8. Rashi on Genesis 38:11.
9. Rashi on Genesis 38:25.
10. Elana Stein Hain, "On Gender, Sexuality, and Derech Eretz," Rabbinic Torah Study Seminar, Shalom Hartman Institute, July 11, 2018.
11. Rashi on Genesis 40:23.

MIKEITZ—GENESIS 41:1–44:17

Emunah—Faith: A Pathway to Patience, Courage, and Acceptance

RABBI LISA D. GRANT, PhD

WHEN WE FIRST MEET JOSEPH in *Parashat Vayeishev*, he is a spoiled and overindulged teenager who flaunts his privilege over his brothers. Though he speaks the truth of his dreams to his brothers, he does so without tact or thought as to how his interpretations may be heard. From the perspective of Mussar, his *yetzer hara* (יֵצֶר הָרָע, "the evil inclination"), which can be understood as the impulse to habitually act selfishly, is more dominant that his *yetzer tov* (יֵצֶר טוֹב, "the good inclination"), the impulse to act with sensitivity and self-awareness. This imbalance produces disastrous consequences. Joseph's brothers throw him into a pit and then sell him into slavery. In *Parashat Mikeitz*, however, Joseph is transformed. Joseph the dreamer becomes a skillful interpreter of dreams. This transformation leads to his salvation and the acquisition of great power, position, and wealth.

The key difference between the Joseph who taunts his brothers in *Parashat Vayeishev* and the more mature and humble Joseph of *Mikeitz* is that he has developed a steadfast faith in God, which helps him to become more aware of the consequences of his actions. His maturation takes place over time, only starting with the time he spends in Potiphar's house when he resists the attempted seduction by Potiphar's wife. Though he is wrongly accused and thrown into prison, he holds fast to his faith, as we see in Genesis 40:8, when Joseph interprets the dreams of his cellmates, the royal baker and the cupbearer.

Here, he says, "Surely interpretations are in God's domain; but go ahead and tell them to me." Joseph correctly predicts the fate of each servant, and the cupbearer, who goes free, promises to remember Joseph to Pharaoh. Yet, as *Vayeishev* closes, we read that the cupbearer has forgotten, and Joseph continues to languish in prison.

Parashat Mikeitz then opens with Pharaoh's dreams, which none of Pharaoh's magicians or priests can interpret. Witnessing their failure, the cupbearer finally remembers Joseph—who is bathed, shaved, clothed, and summoned to interpret Pharaoh's dreams. Immediately, Joseph says, "Not I—it is God who will account for Pharaoh's well-being" (Genesis 41:16). As he offers the details of his interpretation, Joseph repeatedly gives the credit to God, both for his skill and for the content of the dreams. Pharaoh is wowed and exclaims, "Is there anyone like this to be found, a man with *ruach Elohim bo* (רוּחַ אֱלֹהִים בּוֹ, the spirit of God in him)"? (Genesis 41:38).

Abravanel, a fifteenth-century Portuguese commentator, asks us to ponder an open-ended question: What does Pharaoh see in Joseph that leads him to say that he possesses the spirit of God, even before his interpretations come to pass?[1] Is it simply Joseph's repeated mention that everything is unfolding according to God's plan and that he himself is merely the messenger? Or is it because Joseph offers a clear and manageable strategy to stave off the worst? The Netziv, a nineteenth-century Polish commentator, notes that it is precisely these specific details that make Joseph's interpretation so believable.[2] Throughout the narrative, we read that God is with Joseph, and Joseph professes his faith in God, at his darkest times and in his successes.[3] Through his travails, Joseph grows in his practice of *emunah*, "faith," in God. Because of Joseph's faith, Pharaoh trusts him and decides to elevate him to be the chief architect and administrator over all of Egypt.

The cynical among us might think that at this high-stakes moment, Joseph invokes God to deflect attention away from himself, in case Pharaoh would lash out in anger because he predicts a great famine. Yet, Bachya ibn Pakuda, eleventh-century author of *Duties of the Heart*, the first codification of Jewish ethical teachings, notes that faith in God does not mean you should avoid making decisions that result in personal benefit. In a rough paraphrase, he writes that with the clear conviction that affairs are given over to the decrees of the Creator and that the Creator's choice is the best choice, one must pursue means beneficial to oneself and choose what appears to be the best [course of action] in the matter.[4] Joseph's *emunah* leads to a good outcome for himself and all of Egypt.

In the biblical tradition, faithfulness merits divine reward. We see this first with the aged and childless Abram, who sees God in a vision just before he is about to bequeath his wealth to a member of his household. God promises Abram that his seed will be as numerous as the stars in heaven, "And [Abram] put his trust in the Eternal, who reckoned that as loyalty in him" (Genesis 15:6), and he became a father to Isaac. Just like Abram, Joseph learns to trust in God, even in his darkest moments, which eventually leads to his success.

Rabbi David Jaffe draws a direct link between the *middah* of faith in God and an individual's trustworthiness when he describes *emunah* as "that quality of reliability that we engender in others through our sustained honesty and consideration."[5] Joseph becomes trustworthy as an interpreter and as viceroy of Egypt because he has put his trust in God. Thus, he indeed merits Pharaoh's claim that he is endowed with *ruach Elohim*, "the spirit of God."

Bezalel, another key biblical character, is also endowed with *ruach Elohim*. Both he and Joseph can be seen as creators, planners, and builders. Bezalel is entrusted with the design and construction of the *Mishkan*, the portable Tabernacle the Israelites use throughout their wanderings in the wilderness to ensure their spiritual survival. In a parallel move, Joseph builds storehouses for grain to assure Egypt's physical survival. These two biblical characters' *emunah* makes them trustworthy servants and allows the creative work of their hands to flourish.

So how do we translate this lesson for our own lives?

Many of us today may struggle with the kind of faith in God

described in the biblical narrative. Does God truly reward those who believe with *emunah sh'leimah* (אֱמוּנָה שְׁלֵמָה), with "complete" or "perfect faith"? Perhaps our answer to this question depends on how we understand "reward." Faith may not help if material gain is our end goal. Still, if we are seeking to lead a good life, to make good choices, and do what is right and just in the eyes of our loved ones, our community, and God, then faith can play a determining role. Cultivating faith can lead to greater patience, courage in facing hardship and the unknown, and acceptance that so much in life is beyond our control.

Emunah is often confused with "belief." "Faith" is not something to be understood intellectually or rationally; rather it needs to be learned from experience and deep reflection. Faith is not static. Like all other *middot*, it needs to be practiced and renewed constantly. One can grow in faith and one can lose faith. Faith can be seen as a kind of religious courage, as Rabbi Shai Held writes, as "knowing God whether or not one sees Him."[6]

As in the case of other *middot*, we may not see the immediate benefit of cultivating our faith. The inner work of listening for the divine voice as we strive to make good choices takes time. However, the moment we make a choice is the moment in which we consciously negotiate between our inclination to do good (our *yetzer tov*) and our inclination to give into bad habits and irresponsible behavior (our *yetzer hara*). This act of ethical decision-making is at the heart of Mussar. And when we make our decisions in light of the question "How is the divine manifest in me, through me, with me, in this moment?" we are acting in faith.

Questions to Ask

The Babylonian Talmud, in *Shabbat* 31a, connects *emunah* to *Seder Z'raim* (the Mishnaic "order" dealing with agriculture). Rashi explains that for the farmer, faith in God is a prerequisite to planting. Lack of *emunah* leads to stunted growth and even regression.

> What seeds do you need to plant in yourself in order to
> cultivate *emunah*?

How does your experience of the Divine help to shape your choices?

What happens when you stop and ask yourself, where is God for me in this moment? How does asking that question shape your understanding and experience of what may happen?

What are some times in your life when you have felt that *emunah* has helped you to overcome an obstacle or to cope with a challenge?

Practice for the *Middah* of *Emunah*

In the course of daily life, we often find ourselves in difficult or frustrating situations. It could be something as ordinary as waiting in line for a long time or as complex as trying to overcome a thorny problem with a loved one, friend, or coworker. When such moments arise, stop, take a few breaths, and wait a moment before acting. Ask yourself the following question: "How can I respond in this moment with trust and integrity?" Remember, as it says in Proverbs 28:20, "A person of *emunah* is filled with blessings."

Another *Middah* to Consider

M'chilah (מְחִילָה, "forgiveness"): In the latter half of *Parashat Mikeitz*, the sons of Jacob come down to Egypt to buy provisions for their families starving in Canaan. They come before Joseph, whom they do not recognize as their brother. Joseph does not reveal his identity to his brothers. In an elaborate ruse, he plays a trick on them that seems at first to be cruel, but ultimately leads to *t'shuvah* and forgiveness. While we may disapprove of Joseph's manipulative approach, his strategy does allow his brothers' characters to develop, with Judah emerging as a leader with integrity.

Miketz ends mid-story, before Joseph tells his brothers who he is. Several chapters later, he does so with tremendous emotion and assurance, saying, "Don't be troubled, don't be chagrined because you sold me here, for it was to save lives that God sent me ahead of you" (Genesis 45:5). Through these words, Joseph again demonstrates *emunah* and also *m'chilah* ("forgiveness"). First, though, Joseph needs to forgive. At the end of a process, all gain a deeper sense of who they are, and all find some healing of past hurts and harm. How and when we forgive is never a simple matter, but the act of forgiveness almost always relieves a burden on our heart, opening up a possibility for repair and return.

NOTES

1. Abravanel on Genesis 41:38.
2. Netziv, *HaAmeik Davar* on Genesis 41:38.
3. See, for example, Genesis 39:3–5, 39:21–23, 40:8, 41:16, 41:51–52, 42:18, 45:5–8.
4. Bachya ben Joseph ibn Pakuda, *Duties of the Heart*, trans. David Haberman (Feldheim Publishers: Jerusalem and New York, 1996), 401.
5. Rabbi David Jaffe, Tikkun Middot Project Curriculum, Institute for Jewish Spirituality, 147.
6. Shai Held, "On Faith Beyond Perception: The Slonimer Rebbe," in *Jewish Mysticism and the Spiritual Life: Classical Texts, Contemporary Reflections*, ed. Lawrence Fine, Eitan Fishbane, and Or N. Rose (Woodstock, VT: Jewish Lights, 2011), 213.

VAYIGASH—GENESIS 44:18–47:27
Bitachon—Several Models of Trust

RABBI TED RITER

PRIOR TO THE OPENING of *Parashat Vayigash*, Judah's youngest brother Benjamin is found with Joseph's silver cup, which has been secretly planted in his bag. As the new *parashah* begins, Judah approaches his long-lost brother Joseph, whom he still believes to be like Pharaoh. In this new portion, we hear Judah's plea to the disguised Joseph to free Benjamin and thereby prevent the anticipated anguish of their father Jacob. In fact, Judah even offers himself as a replacement for his brother.

I can feel the tension grow as I read his words, "By your leave, my lord, please give your servant a hearing, and do not let your anger flare up at your servant" (Genesis 44:18). I can imagine Judah's heart beating out of his chest, the perspiration starting to show on his face, and the shortening of his breath as he begins to plea for his youngest brother's freedom and life. Or perhaps this is simply a projection of the anxiety I would feel in a similar situation. Perhaps Judah had such great *bitachon* (בִּטָּחוֹן, "trust") that the conversation he was entering barely fazed him.

JOSEPH

Bitachon, traditionally understood as trust in God, is a constant theme throughout the Book of Genesis, and especially apparent in this *parashah*. Mussar sages take at least two approaches to *bitachon*. The Alter of Novardok, Rabbi Yosef Yuzel Horowitz (1847–1919), teaches that *bitachon* is a deep knowing that God delivers what we need in each moment.[1] From this perspective, Judah could have believed it would all work out for good, while he was speaking to Joseph.

On the other hand, the Chazon Ish, Rabbi Abraham Isaiah Kare-litz (1878–1953), teaches that everything we experience in this world has greater meaning, even if it is not immediately or ever apparent to us.[2] From this perspective, Judah could have believed that even if things would not work out for the immediate good, God would ulti-mately provide.

The classic interpretation of this story is that Joseph keeps his identity hidden to test his brothers.[3] Have they grown emotionally since selling him into slavery? Have they developed more compas-sion for their father, more fidelity toward their brothers, more integ-rity as men? This reading brings into question Joseph's *bitachon*. If he trusts that all will be for good, would he need to test his brothers?

JOSEPH'S BROTHERS

The question can be turned to the brothers as well. Is Judah express-ing his *bitachon* in this moment? Does he know that Joseph will refuse his offer? Does he truly worry that leaving Benjamin behind in Egypt will cause the death of his father? Why does he not trust in God to provide help for Benjamin?

Not being able to hold back any longer, Joseph finally reveals him-self: "I am Joseph your brother, whom you sold to Egypt; and now, don't be troubled, don't be chagrined because you sold me here, for it was to save lives that God sent me ahead of you" (Genesis 45:4–5). Not in vain have they sold him into slavery in Egypt! Or, as the Cha-zon Ish will later teach, everything we experience is for good!

Imagine hearing that message: "You, brothers, took out your ret-ribution on me. Out of jealousy and anger and a whole host of other emotions, you threw me into a pit and sold me into slavery. You sent our father into mourning at the loss of me, his favorite son. You caused untold angst for yourselves as you dealt with the shame of your actions. And yet, you could not have known this was all part of a divine plan."[4]

I can imagine a whiplash of the brothers' emotions from an ear-lier anxiety to a stunned disbelief. How can this be happening? And, can they trust that they will really be safe in Joseph's care? This, too, becomes a test of their *bitachon*.

The brothers are sent back to Canaan to gather their father, families, and livestock. As a gesture of generosity from Joseph, or to convince those in Canaan that the move to Egypt would be safe, they are given treasures, food, and clothing for their journey.

JACOB

On their way down to Egypt, Jacob offers a sacrifice to the "God of his father Isaac" in Beersheba (Genesis 46:1). The text does not clarify the intention of this sacrifice. Is it an offering of gratitude? Is it offered out of anxiety, expressing hope that all will go well?

Jacob is a tested veteran of life, highlighted by his name change from Jacob to Israel—transitioning from the "one who catches" into "the one who struggles with God." And yet, here again, God senses that he lacks *bitachon* and needs reassurance: "I am God, the God of your father; do not be afraid to go down to Egypt, for I will make you a great people there. I Myself will go down with you to Egypt, and I will most surely bring you back up as well; and Joseph will lay his hand upon your eyes" (Genesis 46:3–4).

A TRUST-INSPIRING GENEALOGY

To bring home the point that everything will work out in the end, the text continues with twenty verses devoted to the genealogy of Jacob's descendants. Perhaps the authors of this text themselves need reassurance, or want to reassure the doubtful readers, that God's words are indeed true. This genealogy, largely skipped by many readers of this text, hides perhaps one of the greatest reasons to live with *bitachon*.

While most world religions and traditions focus on perfection and deity-like humans, Judaism recognizes that we all have our flaws, sometimes show a lack of integrity, and perform actions we would prefer to ignore or hide. This is apparent in *Vayigash*, too. Jacob, once the trickster, has been worthy of being renamed "Israel" and now of being reunited with his son Joseph. Jacob is redeemed from starvation, the crushing loss of his son, and perhaps even the anguish of knowing the truth that Joseph was sold by his brothers. Jacob, with all of his faults, is worthy of a relationship with God and his place in the divine plan.

The brothers are given descendants, even after their mistreatment of Joseph and Judah's mistreatment of Tamar (Genesis 38). Joseph is promised a lineage, even while indenturing Egyptians during the famine. These brothers too are worthy of divine guidance. The ultimate reason to live with *bitachon* may therefore be the knowledge that as flawed as you and I are today, we are all part of a divine plan for good.

A NEW LIFE IN EGYPT

The narrative picks up again with Joseph reuniting with Jacob and the entire family. Here, Joseph counsels his relatives to tell Pharaoh that they are "breeders of livestock" rather than shepherds, because "Egyptians find shepherds abhorrent" (Genesis 46:34). Is this also a break in Joseph's *bitachon*? Can he not trust that his family will be safe if they speak the truth? Strangely, though, Joseph then tells Pharaoh that they are indeed both livestock herders and shepherds. Does he gather *bitachon* between the two encounters?

In any event, the brothers dismiss Joseph's advice altogether. When questioned by Pharaoh, the brothers offer, "Your servants are shepherds, both our households and our fathers' households" (Genesis 47:3). Is this an effort by the brothers to regain their integrity after creating the tremendous lie of Joseph's death? Is this an act of *bitachon* that has the brothers ignoring Joseph's instructions and putting their fate in the hands of Pharaoh and ultimately God? Or has Joseph told them that Pharaoh did not respond unfavorably to learning that they are shepherds?

Pharaoh directs them to the best land, Goshen, but ignores the fact that they are shepherds and offers them livestock to oversee. May we read Pharaoh's response as evidence that he could indeed be trusted, not only with the fact that they had been shepherds, but to transition them gently into a line of work that would be better received in Egypt?

The *parashah* ends, *Vayeishev Yisrael b'eretz Mitzrayim b'eretz Goshen vayei-achazu vah vayifru vayirbu m'od* (וַיֵּשֶׁב יִשְׂרָאֵל בְּאֶרֶץ מִצְרַיִם בְּאֶרֶץ גֹּשֶׁן וַיֵּאָחֲזוּ בָהּ וַיִּפְרוּ וַיִּרְבּוּ מְאֹד), "Israel thus settled in the land of Egypt, in the region of Goshen. They struck roots in it, were fruitful and multiplied greatly" (Genesis 47:27). After all the trials and tribulations, our ancestors have truly arrived in Egypt.

This happy ending is perhaps one of the greatest lessons of the entire patriarchal-matriarchal narrative: Everything that happens, happens for the best. Without the family's descent into Egypt at the end of Genesis, there would be no enslavement, no foundational Exodus story, no experience at Mount Sinai, and no eventual return to the Land of Israel.

I like to see the practice of Mussar as akin to practicing any new dance step, swing of a racket, or karate punch—it's about creating muscle memory for the soul. We exercise a *middah* muscle when things are good, safe, and controlled, when there is no famine and when we are thriving in the land. Then, in a time of need, when we are Judah standing before our rediscovered brother Joseph and tension is growing, we can call on our *bitachon* muscle with more surety and ease and thus ensure a future of prosperity and peace.

A Question to Ask

When have you doubted a good outcome, only to look back and recognize the value of the experience?

Practice for the *Middah* of *Bitachon*

Note the unexpected turns of events in your life, and give thanks for bringing you to this moment.

Other *Middot* to Consider

G'vurah (גְּבוּרָה, "strength"): Joseph's strength to hold his composure while he tested his brothers.

Rachamim (רַחֲמִים, "mercy"): Joseph's compassion for the dire plight of his brothers and family.

NOTES

1. Daniel Stein, "The Limits of Religious Optimism: The Hazon Ish and the Alter of Novardok on *Bittahon*" in *Tradition: A Journal of Orthodox Jewish Thought*, vol. 43, no. 2, Summer 2010, pp. 31–48.
2. Ibid.
3. See, for example, the Ramban on Genesis 42:6.
4. My midrashic dialogue that could have happened.

VA-Y'CHI—GENESIS 47:28–50:26

Emet—Truth:
Truth and Its Consequences

RABBI BRETT R. ISSEROW

How could he say that? Did Jacob, on his deathbed, really tell his oldest son Reuben that he would "boil up like water" and not excel (Genesis 49:4), and say to Simeon and Levi that he will "disperse them in Jacob, scatter them in Israel" (Genesis 49:7)? Did he call Dan "a snake on the road, a horned serpent on the path biting the horse's heel so its rider tumbles backwards" (Genesis 49:17), and Benjamin "a wolf that rends, in the morning devouring the booty, in the evening dividing the spoil" (Genesis 49:27)?

For Jacob, a person who is often considered to have excelled in deceit, this brutal honesty and frank level of truth-telling appears to be out of character. However, to dismiss his last words to his sons as an aberration contrary to his lifelong reputation for deviousness is to do Jacob a serious injustice.

As we look back over Jacob's life, we see that he wrestles with the truth and its consequences far more frequently than he does with angels. At almost every stage of this saga, "the truth" causes Jacob pain and suffering, either because of his own forthright honesty or because he listens to and believes someone he thinks is telling him the truth.

According to Rabbi Menachem Mendel Levin of Satanov,[1] truth should never be mitigated. In his classic *Cheshbon HaNefesh*, he begins his section on truth with the statement "Lying is a most despicable spiritual illness." He proceeds to condemn any form of falsehood, including flattery, mockery, hypocrisy and slander. Instead, he urges us to work hard at becoming lovers of truth "until our eyes are opened

and we see the beauty of truth, how precious it is to [God] who spoke
and the world came about, who is known as the God of truth."[1]

Most *middot* can be expressed in terms of a continuum. We strive
to achieve a balance somewhere along the line. Instinctively, we
would think that the spectrum of truth would have as its polarities
absolute truth and falsehood. Indeed, Rabbi Levin describes truth as
an absolute value.

By contrast, Alan Morinis teaches, "The Mussar tradition offers
us more mature and down-to-earth guidance based on the recognition that in this complex life, different values can compete with one
another in any situation, and literal truth isn't always meant to be the
victor. It is given over to us, in our humanity, to use our judgment to
define truth and to decide how to apply it."[2] Morinis here suggests
that the continuum may range from sharing to not sharing that truth
with ourselves and others. We must consider when to share, when
not to, as well as how to tell the truth while at the same time mitigat-
ing the consequences that sharing might cause.

If we examine Jacob's life from this point of view, we find that his
struggle revolves around his implicit honesty and his inability to discern when it is best to speak the blatant truth, when to mitigate and
soften it, and when to keep silent.

As a youth he supposedly tricks Esau into giving up his birthright.
Yet there is nothing deceitful in his exchange of pottage for Esau's
birthright (Genesis 25:29–34). Jacob demands and Esau freely relin-
quishes his privileged inheritance for a plate of food. Esau is fully
aware of what he is doing. Only in hindsight does it become apparent
that Esau believes that Jacob took unfair advantage of his weakened
state, fueling his resentment of and anger toward Jacob.

Jacob seems to be unaware of the long-term consequences of his
actions in this scenario. However, the same cannot be said for his
participation in Rebekah's plan to deceive Isaac into giving Jacob the
blessing that is meant for Esau. After listening to Rebekah's instructions Jacob says, "Should my father feel me I will seem to him like
a cheat, and I will bring a curse on myself, not a blessing!" Rebecca
answers, "Any curse that you will get will be on me, son—just listen

to me" (Genesis 27:12–13). He believes she is telling the truth and goes through with the plan; as a result, he is forced to flee for his life in the face of Esau's now murderous anger.

The pattern of the explicit declaration of a truth and then having to suffer its painful repercussions repeats itself throughout Jacob's life. He openly declares his love for Rachel and, after seven years of unpaid work, ends up with both Leah and Rachel and seven further years of unremunerated labor (Genesis 29:15–27). Over a decade and a half later, when Jacob flees Haran without informing Laban in advance, their ensuing verbal confrontation—during which they trade their honest, but hardly flattering, opinions of each other—results in the permanent severing of their relationship (Genesis 31).

In addition, unaware of Rachel's subterfuge over the theft of her father's household teraphim and taking her at her word, Jacob incautiously declares, "But the one with whom you find your gods shall not live" (Genesis 31:32). Is this yet another instance of Jacob's zealous honesty coming back to haunt him? In this case, does his oath lead to the tragic death of his beloved wife, Rachel, as she dies giving birth to Benjamin some months later (Genesis 35:16–20)?

Jacob's failure to realize the consequences of his unmitigated honesty is manifest again in his clearly stated and obviously preferential love for Joseph. His action provokes a dangerous jealousy against Joseph, leading to the plot by his brothers to kill or otherwise dispose of him. And once again, Jacob is deceived by those he thought he could trust, his sons, who lie to him by feigning Joseph's death (Genesis 37:3–35).

Even at the age of 147, it appears that Jacob has not learned. As he blesses the sons of Joseph, Manasseh and Ephraim, Jacob reverses his hands, preferring the younger son over the elder and declaring, "He [Manasseh] too shall become a people, and he too shall be great. Yet his younger brother [Ephraim] shall be greater than he, and his seed shall become a multitude of nations" (Genesis 48:19). We know that Joseph was unhappy. It is not hard to imagine how Manasseh must have felt!

On his deathbed, Jacob addresses each of his sons and expresses his predictions of their future—characteristically without mitigation or taking into account what effect his words may have on them. For some, his words are short and sweet, for others mixed or harsh; but once again, his unabashed preference for Joseph is remarkably obvious by virtue of both the content and the length of his particular blessing (Genesis 49:22–26). What emotions did this clear disparity kindle within the brothers? Did it aggravate old and buried fears of retribution? Would Joseph seek revenge for all that he had suffered at the hands of his brothers?

And so, after Jacob's death and burial, the brothers send Joseph a message claiming that their father had commanded, "Please, I beg of you, forgive the transgression of your brothers and their sin, though they inflicted harm upon you" (Genesis 50:17). Do they really think that Joseph will believe this? After all, would Jacob, who insisted on brutal honesty and who never fully forgave his older children for depriving him of his beloved son, Joseph, for decades, command that son to forgive the others unconditionally?

Jacob's life reflects his consistent struggle with truth—not in terms of whether to be honest or not, but more in terms of how to share that truth with others and how to discern whether others were being truthful to him. Ultimately, "the truth does spring forth" (Psalm 85:12) from Jacob, but its consequences for him and those around him warn us to use the utmost discernment and pay careful attention as to how we share that truth.

Mussar has always emphasized honesty and truth-telling as an essential *middah*. Falsehood and deception should play no part in our relationships. But there is a further dimension to this *middah* that we regularly encounter: How often do we pause to consider how we share the truth and the consequences that our words may have on those we love and respect and who are part of the fabric of our lives? Are we too quick to share? Should we rather consider being silent? Not hitting the send button? Will our words cause more pain than the situation itself? Training ourselves to pause and reflect before talking (in any form) is part of the discipline being honest requires.

Truth is not malleable, but how we share it is!

Questions to Ask

Rabbi Levin regards truth as absolute. Still, many of us struggle with honesty, especially in regard to being totally honest with ourselves. How often does pride or self-deception eclipse honesty when we try to justify our attitudes, opinions, actions, or comments?

Are there times when we need to mitigate the truth? Is it acceptable to fudge the truth when it protects another individual from hurt or distress? How does one discern where the line between truth and dishonesty should in fact be drawn? Does that line fluctuate depending on the circumstances?

Jacob's honesty often seems unkind. Is it ever in someone's best interest to be told the full truth about their shortcomings, at least with no one else present?

Joseph appears to have forgiven his brothers. Can we learn a lesson from his actions? Does forgiving necessitate forgetting and thereafter fully trusting those we have forgiven?

Practices for the *Middah* of *Emet*

Truthfulness is without doubt the foundation of a lasting and stable relationship. It is easy to say, "Be honest and never mitigate that honesty!" but our relationships demand a much more nuanced approach.

Most of us deal with truth-telling instinctively. We blurt it out when upset or angry; we mitigate it unnecessarily or overmuch when afraid of how another person may react. Seldom do we reflect on how we share the truth.

The first part of our practice then is to do a self-assessment for a few days without attempting to change our behavior.

Once we are more aware of our tendencies, we can begin to work on the aspect of sharing. Do we have the courage to ask those we love or those we work with to change aspects of their behavior? What language do we use to do so effectively? When do we personalize the request—"I find myself getting. . . ." And when is it preferable to phrase it as a request for help—"Could you please help me to work this out . . . ?"

Some of us will need to start with minor, easily changeable things and work toward more difficult traits, while others find that they need to prioritize their approach.

Patience and forethought are crucial supplementary *middot* that together with honesty will allow us to build more complete and satisfying relationships.

Other *Middot* to Consider

N'divut (נְדִיבוּת, "generosity"): Joseph shares his material success with his brothers even though they had treated him so deplorably. More importantly, through generosity of spirit he heals the rift between them by forgiving them, proceeding to reestablish a relationship with them and eventually reconciling completely with them after their father's demise.

Kavod (כָּבוֹד, "honor"): Although the relationships between Joseph and his brothers are fraught with difficulty as a result of past actions, in this *parashah* they treat each other with *kavod*. They respond to their father's summons, accept his "blessings" with equanimity, and carry out his wishes after he dies. Joseph and his brothers also provide Jacob with the funeral and mourning period fitting for a person of great stature.

NOTES

1. Menachem Mendel Levin of Satanov, *Cheshbon HaNefesh* (1812), trans. Dovid Landesman (New York: Feldheim, 1995).
2. Ibid., 175.
3. Alan Morinis, *Everyday Holiness: The Jewish Spiritual Path of Mussar* (Boston: Trumpeter, 2007), 170.

Exodus

Ometz Lev—Moral Courage: Women of Moral Courage

RABBI AMY EILBERG

ONE OF MY TREASURED MEMORIES of my college rabbi, Al Axelrad, at Brandeis University, was his tradition of an annual "Shifrah and Pu'ah Award." Each year, on the Shabbat of *Parashat Sh'mot*, Rabbi Al announced the recipient of the prize: someone who had acted with moral courage despite potential danger to their lives or their reputations. Some of the honorees, as I recall, were international human rights heroes, like Archbishop Desmond Tutu. Others were less famous—unsung heroes who had stepped up to act on behalf of people in need, when doing so might well have endangered their personal safety and comfort.

Ever since, I have been fascinated by the story of the midwives Shifrah and Pu'ah. Who were these midwives, and what do they have to teach us about the *middah* of *ometz lev* (אֹמֶץ לֵב, "moral courage")?

Exodus 1 narrates the beginning of the Exodus story. A new Egyptian king arises, who oppresses the Israelites, perceiving them to be a threatening "other." The Egyptian taskmasters force the slaves to produce more and more labor, yet still the Israelites are fertile, making them seem even more menacing to the Egyptians. Pharaoh ordered the "Hebrew midwives," Shifrah and Pu'ah, *B'yaledchen et haIvriyot uriten al ha-ovnayim: im bein hu, vahamiten oto; v'im bat hi, vachayah* (בְּיַלֶּדְכֶן אֶת־הָעִבְרִיּוֹת וּרְאִיתֶן עַל־הָאָבְנָיִם אִם־בֵּן הוּא וַהֲמִתֶּן אֹתוֹ וְאִם־בַּת הִיא וָחָיָה), "When you deliver the Hebrew women, look at the birthstool: if it is a boy, kill him; if it is a girl, let her live" (Exodus 1:15–16).

The story continues:

> The midwives, fearing God, did not do as the king of Egypt
> had told them; they let the baby boys live. So the king of Egypt
> summoned the midwives and said to them, "Why have you done
> this thing, letting the boys live?" The midwives said to Pharaoh,
> "Because the Hebrew women are not like the Egyptian women:
> they are vigorous. Before the midwife can come to them, they
> have given birth." And God dealt well with the midwives; and
> the people multiplied and increased greatly. And [God] estab-
> lished households for the midwives, because they feared God.
> (Exodus 1:17–21)

The story has a number of fascinating features. First, the term
"Hebrew midwives" is ambiguous. Some commentaries understand
it to mean that the midwives were themselves Israelite women.[1] I
think that the context confirms the view of other commentaries,[2]
which say that these were Egyptian midwives who helped Israelite women give birth. They were Pharaoh's own subjects, whom he
expected to obey his command without question. According to this
explanation, these Egyptian women reached across national and
religious divides, feeling human and moral solidarity with their sisters, the Israelite women, in a bond stronger than their allegiance to
their own king.

A second striking feature of the text appears when Pharaoh challenges the midwives' refusal to carry out his order. He summons the
midwives and demands an explanation. Strikingly, the midwives
cry out, *Ki lo chanashim haMitzriyot halvriyot ki chayot heinah b'terem
tavo aleihen hamyaledet v'yaladu* (כִּי לֹא כַנָּשִׁים הַמִּצְרִיֹּת הָעִבְרִיֹּת כִּי־חָיוֹת
הֵנָּה בְּטֶרֶם תָּבוֹא אֲלֵהֶן הַמְיַלֶּדֶת וְיָלָדוּ), "Because the Hebrew women are
not like the Egyptian women: they are *chayot*. Before the midwife can
come to them, they have given birth" (Exodus 1:19). The word *chayot*
(from the Hebrew word *chai*) means "alive" or "vigorous," but also
"animals"—as in the Yiddish expression *vilde chaya* ("wild beasts").
In so doing, the midwives brilliantly mock Pharaoh's view that the
Israelites are subhuman creatures. Oppressors throughout time
have used this view of the "other" as less than human to justify hat-
ing, persecuting, and murdering marginalized populations.

Finally, it is noteworthy that God rewards the midwives for their courageous action. Yet we must remember that the midwives had no way of expecting such a reward in advance. In fact, it would have been more reasonable to assume that they could have been executed if Pharoah learned of their courageous (from his perspective, treasonous) action.

Thus, in a number of ways, Shifrah and Pu'ah serve as exemplars of what the Mussar masters call *ometz lev*, a fascinating phrase, literally meaning "heart strength." The phrase raises a key question for us to ponder: Is "heart strength" always positive, or can it turn into rigidity, stubbornness, or arrogance? How are we to understand the fact that the word *ometz* is also used to describe those who clench their hearts and refuse to give to the poor (Deuteronomy 15:7)?

One classic Rabbinic text about strength of spirit appears in *Pirkei Avot*: "Yehudah ben Teima says: 'Be strong like the leopard, light like the eagle, swift like the deer, and mighty like the lion to do the will of God who is in heaven.'"[3] Rabbi Yehudah ben Teima employs images for boldness, eagerness, and power from the animal world. But as human beings, we are urged to reach for these qualities only in the service of God's will, only when we act for the greater good. Not to be misunderstood, Yehudah ben Teima continues, "The brazen-faced [are bound] for *Geihinom* ['purgatory'], and [the] shamefaced [are bound] for the Garden of Eden." In these striking statements, he warns that strength of will is a complex and sometimes dangerous quality, which can easily drift into conceit and obstinacy, the very opposite of the much-praised quality of humility.

In our own lives, when we sense power and urgency arising in our hearts, how are we to know whether we are acting "for God's will," like the biblical Shifrah and Pu'ah, or whether we are motivated by desire for fame, admiration, or personal gratification? Is the surge of strength welling up in us truly righteous anger for the sake of heaven or for the sake of the world's needs, or is it coming from the powerful force of our own ego desires? How do we discern when to trust the rush of activist energy and when to pause and interrogate it?

Another clue about classical Jewish views of strength appears at the end of Psalm 27, read by traditional Jews each day from the beginning of Elul to Hoshanah Rabbah, throughout the High Holy Day season. The Psalmist cries out to us: *Kaveih el Adonai chazak v'yaameitz libecha v'kaveih el Adonai* (קַוֵּה אֶל־יהוה חֲזַק וְיַאֲמֵץ לִבֶּךָ וְקַוֵּה אֶל־יהוה), "Look to the Eternal; be strong and of good courage! O look to the Eternal!" (Psalm 27:14).

The Psalmist has been describing a range of intense experiences: mortal threats, military enemies, the death of parents, and the fear of abandonment by God. Yet after reviewing this dizzying array of challenges, he calls out an exhortation to strength and courage, surrounded by calls to "hope in God." Clearly, the strength described here is not mere physical strength, and certainly not the willfulness of the egotist. Rather, courage is described as an aspect of a trusting relationship with God.

This leads me to one of my favorite Rabbinic teachings, also in *Pirkei Avot*: "Who is heroic? One who conquers one's own impulse, as it is said, 'Better to be forbearing than mighty, to have self-control than to conquer a city' (Proverbs 16:32)."[4] This powerful teaching turns our usual understanding of "strength" inside out. Surely a person who runs into a burning building to rescue a child or rushes onto the battlefield to save a wounded comrade is heroic. But the Mishnah chooses to praise inner strength, the capacity to work skillfully with the complex energies that move in our hearts. The Mishnah suggests that it is relatively easier (for some of us) to summon physical strength. What is more difficult is responding with courage when what threatens us is the status quo, the assumptions of those around us, or the risk of speaking up when many others prefer to remain silent.

In the Mussar system, no *middah* ("quality of soul") is absolutely good or bad. Every *middah* in its extreme form can be harmful to oneself or others. The path to holiness lies in a middle way, when we experience and draw on a *middah* in a balanced way, depending on the situation.

For *ometz lev*, the key to such balance lies in the term itself. *Ometz lev* is a quality of "strength," power, and willingness to speak truth to power and to defy community expectations. But *ometz lev* is also a quality of the "heart": strength tempered by love, gentleness, and desire for the well-being of all.

We can easily err by leaning toward one extreme or the other. On the one hand, timidity in the face of moral challenge means that we miss opportunities to partner with God in the work of perfecting the world. Allowing the disapproval of others or fear of "getting it wrong" prevents us from doing the work of justice and enables the hand of those who pursue injustice. Becoming lost in fearfulness, uncertainty, or confusion makes us complicit in the evils perpetrated all around us. Lacking trust in ourselves, we fail to imagine how important our intervention can be as a response to the divine call for justice.

On the other hand, the call for justice can be an adrenaline surge, a rush of angry energy born of psychological components, disconnected from the people on whose behalf we wish to act. When we are driven by impulsive boldness that is unsoftened by the energies of the heart, we run the risk of crusading for our own glory rather than for the greater good. Such boldness is propelled by our own needs, rather than devotion to God's desires for the world.

Discerning the path of *ometz lev*, courage born of love and devotion, is a delicate dance for us, especially in times when moral challenges surround us. But the tradition gives us models and directives to guide our determination to boldly do our part in creating a more just and loving world.

Questions to Ask

What difference would it make if the midwives in the biblical text were Israelites or not? How would those different understandings of the text parallel current examples of moral courage?

88   RABBI AMY EILBERG

In our own practice, how do we distinguish between a rush
of energy that is sacred and other-directed, on the one
hand, and one that derives from our own ego needs?
When we are overwhelmed by the challenges in the world
around us, what is the best way to choose a wise response?

Practices for the *Middah* of *Ometz Lev*

The next time you are asked to engage in political action and you
jump to respond, take a moment to consider: What are the components of that excitement moving in you? Do they represent the call
of ego or the call of the sacred? Then, let your reflection guide your
response.

The next time you feel disheartened by the state of the world and
doubtful that you can contribute in any meaningful way, stop and ask
yourself: What might the biblical midwives have done? What would
moral courage look like in this situation?

Other *Middot* to Consider

Pachad (פַּחַד, "fear") versus *bitachon* (בִּטָחוֹן, "trust"), as manifest in
the Egyptians' view of the Israelites.

Rachamim (רַחֲמִים, "compassion") in the action of Pharoah's daughter and in God's hearing the cry of the Israelites.

Moshe's *hitlamdut* (הִתְלַמְּדוּת, "learning, studying, apprenticing") in
the presence of the Burning Bush.

NOTES
1. *Babylonian Talmud, Sotah* 11b, echoed in Rashi, Ibn Ezra, Rashbam, and
   Ramban.
2. Josephus, Abravanel, and Shadal (Samuel David Luzzatto). All cited in
   Nechama Leibowitz, *Studies in Shemot/Exodus*, vol. 1 (Jerusalem: World
   Zionist Organization, 1981), 34.
3. *Mishnah, Pirkei Avot* 5:20.
4. *Mishnah, Pirkei Avot* 4:1.

VA-EIRA—EXODUS 6:2–9:35

Anavah—Humility: Understanding Our Place

RABBI JOSHUA MIKUTIS

WHEN HÉLÈNE CAZÈS-BENATAR was growing up in Tangier, she showed the kind of leadership potential that educators dream of— she became the first Moroccan Jewish woman to receive a bachelor's degree. After earning a law degree from the University of Bordeaux, she became the first female lawyer in Morocco. As if these remarkable achievements were not enough, she could have never known what she would be called to do as the horrors of World War II made their way across the European continent and toward North Africa.

When World War II began, Hélène Cazès-Benatar sprang into action. She volunteered with the French Red Cross and encouraged the Jewish community to support the war effort, resulting in two thousand Moroccan Jews joining the fight against Nazism. When she found herself stuck in Casablanca, she did not admit defeat but worked with the American Jewish Joint Distribution Committee to assist the hundreds of Jewish refugees from Europe flooding the city. Embracing her full potential at an hour of need and connecting with the forces of the Jewish community, Hélène Cazès-Benatar dealt heroically with a reality previously unimaginable.[1] At every step, she forged ahead and refused to surrender to the forces and expectations outside of her.

None of us can know what we will be called to do at a later hour. The world is inherently unpredictable and capricious. As the Yiddish expression goes, "People plan; God laughs." Still, we, like Cazès-

Benatar, are able choose our paths. But when stumbling blocks are placed before us, will we forge on or will we retreat?

I want to suggest that core to navigating any uncertain time is *anavah* (עֲנָוָה, "humility"). Humility is not about lowering one's self-worth but embarking on a deep understanding of the forces that surround us, shape us, and direct our actions. And an ideal engagement with humility is not surrender but a willingness to grapple with those absurd forces beyond our control and to proactively shape our reality into the world we seek to build. Key to *anavah* is knowing how to understand our own place in the world. *Anavah* should not diminish our sense of self but sharpen our understanding of the world to show us that failure is not permanent but a way of pushing us in a new direction.

In *Parshat Va-eira*, Moses's struggles offer several lessons about how to behave when failure stares us down. The *parashah* can help us understand that our stumbles should lead us to reassess how we relate to ourselves, the Divine, and our own narrative. The world is unpredictable—but it is critical that we stay present.

We catch Moses on the cusp of defeat: *Vay'dabeir Moshe kein el b'nei Yisrael, v'lo shamu el Moshe, mikotzer ruach umei-avodah kashah* (וַיְדַבֵּר מֹשֶׁה כֵּן אֶל־בְּנֵי יִשְׂרָאֵל וְלֹא שָׁמְעוּ אֶל־מֹשֶׁה מִקֹּצֶר רוּחַ וּמֵעֲבֹדָה קָשָׁה), "But when Moses told this to the Israelites, they would not listen to Moses, their spirits crushed by cruel bondage" (Exodus 6:9). Despite the fact that he comes wielding a heady promise of redemption from God and that he is able to present himself as God's messenger, something falls flat. The Israelites are simply too overwhelmed by their circumstances to internalize Moses's message. We can empathize with the despair Moses might feel—with prospects for redemption so high, the sting of failure is all the more painful.

Rabbi Menachem Mendel of Kotzk noticed something strange in the text and asked Rabbi Menachem Mendel of Varkaw about an earlier promise God had made to Moses: *V'shamu l'kolecha* (וְשָׁמְעוּ לְקֹלֶךָ), "They [the Israelites] will listen to you" (Exodus 3:18). If this promise did not come true, can it be the case that God's words have failed to come to fruition? Our second Rabbi Menachem Mendel parses the verse carefully. He explains that the text is very specific to say *l'kole-cha* rather than use *b'kolcha*—that is, "to your voice" rather than "in your voice"—implying a looser connection between Moses's words and the people. The text seeks to say, "It is your voice alone that the people will listen to, not the specific content of your words," since, at this point, the people are too spiritually and physically oppressed to understand the fine details of their redemption. However, even if they cannot hear Moses's words, they can hear his voice. They can tell that in their hour of sorrow and pain, God's servant is there for them.[2]

Rabbi Menachem Mendel of Varkaw teaches us how to understand our perceived failings. In times of struggle, we may feel that our words fall flat. Moses may perceive himself as having failed his mission. However, from a different angle, his presence still has a palpable effect. With the right dose of *anavah*, we can see that the results of our work might not be what we expected; but, balanced with the right amount of confidence in who we are, we can still bring good into the world. Moses's effect on the people is not the anticipated one, but it is powerful nonetheless.

Additionally, *anavah* demands that we aim to understand the context of who we are based on the forces larger than we are. This notion of relationality is established at the beginning of the parashah: *Va-eira el Avraham, el Yitzchak, v'el Yaakov b'El Shaddai ushmi Adonai lo nodati lahem* (וָאֵרָא אֶל־אַבְרָהָם אֶל־יִצְחָק וְאֶל־יַעֲקֹב בְּאֵל שַׁדָּי וּשְׁמִי יהוה לֹא נוֹדַעְתִּי לָהֶם), "I appeared to Abraham, Isaac, and Jacob as *El Shaddai*, but I did not make Myself known to them by my name *YHVH*" (Exodus 6:3). From this we can learn about the power of Moses's relationship to the Divine and to the narrative that sets the stage for his life journey and how they both diminish his isolation at this moment. *Anavah* can allow us to understand that fundamentally we are not alone.

The Chatam Sofer sees a linguistic connection between *avot* (אָבוֹת), the word for "ancestors," and the verb *le-evot* (לָאֱבוֹת), "to want or desire." He claims that "the Holy Blessed One connects with those who have longings for God."[3] The Chatam Sofer connects his understanding of the immediate importance of our longing for God to the Ramban's interpretation of God's famous and opaque self-description, *Ehyeh asher ehyeh* (אֶהְיֶה אֲשֶׁר אֶהְיֶה), "I will be that I will be" (Exodus 3:14) as "Just as you are with Me, so I will be with you."[4] The Ramban and Chatam Sofer both suggest that God's presence is directly linked to our capacity to cleave to God. This is an empowering idea—our actions in the world can change the essence of the Divine. Moses may experience himself as alone and useless, but just as earlier he did not necessarily perceive the impact of his words on the oppressed Israelites, here he might miss that his engagement with God has divine repercussions.

When we feel that we are failing, we wallow in our loneliness; but if we look outside of ourselves, we can see those whose legacies sustain us. Here, God also reminds Moses that it is not just God who is in relationship with Moses, but that Moses too is connected to our Patriarchs and Matriarchs before him through God's revelation of God's self in the world. Practicing *anavah* may help us to realize that we are not alone when we attempt to change the world. We are part of a story much larger than our own. When we understand our place within a Jewish story that began thousands of years ago, we can hearken back to those who have handled moments of deep pain and difficulty before us and find strength.

When we find ourselves in moments of difficulty, a practice of *anavah* can push us to ask three questions: How might my impact be different than expected? How can I find the Divine in this moment? How can the story of those who came before me support me at this moment? If we engage in this personal reflection, we can work toward following the path of Moses, who later in the Torah is noted to be "a very humble man, more so than any other human being on earth" (Numbers 12:3).

We may not have a chance to be Moses or Hélène Cazès-Benatar, but everywhere we allow *anavah* to guide our steps, we can navigate our uncertain times.

Questions to Ask

In times of failure, how have you been able to use *anavah* to understand your stumbling?

What forces do you think allowed Moses and Hélène Cazès-Benatar to rise to the occasion at their time of need?

Practice for the *Middah* of *Anavah*

When you struggle at home or at work, use *anavah* to consider unintended, positive consequences of your action.

Another *Middah* to Consider

What roles do you think *emunah* (אֱמוּנָה, "faith") plays in the work that Moses and Hélène Cazès-Benatar did?

NOTES

1. For more, I recommend the masterful *Destination Casablanca* by Meredith Hindley.
2. Menachem Mendel of Kotzk, *Mei-Otzar HaMachshevah shel HaChasidut, Iturei Torah*, 55.
3. Chatam Sofer, *Iturei Torah*, 48.
4. Ramban on Exodus 3:14.

Bo—Exodus 10:1–13:16

Kavod—Honor:
Making an Effort

RABBI NANCY WECHSLER

KAVOD (כָּבוֹד) is usually translated "honor" or "dignity." *Kol hakavod* is enthusiastically exclaimed when someone has done something of worth. The root of *kavod*, כ-ב-ד carries other meanings as well, like "sweeping" (as in sweeping the floors to treat a place honorably), "liver" (the organ credited to purifying the body's blood), and "heavy." This single root contains nuances of purification, cleaning up, heavy lifting—and as a result of the effort, "honor." *Kavod* does not come by osmosis; it takes muscle. *Kavod* demands that we muster our energy, clear away the clutter, and like a weight lifter, breathe into raising the weighted barbell high above our heads.

Moses is instructed by God, *Bo el-paroh* (בֹּא אֶל-פַּרְעֹה), "Come to Pharaoh" (Exodus 10:1).[1] Usually one simply "goes" to interact with another person, but our *parashah*'s name is "Come," making the instruction sound as if it is asking us to make an additional effort: "Come to Pharaoh. For I have hardened his heart" (Exodus 10:1). This additional effort might remind us of the connection between "heavy lifting" and rendering honor.

In most cases, "go" is any movement away from the speaker, whereas "come" is any movement toward the speaker. To whom shall Moses come? To God, we suppose, for "I," the speaker, is God, who has hardened Pharaoh's heart. Does that mean that God is where Pharaoh is? Does that mean that there is a breath of godliness even within Pharaoh, the incarnation of cruelty and arrogance? Does the same spark of God that lives in everyone and everything also live in Pharaoh? Apparently so. Might giving Pharaoh some *kavod* turn things around?

In *Mishnah, Pirkei Avot*, we learn, "Who is honorable? One who honors others."[2] Judaism teaches that honor is something we give to others, which in turn makes us honorable. Why is Pharaoh worthy of being honored? The answer, I believe, can be found in Moses's childhood. Pharaoh's daughter found baby Moses in the basket floating down the Nile. She rescued him to avoid the Pharaonic ruling of killing every male Jewish child. Pharaoh could have kept his ruling in place and decreed Moses's death. Yet, Moses lived and was raised with riches in the palace, guided through life by none other than Pharaoh's daughter (Exodus 2). Apparently, Pharaoh had decided to spare that one little boy and let him live. That single decision made Moses's life and all his deeds possible. It was ultimately Pharaoh, not his daughter, who saved the life of Moses. To give honor to Pharaoh, to "come" to him, requires "sweeping away" everything but that one fact. Merciless cruelty and humiliation to the Israelites—swept aside in that moment; fear of being killed—swept aside: Pharaoh saved his life, and in that moment, nothing else matters.

The *middah* of *kavod* is taught to the contemporary Mussar student through Alan Morinis's key phrase, a positive affirmation, "Each one, holy soul." It would be far easier if the affirmation said, "Each good one, holy soul," rather than insisting that "each" soul, even Pharaoh's soul, is holy. Rabbi Chayim of Volozhin, a forerunner of the Mussar movement, explains that that one should honor all people simply because they are the handiwork of God.[3] Every being, not just the nice ones, are children of God and for that reason alone are worthy of *kavod*.

After the exchange between Moses, Aaron, and Pharaoh, the last deadly plagues are delivered: locusts cover the land, followed by the penultimate plague of darkness, and finally, the killing of the firstborn (Exodus 12:29). Why do all the firstborns of Egypt, "from the firstborn of Pharaoh who sat on the throne to the firstborn of the captive who was in the dungeon," have to die? Such mass killing seems to declare those souls worthless and seems to ignore the fact that all souls deserve *kavod*.

Our traditional commentaries were sensitive to the problematic ethics of the event, culminating in the drowning of the Egyptians in the Sea of Reeds. Midrash depicts the angels about to break into song, when God silences them, declaring, "How dare you sing for joy when My creatures are dying!"[4] God seems to be reprimanding them, "Show some *kavod*!" As the Talmud teaches, "Our personal elation should never make us forget the misfortunes afflicting others." This quote is used by the later *Tosafot* as the source for the custom of breaking a glass at the end of a wedding ceremony and for the custom of spilling out drops of wine at the seder, to remind us that our cup of deliverance and celebration cannot be full when others are suffering.[6]

It seems that our tradition is of two minds when it comes to *kavod*. On the one hand, we are commanded to celebrate our redemption from our enemies, which we might call "*kavod* to self." At the same time, we are commanded to feel empathy for other human beings—including our enemies—and lift them up with *kavod*, too, that is, "honoring others." Therefore, it is possible to learn in Proverbs, on the one hand, "When the wicked perish there are shouts of joy" (Proverbs 11:10), and on the other hand, "If your enemy falls, do not exult" (Proverbs 24:17).

We live with this dichotomy. If we are not happy that evil has been punished, then we do not care enough; but if we are not sad at the loss of life, then our humanity is weakened. From Ezekiel: *Chai ani—n'um Adonai Elohim—im echpotz b'mot harasha ki im b'shuv rasha midarko v'chayah* (חַי־אָנִי נְאֻם אֲדֹנָי יהוה אִם־אֶחְפֹּץ בְּמוֹת הָרָשָׁע כִּי אִם־בְּשׁוּב רָשָׁע מִדַּרְכּוֹ וְחָיָה), "As I live—declares the Eternal—it is not My desire that the wicked shall die, but that the wicked turn from their [evil] ways, and live" (Ezekiel 33:11).

Thus, in the Rabbinic reading of the story of the Reed Sea, Pharaoh does not die, but flees and eventually becomes the king of Nineveh.

When the prophet Jonah arrives in the city, the king of Nineveh (who is the old Pharaoh) immediately initiates a national repentance movement.[7] Thus, Pharaoh becomes the paradigm of change, and an example for all of us on the afternoon of Yom Kippur when we read and learn his story. *Kavod* means to honor someone by lifting them up. Sometimes, the weight is heavy. Still, the process has the potential to purify ourselves and others, raising us all.

Questions to Ask

What has been the result of a situation in which you have shown *kavod* toward another person? What kind of acknowledgment for another person strengthens the best within you?

What is the benefit of showing *kavod* toward another person even when you do not respect them?

How do its various connotations ("sweeping away," "the purifying liver," and "something of weight") change your understanding of *kavod*?

Practice for the *Middah* of *Kavod*

Give *kavod* to someone without expectation to receive in return. Give honor to a person with whom you do not have an easy relationship. Notice what happens.

Another *Middah* to Consider

Linked to the concept of *kavod* in *Parashat Bo* is the *middah* of *hakarat hatov* (הַכָּרַת הַטּוֹב, "gratitude, recognition of the good"). Moses focuses on that which is godly, even good, within Pharaoh in order to have the courage to approach him. Sometimes it takes *hakarat hatov* to give honor to oneself. Rabbi Nachman of Bratzlav suggested that when foundering in a dark place, we seek one spark of good within ourselves, and then another, and then another. With this practice, we build ourselves up toward giving honor to ourselves and others.[8]

NOTES

1. Biblical translations in this volume are generally from W. Gunther Plaut, ed., *The Torah: A Modern Commentary*, rev. ed. (New York: Reform Judaism Publishing, an imprint of CCAR Press, 2005). However, the author's literal translation is offered here.
2. *Mishnah, Pirkei Avot* 4:1.
3. Rabbi Chayim of Volozhin (1749–1821), *Ruach Chayim* (*Pirkei Avot* commentary).
4. *Babylonian Talmud, M'gilah* 10b and *Sanhedrin* 39b.
5. *Babylonian Talmud, B'rachot* 31a.
6. Explanation by Rabbi Dr. Eduard Baneth (German rabbi and scholar, d. 1930), in *Der Sederabend* (Berlin, 1904), p. 29: "We do so because the Egyptians died during Pesach, and it is written 'Do not rejoice at the downfall of your enemy' (Proverbs 24:17)."
7. *Pirkei D'Rabbi Eliezer* on Exodus 14:28.
8. *Likutei Moharan* 1:282.

B'SHALACH—EXODUS 13:17–17:16

Bitachon—Trusting the Path

RABBI CANTOR ALISON WISSOT

DO YOU REMEMBER THAT TOY CALLED A SPIROGRAPH—a circular toy with holes in which to stick a pencil or marker? You would follow the motion of the circle or oval, drawing on the page what looked like an odd series of lines, but concluding in a magical masterpiece of fractals and fragments, all part of a masterful design.

This process is a metaphor for the life we live. Only at its end can we see its patterns. Stories, biographies, and narratives show us the things that have been in the past, where they have led, and even sometimes the reasons behind them. But in the middle of our life? When we are following a path that is as tangled and disconnected as those lines created by a Spirograph, we do not know if we are heading in the right direction. We do not see the pattern at all!

The Israelites surely do not see a thing. They witness massive plagues against their taskmasters, wonders and miracles, and a leader who could bring them out of their enslavement, and yet, we read at the very beginning of *B'shalach*, in Exodus 13:17–18, that God does not lead them on a straight path out of Egypt: "Now when Pharaoh let the people go, the Eternal did not lead them by way of the land of the Philistines, although it was nearer; for the Eternal said, 'The people may have a change of heart when they see war, and return to Egypt.' So God led the people round about, by way of the wilderness at the Sea of Reeds."

How do we know we are heading in the right direction?

Sometimes our path is so winding and long that it feels like we took a wrong turn somewhere. Even the giant signposts that once indicated that we were on the right path ultimately only go to show that up until that moment, we were headed in the right direction. Similarly, the Children of Israel experienced the walls of water, an extraordinary miracle, as a sign that so far, everything had gone well.

But then what? After the experience of an extraordinary miracle, how can we know in which direction to turn now? How do we know how to continue on the right path?

A wise teacher of mine once made a comment to an irate man who missed his flight, "I don't think you were meant to be on that plane." "Why? What do you know?" the man belligerently seethed. "Because . . . you are not on that plane." *Bitachon* (בְּטָחוֹן), the *middah* we translate as "trust," means believing that somehow, the path we are on is the one meant for us.

In *Duties of the Heart*, Bachya ibn Pakuda, one of the foremost Mussar masters, explains *bitachon* as "tranquility of the soul and liberty of the mind." Living with *bitachon* is living with a deep sense of assurance that the things happening in the world are both God's will and for the good. "Trust is the sense of security you feel when you are sure the person you trust will do something for your benefit correctly and to the best of their ability and know-how," Bachya explains. He gives seven criteria for placing one's trust in someone: they must be compassionate; they would never desert you; they must be strong enough to accomplish what you need; they must know what is good for you; they must be responsible for you throughout your life; your well-being must be in their hands alone; and they must be generous and kind. Even before Bachya ibn Pakuda suggests it, we know that God alone can fulfill all of these seven criteria. Therefore, we should place our trust in God alone.

Looking around, we can see a world full of anxious, angry, fearful people. Looking inside, we can "see" the same anguish the Israelites felt after the parting of the sea. Just after Miriam has raised her timbrel and helped to complete the Israelites' song of praise at the sea, just after experiencing this extraordinary rescue, the people grumble against Moses, complaining that they lack water (Exodus 15:24).

They go so far as to say, "If only we had died by the hand of the Eternal in the land of Egypt, when we sat by the fleshpots, when we ate our fill of bread! For you have brought us out into this wilderness to starve this whole congregation to death" (Exodus 16:3). Not much has changed in the intervening millennia. No matter that we have conquered so much, that miracles have been wrought in our lives, diseases eradicated, slavery rejected, technology invented to bring healing to the sick, closeness achieved between those who are separated across worlds . . . so much angst still remains in this world, and we continue to complain in a world of plenty.

We Jews are duty-bound to see not just the broken shards, not just the random lines on the page. We are to see beauty; we are to cultivate gratitude, perspective, and vision. In B'shalach, the road to the sea is roundabout. The Israelites are led "not by way of the land of the Philistines, although it was nearer" (Exodus 13:17). Perhaps there is no straight path to seeing miracles, even if we once saw them before. We need to cultivate the trust of believing that we are in fact on the right path.

We would be mistaken to think of this kind of trust as giving over everything to God. In a post-Shoah age, we know that we cannot fully trust in God's ability to control all things. In fact, this kind of trust has never been easy to cultivate, even for our ancestors who witness the parting of the sea. Would we not think that they of all people would trust in God? And yet, the very thing they do just after experiencing for themselves the most grandiose miracle in history shows otherwise: they begin to complain, out of anxiety, anger, and fear.

Life without trust in God may seem more rational, and it would be if bitachon meant that everything is in God's hands. We know that human beings make choices and that those choices have consequences; therefore, we cannot say that everything is in God's hands. However, Bachya ibn Pakuda taught that some things are in God's hands and some things are in ours.[1]

What are the limits to trusting in God? What is actually in our hands? There is certainly space reserved for human beings to matter, a space in which our own choices have meaning and provoke consequences. Each of us must decide, Bachya explains, to "either serve [God] or transgress, and set out to do and agree to do it."[2] He explains that "it would be wrong and foolish of you to trust God in those areas," meaning, the actions that are fully within your control and subject to your own choices, "for the Creator left serving or rebelling against God up to you, as it is written, 'choose life.'"[3] Bachya sees that it is our choice whether to follow the mitzvot as we understand them, or not. If we do, then we can trust that we have done all we can and that the rest is subject to trust in God.

As a result, our wish to honor what God desires for us does not automatically provide us with *bitachon* to do so. We are placed in a world in which we never know whether we are facing a situation in which we simply need to let go and trust or a situation in which we need to actively resist the direction in which the path ahead of us seems to lead. Our choices determine how we experience our lives. We can assume that God, and Moses, would have found a way to provide food and water for the Israelites in the desert without the grumbling. The Israelites' inability to master *bitachon* determined the way they experienced life, full of pain and fear despite all they had witnessed.

Miriam, on the other hand, understands this. In her own need to hold on to *bitachon*, Miriam takes with her a timbrel (Exodus 15:20). She does not know what the events of life will bring. She only knows that there will come a time to rejoice. Life is full of tragedies, but the events of life do not make up the path of life. The power to rejoice, to celebrate the miracles that have already happened, and to trust that we have done all we can, these things change our experience of events, even if the events themselves do not change.

That child's toy, that Spirograph, with which I opened my essay, visually demonstrates our experience of our life. However, the Mussar emphasis on *bitachon* invites us to consider that the road in front of us is the right path, because God is waiting for us. Even if we take a different turn, God will be waiting there, too. And when we look back at the pattern of our lives, we will see holiness.

Questions to Ask

Augustine is reputed to have said, "Pray as if everything
depended upon God, and work as if everything depended
on you." How can this practice support you in cultivating
bitachon?

Metaphorically, where can you bring your timbrel, trusting
that you will need it? Where can you bring the story
of someone else who was a master of this *middah*, like
Joseph? (How is Joseph an exemplar of this *middah*?)

Do you sometimes find yourself grumbling, even when you
have just witnessed something especially wonderful? How
can you become more appreciative of the wonders occur-
ring at the path you are on?

Practice for the *Middah* of *Bitachon*

Play with a Spirograph. Which line are you on right now? Can you
see the pattern of your life thus far? Or is it time to just keep walking
until you know more?

Other *Middot* to Consider

Emunah (אֱמוּנָה, "faith"): Faith is the knowledge that God is
present, whereas trust is the knowledge that God intends
all that happens for our good.

Ometz lev (אֹמֶץ לֵב, "courage"): In this portion, Moses, Miriam, Nachshon, and the people of Israel all have to make
choices that contain risk, in order to leave behind slavery
and enter something unknown.

Anavah (עֲנָוָה, "humility") can be explored in this portion in
the interaction of each of the leaders. None of them is responsible for the whole story, but each plays an important
part. Moses, for example, is not the one to first set foot
into the water, but he leads the Israelites on their journey.
Miriam does not lead the people out, but her celebration
with music is crucial to their journey.

NOTES

1. Bachya ibn Pakuda, *The Duties of the Heart*, trans. and with commentary by Yaakov Feldman (Northvale, NJ: Jason Aronson, 1996), 207.
2. Ibid., 206.
3. Ibid., 207.

YITRO—EXODUS 18:1–20:23
Emet—Truth: Emet as a Way of Being

RABBI CAROL GLASS, BCC, SD

"A fact is always the same. Once you learn it, you have it forever. But truth is different. Once you understand it, you are forever changed and 'the truth' disappears. And because you are now someone else, you must learn it all over again."
—Lawrence Kushner, *The Book of Words*

AS AN ASPIRING RABBI trying to support my cousin Celeste (not her real name), I visited her in the family room of the Jewish funeral home where her twenty-six-year-old son had been eulogized only fourteen months before. This time, we gathered to honor and eulogize her beloved husband, who had died unexpectedly two days earlier. As the funeral director approached to pin on Celeste's *k'riah* ribbon, my cousin looked me straight in the eye and blurted out with bitter accusation, "Where's your God now? What's His truth in *this* moment?" I understood Celeste's veiled reference to *Baruch Dayan ha-emet*, or "Blessed is the Judge of truth," a phrase commonly repeated after putting on a mourner's ribbon; and I fell silent. I said nothing, not only in order to validate and provide space for Celeste's anger and pain, but even more because I was silenced by the question itself. I had no reasonable response.

At that time, I didn't yet understand that *emet*, most often translated as "truth," is not primarily about the correctness of one's vision of the world; nor is it the opposite of falsehood, nor that which can be substantiated with facts. *Emet* is a way of being in the world. It is as much an exercise of the heart as it is an exercise of the mind. Pure or absolute *emet*, however, is not humanly attainable; it is, as Rabbi Kushner puts it: "God's way of seeing the world."[1] Based on such teachings, *emet* became one of the Jewish names for God. Within the world of Mussar, there is more than one approach to the *middah* of *emet*. Some teachers favor what I'd call a classical definition of *emet*, teaching that the *middah* focuses on honesty and reliability.[2] Other teachers understand *emet* to be the *middah* of inclusive, respectful regard both for what is apparent and for what remains undetected— for what is obvious, as well as that which may elude us or be hidden from us. Another way of saying this is offered by Batya Gallant, a scholar and teacher at the Darchei Binah Seminary in Jerusalem:

> She notes that "truth-perception" (her name for *emet*), demands of us the ability and effort to perceive reality in its fullness, taking in all that we can, so that we live our lives based on an openness. She writes:
>
> *Middas ha'emes*, truth-perception requires the ability to perceive reality as it really is, and to live one's life based on that reality. . . ." Growth in *middas ha'emes* requires recognizing the illusions we may be holding onto, and discarding them. . . . The shedding of illusions is a lifelong struggle that, like all spiritual growth, requires one's courage to move beyond one's natural inclinations . . . and ultimately, to perceive the finite as thoroughly informed by the Infinite."[3]

This rather different interpretation of *emet*, which I embrace, requires us to hone our powers of observation and to listen to our hearts in addition to the "facts." It is based on the word's very composition. In Hebrew, the word *emet* is spelled א-מ-ת (*alef-mem-tav*)—*alef* being the first letter of that alphabet, *mem* occupying the middle position, and *tav* bringing up the rear as the final letter. In short, *emet* embraces a "from A to Z" perspective. It encompasses the complete picture, the fullness of reality. The *middah* of *emet* asks us to assess, judge, inform, teach, speak, observe, listen, and incline all our thoughts and behavior toward acknowledgment of the fullness of life in all its complexity—as we see it and as others might see it.

We find several examples of this inclusive, all-encompassing, heart-and-vision-directed type of *emet* in the opening sections of our *parashah*.

At the very beginning of the portion, in Exodus 18:3–4, we learn the derivations of the names of Moses's sons, Gershom and Eliezer. The choice of the names Gershom (meaning "I have been a stranger in a foreign land") and Eliezer (meaning "My ancestors' God was my help, delivering me from the sword of Pharoah") reveals Moses's ability to accept and embrace his life in its entirety and to derive meaning not only from the grand highpoints but also from the risky challenges. His children's names reflect an honest appraisal of a life that includes separation, alienation, and danger, as well as spiritual intimacy, significant familial relationships, and gratitude.

Moses again applies *emet*—"whole-picture awareness"—as he reports to Jethro regarding all God has done for the Israelites in Egypt, during the Exodus itself, at the Reed Sea, and during the journey so far. Moses could have focused only on God's miraculous, redemptive actions, as Jethro did when he noted "all the kindness [*tovah*] that the Eternal had shown Israel when delivering them from the Egyptians" (Exodus 18:9). But Moses does not whitewash the history or describe only what is exciting or beneficial or safe to say. Instead, Moses mentions "all the hardships" (Exodus 18:8) before sharing the story of deliverance. In this way, Moses is teaching us that when we benefit, it behooves us to take note and acknowledge the possible losses that occur as a result of our gains. This type of mindfulness can be applied to numerous other trade-offs in life—for example, when we are given an honor, others who were passed over may have lost an opportunity that could have changed their lives; or when our clothing is inexpensive, it might be because the people who are making it are not paid fairly.

Later in our *parashah* we read the Ten Commandments. One of the commandments in particular invokes *emet*, signifying it as a central Jewish principle. We are instructed, "You shall not bear false witness against your neighbor" (Exodus 20:13). Testimony that is completely truthful, "A to Z," is required. One may not be selective about which testimony to provide when asked to provide a full picture.

We end our exploration of the *middah* of *emet* with a fabulous poem about the nature of the realization of truth, or what Batya Gallant calls the moment of Truth-perception.[4]

Sit with this poem. Read it through and read it aloud. Pick out one line to repeat throughout your day. Enjoy!

Truth Is

Truth is only discovered in the moment.
There is no truth that can be carried over
to the next moment, the next day, the next year.

Truth comes into the non-seeking mind fresh and alive.
It is not something you can carry with you, accumulate, or
   hold onto.

Truth leaps into view when the mind is quiet, not asserting
   itself.
You cannot contain or domesticate truth, for if you do, it
   dies instantly.

Truth prowls the unknown waiting for a gap in the mind's
   activity.
When that gap is there, the truth leaps out of the unknown
   into the known.

Instantly you comprehend it and sense its sacredness.
The timeless has broken through like a flash of lightning
and illuminated the moment with its presence.

Truth comes to an innocent mind as a blessing.
Truth is a holy thing because it liberates thought from itself
and illumines the human heart from the inside out.

—Adyashanti

Questions to Ask

How do you feel when you hear a report about someone or something that leaves out vital details pertinent to your viewpoint regarding the same event or person?

When are you tempted to leave "the other side of the story" uninvestigated?

Can you recall learning new details about someone's life that turned your understanding of them from negative to positive? How was your negative judgment formed in the first place?

How has encountering a new truth changed you? Explain.

Practices for the *Middah* of *Emet*

Set a fixed amount of time (twenty minutes?) each day to notice when you make a negative judgment about yourself. Once you notice that you're doing that, stop and breathe. Ask yourself: What am I not seeing? What have I left out? During week two, apply the same exercise to your judgments of others.

Notice if you're saying one thing with your mouth and another with your heart.[5] How would it feel to say both out loud? How would it feel to align your mouth with your heart, or vice versa? Journal using these questions as prompts.

Explore the potential meaning(s) for you of *Karov Adonai l'chol korav, l'chol asher yikra-uhu ve-emet*, "The Eternal is near to all who call God, to all who call God with *emet*" (Psalm 145:18).

Practice saying, "I don't know, but I'll try to find out."

Other *Middot* to Consider

Kavod (כָּבוֹד, "honor"): In the Ten Commandments, we read, "Honor your father and your mother" (Exodus 20:12). We are not given any specifics in Torah as to what this injunction means. Mussar teaches us that the Hebrew for "honor" comes from the Hebrew root meaning "heavy"; thus, we learn that to show *kavod*, one should convey an appropriate amount of "weightiness" toward the person or event involved. Also, we see in Exodus 18:7 how Moses shows *kavod* to Jethro by bowing low and kissing his father-in-law.

Bitachon (בָּטָחוֹן, "trust"): For the most part, the people held a great deal of *bitachon* in their hearts for Moses during their sojourn with him. In our *parashah*, at Sinai, they trust him enough to be able to say without equivocation that they are ready to accept the word of God that Moses has transmitted to them (Exodus 19:8).

NOTES

1. Bachya ibn Pakuda, *The Duties of the Heart*, trans. and with commentary by Yaakov Feldman (Northvale, NJ: Jason Aronson, 1996), 115: "How matters appear to God, that is true."
2. Menachem Mendel Levin of Satanov, *Cheshbon HaNefesh* (1812), trans. Shraga Silverstein (New York: Feldheim, 1845), 172–75.
3. Batya Gallant, *Stages of Spiritual Growth: Resolving the Tension between Self-Expression and Submission to Divine Will* (Jerusalem: Urim, 2010), 107–13, 161.
4. Ibid.
5. *Babylonian Talmud Bava M'tzia* 49a.

Mishpatim—Exodus 21:1–24:18

M'nuchat HaNefesh—Equanimity: Finding Peace in Responsibility

Rabbi Dr. Shmuly Yanklowitz

Naaseh v'nishma (נַעֲשֶׂה וְנִשְׁמָע), "We will do and we will obey" (Exodus 24:7). How tense must one be, accepting responsibility before knowing the extent of one's commitments?

In our complex world, we often feel overwhelmed and anxious. The cost of living is high, our moral responsibilities are great, the demands on our time are substantial, the spiritual challenges are heavy, and relationships are complex. However, we strive for happiness and peace within that race. It seems like we can choose either complexity and anxiety or simplicity and happiness. But, must that be so? Can we choose a path of actualizing our unique potential and living with joy and inner calm? Indeed, can we find balance in the disarray of modern living?

The Jewish tradition contains within it a rich literature that provides inspiration about tackling the complexities of life's challenges. As a people concerned with the minutiae and exactitude of wisdom for its own sake, it makes sense as well that Jewish ethics evolved in tandem with a sense of creating opportunities that allow us to transcend mundane tasks by pairing them with a divine purpose. Such is the case that we will follow in these succeeding pages.

The Torah portion of *Mishpatim* is as inspiring as it is overwhelming and anxiety provoking. It is a *parashah* packed with ethical responsibilities and societal demands that establish order, as well as ways to handle those who transgress that order. The scope of the *parashah* encompasses all sorts of human ills and remedies, including murder, property damage, theft, self-defense, loans, judicial process, and more. And while *Mishpatim* deals with concrete societal problems, it also raises a deep and disturbing question: Why is it so hard to live an ethical life? Why does the Torah add to our already hard and anxiety-provoking reality?

How can we enable ourselves to face both the challenges of contemporary American life and the ancient challenge of living an ethical life of Torah?

For me, a first step to answering these questions is to recognize our own limitations and to be vulnerable even at the most trying of times. If we have not addressed the messiness of our inner life, we will have limited capacity to address the messiness of our outer life. Therefore, it is crucial to first achieve emotional health and spiritual clarity on our life mission.

The character trait—*middah*—that is required to obtain this balance is *m'nuchat hanefesh* (מְנוּחַת הַנֶּפֶשׁ, "equanimity"). Cultivating equanimity is the crucial ingredient to living a meaningful, passionate, purposeful life in joy, peace, and inner calm.

How to Deal with Worries

Traditional thinkers tell us to cultivate the *middot* of trust and faith—*bitachon* and *emunah* (אֱמוּנָה וּבִטָחוֹן). We need not worry too much, they suggest, since ultimately God is in control. Everything happens for a reason. So much is beyond our control. We should not get too worked up in worry, fear, and anxiety.

Years ago, Alan Morinis and Avi Fertig of the Mussar Institute shared, in a program where I was learning, that the word for worry, *d'agah* (דְּאָגָה) has four of the first five letters of the *alef-bet*. The one missing is *bet* (ב), which represents *bitachon*. One who is lacking trust will end up with worry.

Rabbi Shalom Noach Berezovsky—the Netivot Shalom, a late Chasidic thinker—explains that there are two types of trust: (1) we learn from the Exodus from Egypt how to give up control, be patient, and wait; and (2) we learn from the splitting of the sea how to rise up and transcend our limitations. These are two different spiritual truths we can embrace at different moments of our journey. Each day, we must ask ourselves: In what area of my life do I need to just stay the course, let go of control, and stop wasting so much of my physical and spiritual energy in anxiety about that which I cannot control? Each day, we must also ask ourselves: In what area of my life do I need to rise up, become more active, take control, and create change?

Worry can be holy when it is about something profound and warranted. It can be channeled, refined, and even appreciated. But worry also allows us to push our bodies and our minds to be their best. If we are worried about a college placement test, or an interview for a dream job, or whether someone wants to be our partner in marriage, then the reward when seeing such goals achieved is all the sweeter and consequential to our identity in this life.

Recognizing One's Own Limitations
While we must do all we can to strive forward, we also remember, with humility, that we are limited beings. The Rabbis taught, "You are not obligated to complete the work, but neither are you free to desist from it."[1] We are not angels perfectly prepared to fulfill God's will. No. We are human beings, profoundly imperfect and limited. This sensibility should not lower our self-esteem, but give us a healthy sense of balance and perspective.

Rabbi Avraham Isaac HaCohen Kook taught that we must repent for being overly obsessed with details and for missing the big picture:

> When a great man involves himself too much with details, whether by studying them or by anxiety about them, he is diminished and his stature lessened; he must return and repent with love, with greatness of soul, and bind that contents of his spiritual life with great and sublime ideas. Certainly, he must not slight any detail, and always expand force and holiness in his deeds as well.[2]

This is one of the crucial points of *Parashat Mishpatim*. Laws and ethics are complex. It is easy to get lost within the minutiae of the rules and fail to zoom out to the broader principles guiding our moral lives. To be clear, Rabbi Kook deeply valued details. Furthermore, there are too many today who are clearly not concerned enough about facts and the process of truthful inquiry. However, Kook was aware that we can easily begin to worship details in a way that is paralyzing for our broader spiritual vision and for actualizing our most cherished values in the world. Complexity should lead us to pause and reflect, yes, but complexity should also guide us to our moral and societal responsibilities.

The Rabbis teach, "Three things sap a person's strength: anxiety, travel, and sin."[3] To be a Jew means one is to think critically and openly about life, to seek and find a proper balance in everything. No matter how strongly we are pulled in one direction, we must always pause and ask ourselves if this is indeed the direction we should be going in. The path that we follow determines so much in our life.

CREATING CHANGE: ONE STEP AND ONE MITZVAH AT A TIME

For me, creating change is based on Jewish spirituality. Jewish spirituality is not a one-time-a-day act. We do not simply meditate or pray in the morning and declare ourselves done. Rather, Jewish spirituality is about carrying a spiritual consciousness throughout our day. Our child is screaming in the middle of the night, and we center ourselves. Our colleague at work is being obnoxious and triggering us, and we reground ourselves. We want to scream and complain to our life partners, but we internally calm ourselves rather than externalize our aggravations. We see a multitude of options ahead of us, and we take the time to inquire which of them might be the path guided by the mitzvot of *Parashat Mishpatim*. Rather than being ruled by outer stimuli, we contain them. There is a quiet inner stillness that helps us steer through the messiest storms around us.

M'nuchat hanefesh provides us with spiritual clarity. As we journey from darkness to light, from uncertainty to clarity, from the oppression of Egypt to the freedom of the Promised Land, each of us will need to take some time to discern between the urgent and the unimportant. May the values embedded within *Parashat Mishpatim* help us to achieve the inner calm, the equanimity, we need for this task. With cool-headedness, we can cultivate the empathy to see beyond ourselves to others, and the wisdom to determine our next steps on our paths.

In *Parashat Mishpatim*, we read that "when Moses had ascended the mountain, the cloud covered the mountain" (Exodus 24:15). The Kotzker Rebbe shares that it is easy for the masses to stand afar and tremble at the sight, but Moses entered the dark cloud knowing that the deepest spiritual treasures are found not in seemingly perfect certainties, but rather in humble places that are often quite blurry and uncertain. And so, we should prepare ourselves—our hearts and our souls—for a life on earth and in the midst of the clouds.

Questions to Ask

What does it feel like when you are living with *m'nuchat hanefesh*? What does it feel like when you are living with inner turmoil? How can you become more aware of what is happening in your inner world?

In what ways would your life change if you were able to live with more *m'nuchat hanefesh*?

What is a fast-paced experience in your life to which you could bring a slow-paced inner presence and stillness?

Parashat Mishpatim concludes with the *chagim* (holidays). How can holidays (and the weekly Shabbat) become transformational experiences for you? How can holidays decrease stress and help you cultivate more *m'nuchat hanefesh*?

Practices for the *Middah* of *M'nuchat Hanefesh*

Kavanah (כַּוָּנָה, "intention"): Meditate, clear your mind from stress, release your body from anxiety, and regain your focus and energy.

T'filah (תְּפִילָה, "prayer"): Fill yourself with prayerful words of gratitude and positivity.

Hitbod'dut (הִתְבּוֹדְדוּת, "self-isolation"): Pick a verse that is relevant and resonates for you, and chant this mantra in solitude.

B'rachot (בְּרָכוֹת, "blessings'): Recite one hudred blessings in a day (or a number that works for you) to snap yourself out of the current mood and zoom out to your bigger values.

Cheshbon hanefesh (חֶשְׁבּוֹן הַנֶּפֶשׁ, "self-assessment"): Make a list each day of how much good you have in your life.

Another *Middah* to Consider

Consider *hakarat hatov* (הַכָּרַת הַטּוֹב, "gratitude, recognition of the good") as an attempt to cultivate a deeper sense of gratitude. This gratitude will help you to feel a sense of sufficiency and calm.

NOTES

1. *Mishnah, Pirkei Avot* 2:21.
2. Avraham Isaac Kook, *Orot HaKodesh*, 3:259; See also Benjamin Ish-Shalom (trans. Ora Wiskind-Elper), *Rav Avraham Itzhak Hacohen Kook: Between Rationalism and Mysticism* (Albany, NY: State University of New York Press, 1993), 220.
3. *Babylonian Talmud, Gittin* 70a.

T'RUMAH—EXODUS 25:1–27:19

N'divut—Generosity:
"Let a Generous Spirit Sustain Me"

Psalm 51:14

RABBI JOSEPH B. MESZLER

WHEN HEBREW SCHOOL STUDENTS are asked about what the most important values in Judaism are, giving *tzedakah* usually is near the top of the list. *Tzedakah*, imperfectly translated as "charity," "philanthropy," or even "righteous giving," means giving a material good for someone in need. But what motivates someone to give? What *middah* does *tzedakah* embody? Several answers may be found in *Parashat T'rumah*, which can be read as a meditation on the virtue of *n'divut* (נְדִיבוּת, "generosity").

The first instance of *n'divut* is found at the very beginning of the Torah portion: "The Eternal One spoke to Moses, saying: 'Tell the Israelite people to bring Me gifts; you shall accept gifts for Me from every person whose heart is so moved'" (Exodus 25:1–2). God tells the Israelites to bring these gifts in order to make a Tabernacle ("sanctuary") so that God "may dwell among them" (Exodus 25:8). The phrase *yidvenu libo* (יִדְּבֶנּוּ לִבּוֹ, "whose heart is so moved") literally means "generous of heart." Unlike taxes or other requirements of the people, the gifts in this portion are to be offered freely, without coercion.

While generosity can mean much more than giving money, we can begin learning about this attribute by focusing first on what it meant for the Israelites to give their "gold, silver, and copper" (Exodus 25:3). In Moses Maimonides's famous scale of *tzedakah*, the lowest rung is to give begrudgingly, and the highest levels are to give anonymously and with the goal that the recipient becomes self-sustaining.

To give reluctantly or only after coercion may count as *tzedakah* (the money did change hands), but it does not count as *n'divut*. Maimonides wrote, "Anyone who gives *tzedakah* to the poor with a scowl and causes them to be embarrassed, even if the donor gave them a thousand *zuz*, has destroyed and lost any merit thereby." Rather, a sign of generosity is to give *b'simchah*—"gladly."[1]

Being generous is not merely a human virtue, but a divine attribute. When we give, we imitate God. Just as God sustains the world unselfishly, so should we strive to be generous like God.[2] Maimonides taught that when we give solely because of "our noble nature and excellent character," we "become like God."[3]

A habit I have tried to cultivate is that, when I travel downtown in Boston, I bring a box of granola bars with me to hand out to people experiencing homelessness. I have learned that a simple act of generosity can have unexpected results. On one occasion, when I gave a man a granola bar, his eyes lit up, and he exclaimed, "Chocolate chip! My favorite!" In that act, we were elevated from being indifferent strangers to being two people who liked chocolate. The light in the man's eyes could be seen as the spark of the Divine.

Beyond giving *tzedakah*, we can think more expansively about *n'divut*. Visiting the sick, hospitality, or simply having patience requires generosity. If we look at the *parashah* as a whole, we see that building the Tabernacle took more than just donating precious metal and other expensive items. Such is the case with constructing a generous spirit. *Yidvenu libo*—willingly giving whatever you have and from your heart—is an act of loving-kindness. Whereas *tzedakah* is about someone who has the financial wherewithal to give donating to someone else in need, *g'milut chasadim*, "acts of loving-kindness," are forms of generosity that can be given between all people.[4] Time and attention are both universal and precious commodities.

In this vein, our portion indicates that each of us has unique gifts of the heart to give. The Torah describes the construction of the Ark of the Covenant in detail, and we read that the Ark needed to have gold *mibayit u'michutz* (מִבַּיִת וּמִחוּץ), "inside and out" (Exodus 25:11). Rava in the Talmud reads this symbolically and likens each person to the Ark.[5] Figuratively speaking, we are supposed to produce our personal gold "inside and out" as well. This might mean taking what is in our heart "on our inside" and giving it to others "on the outside."

Just as each person can be likened to the Ark, our tradition also compares each one of us to a Torah. Rabbi Menachem Nachum of Chernobyl, a student of the Baal Shem Tov, taught, "We must know that the Torah is in every person; each of us is a complete Torah, as is written, 'This is the Torah—a human being (*adam*)' (Numbers 19:14)."[6] Generosity can be shown through the sharing of wisdom. Each person has something to give and teach.

During a downturn in the economy, a friend who works as a teacher felt like he wanted to do something that could be helpful. He posted a video saying that he didn't really have money to give, but he could teach. Therefore, he offered free tutoring for certain subjects at the library. This example shows how, with a bit of creativity, acts of generosity can be very individual.

We can also learn a lesson about *n'divut* from the construction of the Tabernacle itself. The sides of the sanctuary were to be made of planks of acacia wood, and "each plank shall have two tenons, parallel to each other; do the same with all the planks of the Tabernacle" (Exodus 26:17). A tenon is a jutting piece of wood, so the planks would interlock with each other and be secure. The planks would click into place on both sides. The Hebrew word for these interlocking projections is *yadot*—literally, "hands." In other words, the planks need to "hold hands" in order to stand together. The tenons may be compared to the hands of one who gives *tzedakah* and the hands of the recipient. Both are the hands of God. They reach out and connect, the same way the planks "hold hands." Generosity connects us with each other, and the One God can be found on both sides of the connection. Just like the planks need each other to stand up and be stable, so are donor and recipient interdependent. Through the Hebrew word *v'natnu*, which means "they gave," Alan Morinis teaches about the mutuality of generosity. In Hebrew, the word *v'natnu* is a palindrome. Read right to left or left to right, it is the same. Generosity flows both ways.[7] We might add: through the tenons, generosity flows from one plank to the other and back again.

A final thought: In the Psalms, we read, *V'ruach n'divah tism'cheini* (וְרוּחַ נְדִבָה תִסְמְכֵנִי), "Let a generous spirit sustain me" (Psalm 51:14). Like the two sides of the planks, this verse can be understood two ways. Either we receive, and therefore someone else's generous spirit sustains us; or we give, and our own acts of generosity make our life worthwhile. Either way, "a generous spirit sustains me."

Why should we be generous? Because generosity elevates our behavior and interactions, it enables our unique gifts to come into the world, and it reveals the truth of our interdependence. Striving to live with *n'divut* is an aspiration to go through life hand in hand and in God's image, sustained by each other.

Questions to Ask

With whom in your life are you easily generous? With whom is it difficult to be generous? Why is there a difference?

Some people have a hard time accepting another person's generosity. Considering how Judaism teaches that God is found in both the giver and receiver, how can accepting someone else's gift be an act of *n'divut*?[8]

What small, achievable step can you take to be a bit more generous?

Practice for the *Middah* of N'*divut:*

There are many ways to remind yourself of character traits you wish to cultivate. You can tape them to your bathroom mirror; write down a word or phrase, take a picture of it, and use that as the lockscreen on your phone; or even use a phrase as your password to log on to your computer. Consider one of these options, and use the verse "Let a generous spirit sustain me" (Psalm 51:14) as a spiritual prompt.

Another *Middah* to Consider

Concerning the Ark, we have read, "Overlay it with pure gold—overlay it inside and out" (Exodus 25:11). In the Talmud, Rava taught,

"Any student of the wise whose inside is not like their outside is not really a student of the wise."[9] In other words, according to Rava, this verse means your feelings inside should match your actions and words "outside." What does this saying teach you about the nature of *emet* (אֱמֶת, "truth" or "integrity")?

NOTES

1. Maimonides, *Mishneh Torah, Hilchot Mat'not Aniyim* 10:4, 7–14.
2. *Babylonian Talmud, Sotah* 14b.
3. Maimonides, *Guide for the Perplexed* 1:72, 192.
4. *Babylonian Talmud, Sukkot* 49b.
5. *Babylonian Talmud, Yoma* 72b.
6. Menachem Nachum of Chernobyl, *Me'or Einayim Song of Songs* #3.
7. Exodus 30:12, repeated uses in Numbers 4:6–14, etc. Alan Morinis, *Everyday Holiness: The Jewish Spiritual Path of Mussar* (Boston: Trumpeter, 2007), 161.
8. See the chapter in this book on *Parashat Eikev* by Rabbi Yair Robinson.
9. *Babylonian Talmud, Yoma* 72b.

T'TZAVEH—EXODUS 27:20–30:10
Anavah—Humility:
The Breastplate of Anavah

RABBI LEAH LEWIS, MAJS

WHEN WILLIAM SHAKESPEARE wrote *Hamlet* at the turn of the seventeenth century, much of the worldly yet pithy advice that Polonius gave to his son Laertes—"The apparel oft proclaims the man"—had already been proved to be true.

In many ways, the idea that "clothes make the man" takes its root in *Parashat T'tzaveh*. In painstaking detail, the Torah describes how the *Mishkan* and all its ritual items were to be constructed. Among those ritual items was the *choshen*, the "breastplate" worn by the High Priest while serving in the *Mishkan*. The breastplate, with its four rows of three precious gemstones each, was designed to represent the twelve tribes of Israel. Every stone had its place. Only when every stone was in its place would the priest be able to don the breastplate and thus be fully ready to fulfill his service to the Divine. The instructions for the *choshen* ensured that there was a place for every tribe and that none's space dominated any other. By divine design, all of Israel was given their rightful space. As a result, this elaborate accessory was, from the outset, a lesson in the *middah* of *anavah* (עֲנָוָה, "humility") for the tribes, lest one try either to dominate the space of the others or to wither into the background.

The lesson in *anavah* shone through for the tribes, as the stones of the *choshen* representing them were placed in exactly their rightful spaces. At the same time, those instructions were also a reminder for the High Priest to occupy his rightful space only and to remain mindful of his role. Leading the ritual life of the people, the High Priest could easily develop an inflated sense of self. Yet the mere structure of the *choshen* made it impossible for his hubris to take over. After all, only when he was wearing the jewel-studded piece representing the entire people—its weight literally and figuratively pressing on his shoulders—was he able to fulfill his sacred duty. By placing the breastplate over his chest, he was reminded of his proper role—a role of service and responsibility to others.

According to the nineteenth-century Netziv (Rabbi Naftali Tzvi Yehudah Berlin in *Ha'amek Davar*), the *choshen* lay over the High Priest's heart to remind him that it was his duty to pray and offer sacrifices on behalf of the whole community. Power and prestige were given to the *Kohein Gadol* ("High Priest") with the express purpose of serving God and others—and not to bolster the self.

To act with *anavah* does not simply mean to refrain from standing out. Instead, to act with *anavah* means to limit "oneself to an appropriate space while leaving room for others."[1] Identifying our "appropriate space" in different contexts is the first step of this Mussar challenge. What follows is the task of filling that space—no more and no less.[2]

Shakespeare's tragic character believed that his son needed to take up more space. In a remarkably direct and clear way, *Parashat T'tzaveh* teaches that occupying one's rightful place requires finding a divine balance. The finest fabrics, metals, and gems were reserved for the High Priest, yet they were used to remind him that there was a place and need for every tribe and every person. To adorn him with this accessory meant to burden him with his responsibility for others. Four rows of three stones leave no single center point, just as there is no single individual at the center of *Am Yisrael*.

This image of absolute equality seems to stands in stark contrast to the social dynamics of our contemporary Western societies. Self-promotion is rewarded, and self-aggrandizement is expected. Elected officials campaign by bolstering themselves and cutting down their opponents. Celebrity culture enhances the image of celebrity life. We find affirmation in how many "likes" or "followers" we can attract on social media. "Selfies" ensure that we are always front and center in the world as we perceive it.

There is some truth to the adage: clothes do "make the man." But as *Parashat T'tzaveh* suggests and Mussar confirms, it is not the size of our closets or the labels sewn on our garments that define us. Rather, the things we wear on the outside have the potential to function as instigators of internal, spiritual exercises. Like the stones on the breastplate and its placement, each of us bears a sacred duty. We must consider where we fit into the broader world, and occupy our rightful space—no more and no less.

Questions to Ask
Do the clothes you wear on any given day impact your behavior? How is this behavior similar to or different from your behavior when you are wearing something else?

Practice for the *Middah* of *Anavah*
If you are accustomed to wearing clothes that make you stand out, experiment with wearing clothes that are easily overlooked. If you are accustomed to wearing neutral clothes, experiment with wearing something that makes you stand out. Notice any changes in how you feel, how you behave, and how people respond to you.

Another *Middah* to Consider
The *choshen* of the High Priest was part of an elaborate eight-piece decorated uniform for his ritual work. Consider the "courage" (*ometz lev*, אֹמֶץ לֵב) that he had to show by stepping into this highly visible role, and consider the comfort given by the uniform. What would it be like if he did not wear a uniform?

NOTES
1. Alan Morinis, *Everyday Holiness: The Jewish Spiritual Path of Mussar* (Boston: Trumpeter, 2007), p. 49.
2. Alan Morinis, "Seeking Everyday Holiness," curriculum notes.

Ki Tisa—Exodus 30:11–34:35
Kaas—The Value of Anger

RABBI MARI CHERNOW

V'atah hanichah li v'yichar api vahem vaachaleim (וְעַתָּה הַנִּיחָה לִּי
וְיִחַר־אַפִּי בָהֶם וַאֲכַלֵּם), "Now, let Me be, that My anger may blaze
forth against them and that I may destroy them!"
—*Exodus 32:10*

TO BE FAIR, the Golden Calf is the most egregious offense in the
Torah. It will become the prototypical sin in Jewish tradition. To be
fair, the description of the idol, *Eileh elohecha Yisrael asher he-elucha
mei-eretz Mitzrayim* (אֵלֶּה אֱלֹהֶיךָ יִשְׂרָאֵל אֲשֶׁר הֶעֱלוּךָ מֵאֶרֶץ מִצְרָיִם), "This
is your god, O Israel, who brought you out of the land of Egypt!"
(Exodus 32:4), is an outrage. To be fair, it was not long ago that God
lovingly promised, *V'lakachti et-chem li l'am v'hayiti lachem leilohim*
(וְלָקַחְתִּי אֶתְכֶם לִי לְעָם וְהָיִיתִי לָכֶם לֵאלֹהִים), "I will take you to be My
people, and I will be your God" (Exodus 6:7); and here, the people
respond with disloyalty and distrust.

God's anger (*kaas*, כַּעַס) may not be surprising, but it is shocking
nonetheless. It is wrathful, ruinous, and terrifying as God threatens
nothing short of calamity. This is precisely the anger that teachers
of Mussar warn against. The Talmud cautions us about anyone who
"tears his garments or scatters his money or breaks his vessels in
his anger."[1] These actions are mild and restrained compared to the
destruction that God intends to bring upon the people of Israel in
Ki Tisa.

Thankfully, that destruction does not come to be. In several midrashim the Rabbis read God's words "Now, let Me be" (Exodus
23:10) as intending the exact opposite of their face-value meaning.[2]

That is, in supposedly telling Moses not to intervene, God is inviting Moses to intervene! If so, the phrase reveals God's own misgivings about the force of God's own rage. Before Moses so much as raises an eyebrow in objection, God suggests that there is reason to object.

Moses takes the opportunity and convinces God to relent. Had that not been the case, *Ki Tisa* might have been an illustration of the teaching of *Orchot Tzadikim*, "It is impossible for the angry one to escape great sin,"[3] and that of Abraham ibn Hasdai, "Anger begins with madness and ends with regret." It seems that God teeters just on the edge of both madness and regret.[4]

Must anger lead to regret? As an emotion, no. But as a momentary justification for behavior we would not otherwise condone, perhaps. As the Talmud explains, the problem with tearing one's garments in anger is "that is the work of the evil inclination. Today it tells one to do this, and tomorrow it tells one to do that."[5] In other words, emotions are fleeting. They come and go. But anger has a particular power to drive us to make reckless decisions.

To highlight anger's toxic potential, the Talmud compares the one who acts rashly in anger to an idol worshiper. Alan Morinis explains:

> This association of anger with idolatry also reveals why anger is such a frightful power. When a person loses his or her temper, he or she becomes overwhelmed and overpowered by the emotion of anger. By allowing that to happen, a person yields authority over their life to the raging emotion, and it is then the power of anger [i.e., rather than God] that the angry person serves.[6]

Comparing anger to worshiping idols seems nonsensical when the anger is God's. However, in *Ki Tisa*, the seemingly nonsensical makes perfect sense. The Golden Calf, of course, is the quintessential idol. By worshiping an idol, the Israelites very nearly provoke God to an anger that is equated with idol worship! Anger is almost always triggered by a breach in a relationship. Here, the Talmud creates an equivalency between the original breach caused by the Israelites and God's reaction to it.

Once anger leads us to regrettable action, we can no longer speak of one injured party and one injuring party. Anger has the potential to make it impossible to claim that one is holding righteous high ground. It ensures that both parties will bear responsibility for a damaged relationship. In this case, if God had given into rage, there would be little difference between God and the brazen Israelites. Both sides would be, as it were, idol worshipers.

How interesting, then, that this *parashah* includes God's well-known self-description: "*Adonai! Adonai!* God compassionate and gracious, *slow to anger*, abounding in kindness and faithfulness" (Exodus 34:6). This verse will be repeated throughout the *Tanach* and ultimately included in holy day liturgy. It lays out God's admirable qualities, those that we human beings are to notice and emulate. Perhaps God's words are aspirational here, and instructive. Perhaps, once the emotion has subsided and forgiveness has occurred, God vows to behave differently in the future. These words may then be understood as a reflection on how anger ought to show up in a relationship. They do not describe how God has recently acted, but rather prescribe, with optimism and hope, how God will control divine anger in the future.

It is critical to note that the text does not say "never angry," but rather "slow to anger." Anger, in the right measure, is actually a teacher. It can function like a bright red-flashing indicator light on our emotional dashboard, alerting us to a matter in need of attention. As a signal to our souls, anger can be holy. It can reveal a deep passion or perhaps a wound, a longing or a regret. It can help us clarify and prioritize.

Imagine if God had said to the Israelites, "I didn't even realize how important your loyalty was to Me until so much anger rose up that I actually wanted to kill you!" What are the parallels for us? Where can we notice anger and learn from it?

On a societal level, too, anger can indicate that transformative change is necessary. Consider social movements, such as Me Too and Black Lives Matter. The issues at their heart, sexual violence and racial inequality, have long been critical and worthy of our attention.

However, they did not gain the national spotlight until anger fueled a sense of urgency.

As with every *middah*, we are in search of the appropriate place and space for anger, too. The ideal presented in *Ki Tisa* is "slow to anger," that is, anger that is tempered by thoughtful consideration. Our goal is to avoid either underreacting or overreacting to anger.[7]

If we tend to overreact, then we might consider the wisdom found in Proverbs, "Better to be slow to anger than mighty, to have self-control than to conquer a city" (Proverbs 16:32). We might seek strategies that help assuage our anger before we react. Several possibilities may be found in *Ki Tisa*, in Moses's approach to calming God down.

If we tend to underreact, then we might examine how to prioritize our own needs. If we never get angry, we may have an overabundance of humility or compassion. If we never get angry, there may be anger under the surface with the power to control us just as much as overt anger does.

The teachings of the Talmud, Ibn Hasdai, *Orchot Tzadikim*, Proverbs, and *Ki Tisa* itself guide us to identify anger and give it healthy space to breathe. They warn of the danger of unmanaged rage. They invite us to learn from anger as we strengthen our emotional and spiritual health. Anger contains great wisdom. Our task is to give it honor but not too much power, to listen to it carefully without wholly deferring to it, and to find within it sparks of holiness.

Questions to Ask

Mussar practitioner Nancy Weiss has compiled a list of antidotes to anger. These include gratitude, perspective, humility, compassion, and taking responsibility. What strategies does Moses employ in Exodus 32:11–13? Do you believe that they would be effective with human anger?

How comfortable are you with considering God to be nearly out of control in anger? Does this interpretation conform to your beliefs about God? Alternatively, are you drawn to the idea that God is in a process of reflecting and learning?

Is there someone in your life to whom you can say, *V'atah hanichah li* ("Now, let me be")? In other words, is there someone who might help you reconsider an action you are considering taking in a moment of fury? What about that relationship makes it safe enough to do so? If not another person, what else gets you to a calmer, more reasoned space following great anger?

Practices for the *Middah* of *Kaas*

Keep a journal in which you make note of times when you encounter anger (yours and that of others). Notice both your internal experience and any reactions that you have that would be observable to someone else. Reflect back from time to time on what you have written in your journal and on whether you would like to handle anger differently in the future.

If you agree with Proverbs 16:32, "Better to be slow to anger than mighty, to have self-control than to conquer a city," consider learning that verse in English or Hebrew. You might also use *erech apayim* as a phrase to keep you connected to this concept. *Erech apayim* is translated as "slow to anger" and is a key phrase in both the Proverbs verse and the list of God's attributes from Exodus 34.

Work to develop a respectful relationship with your anger. Ask it what it wants to teach you. Listen carefully for nuggets of wisdom and holiness.

Other *Middot* to Consider

Compassion (*rachamim*, רַחֲמִים) is the flip side of anger in *Ki Tisa*. Both God and Moses hold the people accountable but ultimately respond with love and compassion. What drives their compassion as the story develops? Does their compassion come in the right measure?

Trust (*bitachon*, בִּטָּחוֹן): The crisis of the Golden Calf comes about because of the people's overwhelming anxiety as they wait at the bottom of Mount Sinai. What, if anything, could have helped them become more trusting?

NOTES

1. *Babylonian Talmud, Shabbat* 105b.
2. In *Sh'mot Rabbah* 42:9, the Rabbis compare God to a king who is so angry with his son that he is about to become violent with him. They compare Moses to the boy's instructor, who is in the room next door. When he hears the king cry out, "Let me be!" he realizes that no one is in the chamber besides the king and his son, that is, there is no one else to whom the king might be talking. The instructor concludes that the king must be calling out so that he will go in and plead on the boy's behalf.

   In *D'varim Rabbah* 3:15, God has previously set up a system to manage divine emotions, telling Moses, "Let not the two of us be angry, but when you see Me pour hot [water], you pour cold, and when you see Me pour cold, you pour hot."

   These texts were highlighted by Dr. Christine Hayes in a Hartman Institute webinar, "Moses at Sinai: God's Partner or Adversary."
3. From a course of the Mussar Institute, though I cannot find a specific citation.
4. Ibid.
5. *Babylonian Talmud Shabbat* 105b.
6. From a course of the Mussar Institute, though I cannot find a specific citation.
7. Here my view contradicts Maimonides, who argues (*Hilchot De'ot* 2:3) that anger should be avoided entirely.

VAYAK'HEIL—EXODUS 35:1–38:20

Z'rizut—Alacrity:
With Joy in His Heart

RABBI ELIZABETH BAHAR

Vayomer Moshe el b'nei Yisrael r'u kara Adonai b'shem B'tzaleil ben Uri ben Chur l'mateih Y'hudah (וַיֹּאמֶר מֹשֶׁה אֶל-בְּנֵי יִשְׂרָאֵל רְאוּ קָרָא יהוה בְּשֵׁם בְּצַלְאֵל בֶּן-אוּרִי בֶן-חוּר לְמַטֵּה יְהוּדָה), "And Moses said to the Israelites: See, the Eternal has singled out by name Bezalel, son of Uri son of Hur, of the tribe of Judah."
—*Exodus 35:30*

WHAT WAS SO SPECIAL about Bezalel? Why was he singled out by name? This *parashah* is one of five portions telling of the construction of the Tabernacle. At times, it appears repetitive, offering an almost verbatim copy of the instructions that God gives to Moses in Exodus 25–31. These divine directives are subsequently carried out in Exodus 35–40 by the people and overseen by Bezalel and a second select individual, Oholiab.

Who were these two individuals? We know almost nothing about their origins, except that Oholiab is from the tribe of Dan in the north, and Bezalel from the tribe of Israel in the south. Neither of them is a priest or from a ruling family, clans we might expect to lead in the building of the Tabernacle.

The Rabbis who commented on this *parashah* noticed that a new type of leader is being recognized here. In the second century, when leadership was a hereditary rite under Roman rule, the Rabbis understood that Israelite leadership had not derived from heredity right, but instead from merit and wisdom.[1] Great leaders earn power from their followers, and not the other way around.[2]

So what exactly did Bezalel do to rate his prominent place? How did he engage in the task at hand? What can we glean from his actions and words that might be applicable to our own lives?

Bezalel was charged with precise and specific instructions to create the Tabernacle in which God would be able to take residence among humanity. This would be the first time God would be residing with humans since the Garden of Eden. Such an immense and ambitious vision must have seemed daunting and nearly impossible. The overwhelming responsibility might have left him eager to avoid the assignment. It requires no great leap of the imagination to empathize with the challenge Bezalel faced. I can't do it. I don't have the necessary resources. What if I mess it up? What if I can't get the help I need? But Bezalel persevered with joy in his heart. The Rabbis understood that despite his fears, Bezalel chose courage every day. He chose leadership and openness and humility and joy. He did not cower away from the grand mission, but instead he attacked it with alacrity, all the while knowing that the greatest undertakings bring the greatest rewards.

How do we know that he attacked this project with determination?

There are two different Rabbinic ideas about the reasons Bezalel was chosen by God to build the Tabernacle: his appointment as a leader by the people and his youthfulness. Rabbi Yitzchak shared a story in the Talmud: There was something so special about Bezalel, that the people specifically desired him to lead.[3] The Gemara imagines Bezalel to be merely thirteen when he leads the other artists to direct Moses to stop the people from offering further donations, since they were inundated with materials.[4] He did not quash their enthusiasm, but harnessed it from the beginning until its completion.

Z'rizut is the trait motivating us to get up and get going with cheer and joy. Moshe Chayim Luzzatto devotes four chapters in his book *M'silat Yesharim* (*The Path of the Upright*) to this trait. When the opportunity to act positively presents itself, only zeal will answer the call.[5] Our life demands that we engage. We can choose to engage with zeal or choose to sit and be lazy. The path of laziness, Luzzatto warns, leaves an opening for the *yetzer hara* to enter, allowing us to make unwise choices and fail to achieve a level of happiness or satisfaction.[6]

The possibility of filling our life, or overfilling it, with the insipid "110 percent," with one singular vision above all others, distorts our ability to live a life of balance as God commands. We know that we cannot carry out a task to excess without becoming a slave to the task.[7] The balance must be found between laziness and compulsion, between sloth and vigor. When we make excuses or practice avoidance, we create a scenario in which fear can be paralyzing. Fear of failure. Fear of success. Fear of mediocrity. And that paralysis comes at the expense of every other aspect of a full and balanced life.

According to a midrash, Bezalel had a reputation for hard work,[8] skill, and caring. The Rabbis teach that people are known by three names—"one given by their parents; one, by other people; and one they acquire wholly on their own"—the last being the most important,[9] and that Bezalel received the call to build the Tabernacle because of the good name he had acquired.[10] Ibn Ezra notes that not all scholars are capable of teaching. Not all builders are capable of instructing, and not all leaders are capable of bringing people in.[11] Possessing the skills required to lead, teach, or build does not guarantee that one will fulfill that potential. But through knowledge, experimentation, and patience,[12] Bezalel did.

Devotion to a task requires resiliency. We may choose to drift from our chosen path, reverting to laziness and using rationalizations as excuses. Living a life of alacrity means engagement even when we might wish not to engage. Rashi understood that this trait of commitment is one of the characteristics that ensured the project would be completed. In his commentary on Exodus 37:1, Rashi states that Bezalel did so because *shenatan nafsho*, "he gave his life."

Countless small businesses fail within the first few years. Craft projects are abandoned in basements all over America. Backyard gardens languish and die from lack of attention. So many ideas and dreams remain incomplete, abandoned because of a sprinkling of procrastination and excuses. Alaracity helps us to push through the initial urge of facing a hardship and enables us not to allow laziness to creep in as a result. Giving ourselves to a project, like Bezalel, prompts us to tackle our goals and recognize opportunities as they present themselves. It is our obligation to begin building a sukkah as soon as Yom Kippur has ended, so that the upcoming mitzvah will not be put off and therefore overlooked through laziness.

The Ramban offers an interesting take: When the slaves left Egypt, they had been crushed under the work of mortar and brick. They had acquired no skill set or knowledge with which to create or build a fine structure including melting of metal, cutting precious stones, sewing fine cloths, or carving wood. Still, when Bezalel saw the people's generous, charitable hearts that moved them to give, he concluded that the same spirit would also inspire their courage to engage in skills new to them. This is the true genius and leadership of Bezalel: his ability to see the potential of his people and then convince those same people of their own worth and abilities. He was able to harness the energy of the people to construct a Tabernacle on earth linking the mystery of the heavens above to the physicality of the present. The true artistry and genius of Bezalel was his ability to move from the repetitive drudgery of Egypt to the vast creativity of building the Tabernacle, without prior training or vision.

As Avivah Zornberg points out, based on a midrash: "One might even say that he most purely fulfills God's project in creating human beings: 'Let us make human beings in our image [be-tzal-menu] . . .' (Gen 1:26). To be the 'image of God,' the tzelem, perhaps invokes a 'shadowing' ability (tzel)."[13] In the shadow of God, Bezalel was able to intuit from the words of Moses how to create the phenomenal and sacred Tabernacle where God would reside. He was able to see beyond the words. He was able to take the instruction manual, with limited tools, limited knowledge, and limited ability from the people to create something that lasted as the home for God until King Solomon built the Temple in Jerusalem. Without an intimate knowledge or having ever seen such a tabernacle previously, Bezalel was able to intuit the divine intent. He was, if you will, able to take a manual from Ikea, not see the furniture, and improve it beyond the engineers' vision.

How many times have we started on a path only to abandon our journey halfway through because we couldn't see the finish line? How many times have we faced obstacles and retreated using rationales such as lack of time and resources? How many times have we faced the unknown and shrunk, unsure how to best finish the task or what the project should look like? When we open our hearts to possibility and hope, we create a path for options and success. By embracing the task at hand with alacrity and joy, we can find the energy and motivation to keep going.

Questions to Ask
How have you used excuses or rationalizations to prevent yourself from completing a task?
How have you pushed through and met a goal? Do you think it can become a habit?

Practice for the *Middah* of *Z'rizut*
Create a plan of action when faced with a project that overwhelms you, perhaps by identifying small bits to accomplish first. Accept that you will stumble, but know that you can get back up.

Another *Middah* to Consider
Bezalel takes the vision presented to him with grace. While he might be a more accomplished artist, he does not allow his skill to put others down. He does not use his ego. Instead he acts with humility (*anavah*, עֲנָוָה). Please consider how to be a leader and still act with humility.

NOTES
1. *Tanchuma, Vayak'heil* 2.
2. *Babylonian Talmud, B'rachot* 55a.

3. "With regard to Bezalel's appointment, Rabbi Yitzchak said: One may only appoint a leader over a community if he consults with the community and they agree to the appointment, as it is stated: 'And Moses said unto the Children of Israel: See, the Eternal has singled out by name Bezalel, son of Uri son of Hur, of the tribe of Judah' (Exodus 35:30). The Eternal said to Moses: 'Moses, is Bezalel a suitable appointment in your eyes?' Moses said to God: 'Sovereign of the universe, if he is a suitable appointment in Your eyes, then all the more so in my eyes.' The Holy One, Blessed be God, said to him: 'Nevertheless, go and tell Israel and ask their opinion.' Moses went and said to Israel: 'Is Bezalel suitable in your eyes?' They said to him: 'If he is suitable in the eyes of the Holy One, Blessed be God, and in your eyes, all the more so he is suitable in our eyes'" (*Babylonian Talmud, B'rachot* 55a).
4. *Babylonian Talmud Sanhedrin* 69b:18, Exodus 36:4.
5. In his commentary on *M'silat Yesharim*, Ira Stone writes, "Only when we learn through watchfulness to inhibit ourselves from choosing the *yetzer ha-ra* [evil inclination] can we begin to contemplate how to choose the *yetzer ha-tov* [good inclination]. It is at this point that zeal can enter the equation" (Moses Hayyim Luzzatto, *Mesillat Yesharim: The Path of the Upright*, trans. Mordecai Kaplan, commentary by Ira Stone [Philadelphia: Jewish Publication Society, 2011], 82).
6. Ibid.
7. Eugene B. Borowitz and Frances Weinman Schwartz, *The Jewish Moral Virtues* (Philadelphia: Jewish Publication Society, 1999), 87–88.
8. *Tanchuma Vayak'heil* 1.
9. Ibid.
10. Ibid., 2–3.
11. Ibn Ezra commentary on Exodus 35:34.
12. *Tanchuma Vayak'heil* 4. Also Rashi on Exodus 38:22: "God commanded"—So great was Bezalel that he not only act as Moses commanded, but he intuited instructions from God that Moses had not conveyed to Bezalel. Moses taught Bezalel the order of the construction as it is found in chapters 25–26, where the Ark is mentioned before the structure, to which Bezalel argued that a building (the Tabernacle) must be erected before its contents (the Ark). Moses answered that not only was Bezalel right, his name reflects that he is in the shadow of God. (There is a similar commentary in *Babylonian Talmud, B'rachot* 55a.) Furthermore, Bezalel knew the order of building things based on how things were built in the real world and did not rely solely on instruction from Moses.
13. Avivah Gottlieb Zornberg, *The Particulars of Rapture: Reflections on Exodus* (New York: Schocken Books, 2001), 477.

P'kudei—Exodus 38:21–40:38
Emunah—Regaining Faith

Rabbi Cheryl Rosenstein, DD

At long last, the *Mishkan*, the Holy Tabernacle, becomes a reality. Moses has collected all the gifts and delivered the divine pronouncements for the specifications of its construction. Bezalel and his team of artisans have executed the divine orders. *Parashat P'kudei* commences with Moses's careful accounting of the bounty that the Israelites have donated with great zeal.

Where the Golden Calf symbolized their lack of faith, the *Mishkan* stands for the *emunah* (אֱמוּנָה, "faith") of the Israelites. However, such faith did not come easily to our ancestors, and it does not come easily to us today, either.

Enslaved and oppressed for four hundred years, the Israelites' faith was understandably weak. It was for their sake that God sent the plagues against Egypt, that they should witness God's power and faithfulness. In flight, flanked by Pharaoh's army on one side and the Reed Sea on the other, our ancestors' newfound faith flagged. Only after they had crossed the sea on dry land and had seen the waves close over their pursuers did their faith revive: "Who is like You, Eternal One, among the celestials?" (Exodus 15:11). Their faith reached a pinnacle at Mount Sinai—only to disintegrate in the debacle of the Golden Calf, when Moses's prolonged absence on the mountaintop enflamed their fears and doubts. The Israelites' crisis of faith precipitated God's reciprocal if momentary loss of faith in the people of Israel: "Now, let Me be, that My anger may blaze forth against them and that I may destroy them" (Exodus 32:10).

In the aftermath of the Golden Calf, when the remnant of the people stood punished, shattered, subdued, and repentant, God restored their dignity by asking something of them.

> Then they brought the Tabernacle to Moses, with the Tent and all its furnishings: its clasps, its planks, its bars, its posts, and its sockets; the covering of tanned ram skins, the covering of dolphin skins, and the curtain for the screen; the Ark of the Pact and its poles, and the cover; the table and all its utensils, and the bread of display; the pure lampstand . . . the altar of gold . . . the oil for anointing . . . all the furnishings for the service of the Tabernacle, the Tent of Meeting.   —*Exodus 39:33–40*

The gifts the Israelites bring for the construction of the *Mishkan* help them not only to create the sacred structure, but also to rebuild their faith in the invisible Deity. God has motivated and inspired the people with the promise "And let them make Me a sanctuary that I may dwell among them" (Exodus 25:8)—a sort of "if-you-build-it-I-will-come" divine recognition that the fragile faith of the people requires presence, both God's and their own.

> For over the Tabernacle a cloud of the Eternal rested by day, and fire would appear in [the cloud] by night, in the view of all the house of Israel throughout their journeys.   —*Exodus 40:38*

With their wholehearted contributions to the *Mishkan*, the people of Israel brought themselves wholeheartedly into the covenant. Their *emunah* is rewarded with God's *emunah*—their presence is met and accompanied by the Divine Presence.

Another story, elsewhere in our tradition, builds on the notion of the fragility of our faith, while also adding a new layer of theology. In the biblical story, acts of *emunah* lead to renewed and strengthened faith of the people in their God. In the Rabbinic imagination, we learn that acts of faith also renew God's presence in this world. Rabbi Shimon bar Yochai, the first-century mystic credited with writing the *Zohar*, taught:

> It is written: "This is my God and I will enshrine Him" (Exodus 15:2). This means: "When I acknowledge God, God is glorified,

but when I do not acknowledge God, God is glorified only in name." It is written: "For the name of the Eternal I proclaim; give glory to our God" (Deuteronomy 32:3). [This means:] "When I call God's name, God is great, but when I don't . . . [it is as if God is not great]." It is written: "You are My witnesses, said the Eternal . . . and I am the One" (Isaiah 43:10). This means: "When you are My witnesses, I am God, but when you are not My witnesses, it is as if I am not God." It is written: "To You, enthroned in heaven, I turn my eyes" (Psalm 123:1). This means: "If it weren't for me, it is as if You would not be sitting in the heavens."[1]

No wonder, then, that the words of the *Sh'ma*, affirming our faith, are embedded in our daily prayers: "Hear, O Israel, *Adonai* is our God, *Adonai* is One!" (Deuteronomy 6:4). And no wonder that, by scribal tradition, the last letters of the first and last words of the *Sh'ma* (שְׁמַע)—the *ayin* (ע) of *sh'ma* (שְׁמַע) and the *dalet* (ד) of *echad* (אֶחָד)— are written larger than all the other letters, those two oversized letter spelling the word *eid* (עֵד—"witness").

The paragraph that follows Deuteronomy 6:4, popularly referred to as *V'ahavta*, asserts that it is by our deeds, our adherence to the mitzvot, that we bear witness to God's Being. Rabbi Shimon bar Yochai might say that by proclaiming our faith with our recitation of these sacred words and by evidencing our faith by fulfilling God's commandments, it is as if we unify and enthrone God in our world.

Faith appears to be both tender and transitory, while doubt and critical thinking seem to be built into the human genome.

We pride ourselves on being rational beings. The Talmud itself may be read as a testament to Judaism's celebration of the mind and its power of inquiry. Our tradition encourages us to ask questions and to challenge our perceptions. In medieval Spain, Jews adopted the rational thought of Greek philosophy; Maimonides worked to reconcile the ideas of reason and revelation. Ours is a generation defined by an avid, almost insatiable, growth in science and technology. We mock the people who have faith as buying into make-believe. We require the "proof" brought by mathematics, science, and logic.

Yet ours is also an age in which information and misinformation are both readily available and even marketed to us; we struggle to discern truth from lie and fact from opinion. We "believe" whatever sources are most comfortable or conform to our worldview, even if doing so requires disregarding science or logic.

As the story of our people shows, the thirst for faith is also part of our DNA. Faith is the product of experience and presence—not of proof. Faith is encountered by the soul, not "known" by the brain. Abraham and Sarah, Isaac and Rebekah, Jacob and Rachel and Leah traveled their respective paths to faith.

Our experience in utero is that the universe as we know it will protect and provide for us. When we leave that safe space, the world assails us. Our experiences may contrive to erode our nascent *emunah*. Yet in our deepest hearts, we long to be faithful, to commune with an Entity deserving of our faith. Alan Morinis quotes the late Lubavitcher Rebbe, who wrote the following to a struggling student: "It is only due to an inner conviction in our hearts, shared by every human being, that there is a Judge, that there is right and there is wrong. And so, when we see wrong, we demand an explanation: Why is this not the way it is supposed to be? That itself is belief in God."[2]

Just as God makes space for Creation by an act of *tzimtzum* (צִמְצוּם, "contraction"), the ultimate act of humility, so does God perform *tzimtzum* in granting the Israelites permission to build the Tabernacle. God's *emunah* in us is manifest when God empowers us to build God's "house." Our ancestors' *emunah* was strengthened by the act of building that house, the physical space that reminded them that the Divine would reside in their midst. The narrative of the *Mishkan* teaches us that we build our faith not by means of spiritual encounters, but through the works of our own hands.

Perhaps *emunah* is built through acts of faith. Our faith grows when we work to make space for God in our lives. Whether we do this through prayer or meditation, or by performing acts of *tzedakah* or *chesed*, each of us has the ability to construct a space in which faith can be nurtured.

Questions to Ask

What tools do you have in hand to build, grow, or strengthen
your own *emunah*?
Have you ever felt a deep connection with a "Greater Whole"?
When was that?
How might you create, or re-create, that sense of connection?
Martin Buber taught that "God is between us." Is it possible
to experience *emunah* in the mundane—for example, in
(but not only in) nature?

Practices for the *Middah* of *Emunah*

Close your eyes. Imagine the face of someone you love. Feel that person's loving presence. Rest in that feeling. That feeling is *emunah*.
As you go through your day, strive to be more present. Bring more of
yourself. Be fully present when you are with others. Give something
of yourself in each encounter, even if it is just a smile.

Another *Middah* to Consider

What role does generosity (*n'divut*, נְדִיבוּת) play in *Parashat P'kudei*?
What is the relationship between the Israelites' *n'divut* and their
emunah?

NOTES
1. *Sifrei D'varim* 34:6; *P'sikta D'Rav Kahana* 12:6.
3. Alan Morinis, *Everyday Holiness: The Jewish Spiritual Path of Mussar*
   (Boston: Trumpeter, 2007), 223.

LEVITICUS

VAYIKRA—LEVITICUS 1:1–5:26

N'divut—Generosity: Giving Away, Bringing Close

RABBI DAVID JAFFE

"When any of you presents an offering of cattle to the Eternal: You shall choose your offering from the herd or from the flock. If your offering is a burnt offering from the herd, you shall make your offering a male without blemish. You shall bring it to the entrance of the Tent of Meeting, for acceptance in your behalf before the Eternal." —*Leviticus 1:2–3*

THE BOOK OF LEVITICUS opens with a detailed description of the sacrificial system that will become central to Israelite worship until the destruction of the Second Temple in 70 CE. If we take a step back from the details of cattle and blood and fat, an important progression emerges in the last *parashiyot* of the Book of Exodus and the first *parashiyot* of Leviticus. After the incident of the Golden Calf at Mount Sinai, the Israelites needed a way to repair and then remain in right relationship with God. The *Mishkan* ("the Tabernacle"), with its carefully constructed walls and vessels, was established as the setting for this relationship.

Our *parashah* begins the description of how to engage in this relationship. Indeed, the Hebrew word for "sacrifice" is *korban*, from the root ק-ר-ב, meaning "to draw close." The entire sacrificial system is an exercise in drawing close and being in relationship with God—and, by extension, with oneself and others. Embedded in the details of the sacrificial system are clues to having successful relationships. The *middah* of generosity (*n'divut*, נְדִיבוּת) is central to the process.

The sacrificial system presents a nuanced interplay between "free-will giving," responsibility, and obligation. *Parashat Vayikra* describes the types of offerings one brings when desiring to make a sacrifice, which include cattle, sheep, birds, and grain. Some offerings are completely burned on the altar (*olot*, עֹלוֹת), while others are only partially burned, with other parts given as gifts to the priests and yet other parts eaten by the owner (*sh'lamim*, שְׁלָמִים). The *parashah* concludes with detailed descriptions of the different sacrifices brought for atonement for a wide variety of accidental transgressions (*chatat*, חַטָּאת). Rashi points out that the sacrifices described at the beginning of our *parashah* are "freewill" offerings (*n'davah*, נְדָבָה; from the same root as "generosity," *n'divut*, נְדִיבוּת).[1] These must be offered with open-hearted desire so that they are pleasingly acceptable to God. They cannot come from a sense of obligation. On the other hand, the sacrifices to achieve atonement include no such reference to being pleasing before God. If offered properly, they effect atonement, but they have an obligatory quality to them.

Even within the category of "freewill offering," there is a subtle interplay of responsibility and generous, open-hearted giving. Rashi writes:

> "He shall offer it": . . . They [the *beit din*, or "court"] must put pressure upon him to bring it if he is remiss in bringing the sacrifice he had promised. One might think that this means that they shall force him against his will! Scripture, however, states, לרצונו "[he must bring it] so that it shall be favorably accepted for him." How is this possible? They press him until he says, "I wish to do it."[2]

What happened here? A person desired to draw close to God through a sacrifice, perhaps as a sign of gratitude. They generously committed to offer a cow, sheep, or other animal. However, some time passed and they did not fulfill their pledge. At this point, their free-will act has obligated them to follow through, just like a pledge to a charity. The Jewish court has the license to compel them to fulfill their pledge. Now, we are in the realm of obligation. Still, this offering must have the quality of *ratzon* (רָצוֹן), "desire" and "favor," which is associated with "desiring to give out of free will." For the gift to be favorable to God, its receiver, it needs to be given out of a desire to give, not out of compulsion. The *beit din* is charged with the difficult task of working with the giver until they realize that they actually desire to give. While this scenario may evoke images from B movies of henchmen shaking down a debtor, at a deeper level we are back in the realm of open-hearted free will. This may be a low level of free will, brought about through external compulsion, but there must be at least some desire for the offering to be accepted.

This same interplay of responsibility and open-hearted giving is a feature of many healthy human relationships. Strong relationships cannot rely only on freewill desire to give and connect. Such relationships, while feeling good in the moment, are undependable. I want to know that good friends feel committed to me and that they do not base their involvement in the relationship only on how they feel in the moment. On the other hand, relationships must be more than just obligations.

Think of relationships you are in that feel like obligations. You do what is necessary—make the phone call, show up for certain events—but an important life-force is missing from those relationships. Do you want to be treated as an obligation? How does that feel?

Ideally, a good relationship is built on both—a sense of obligation that binds you to the other person, and the free will to want to be in the relationship and get closer with each interaction. We can apply the same principle to friends and to more intimate relationships with our partners, children, and even parents.

The *middah* of *n'divut*, "generosity," as described in the sixteenth century in the anonymously authored Mussar classic *The Ways of the Righteous*, captures this nuanced way of giving that is so essential to lasting relationships.[3] The author cites Abraham as the paradigm of generosity, giving of his material goods while hosting his guests, giving of his very self while fighting to save his nephew Lot, and giving of his wisdom when teaching his people about the Creator. This analysis may make *n'divut* sound a lot like *chesed* (חֶסֶד, "loving-kindness"), Abraham's primary soul trait. Indeed, the author writes, "He who gives a great gift to him who asks is half generous. The truly generous man is he who gives always, little or much, before he is asked." Giving before being asked is a hallmark of *chesed*. The author then makes an interesting move, arguing that giving must become a habit. He quotes from Maimonides's interpretation of *Mishnah, Pirkei Avot* 3:15, according to which it is better to give one dollar a thousand times than to give $1000 once as a gift. The repetitive giving builds a habit, and this habitual giving changes the heart. Here we see giving becoming an internal obligation.

The author continues the discussion of the nuanced interplay of obligation and freewill giving by combining *tzedakah* (צְדָקָה) with *chesed*. Giving *tzedakah* is a responsibility incumbent on every member of the community. Indeed, some scholars argue that a portion of our wealth does not belong to us at all, but is intended by God to be the rightful property of those in need.[4] However, there are many ways to give *tzedakah*. According to *Orchot Tzadikim*, "And when you give charity, you should accompany it with loving-kindness, such as buying with money something that the poor need in order to spare them the bother of buying it themselves."[5] This is generosity— knowing you are obliged to give and thinking well about the person to whom you are giving. The author further emphasizes this connection between *n'divut* and responsibility by connecting this *middah* to mitzvot, the guidelines for personal and communal life. Quoting the Talmud, *Orchot Tzadikim* says, "One must be generous with one's wealth to acquire mitzvot, as in the case of Rabban Gamliel, who purchased an *etrog* for a thousand *zuz*."[6] Generosity is not just a *middah* playing out between people. It is also a spiritual dimension of one's relationship with God. In Rabban Gamliel's case, *n'divut* emerges from commandment. Not only does he fulfill the basic minimum of the mitzvah, but he opens his heart to beautify the mitzvah. This is exactly the point of sacrifices described in such detail in *Parashat Vayikra*. Obligation and open-hearted free will coexist to grow the relationship.

The sacrificial system, so prominent in Leviticus and Numbers, is a model for being in relationship, for drawing close. *Ratzon*, "desire," may be the most important element of becoming close to God and others. However, *ratzon* can be fleeting. We may feel a connection one day and not on the next. Through concrete acts of thoughtfulness, giving, and love, *n'divut*, "generosity," helps us turn our *ratzon* for closeness into habitual behavior. From this internalized sense of responsibility for each other and for God, we create real closeness.

Questions to Ask

When do you give out of pure freewill desire? When does giving feel like an obligation?

What are some things that you or others do that help you feel close to them? What helps you feel close to God? To yourself?

What would being generous with yourself look like?

Practice for the *Middah* of *N'divut*

Identify a way to give that feels like a responsibility or obligation—to your children, your parents, your spouse, or your friend. Bring a spirit of "freewill offering" when you give to this person the next time. Notice how this type of giving leaves you feeling about the person to whom you give.

Another *Middah* to Consider

The sacrificial system, like the system of the *Mishkan*, is full of rules and precision. These are aspects of the soul trait of *seder* (סֶדֶר, "order"). *Seder* is also related to *ratzon*, "desire." Twentieth-century Mussar master Rabbi Shlomo Wolbe teaches that if our desire is strong enough, we will create *seder* to accomplish our desire. In this way, *seder* contributes to the presence of deeply felt will and desire. What *seder* ("order") do you have in your life? Does it actually reflect what you really care about?

NOTES

1. Rashi on Leviticus 1:2.
2. Rashi on Leviticus 1:3, quoting *Sifra*.
3. *The Ways of the Righteous*, ed. Gavriel Zaloshinsky, trans. Shraga Silverstein (New York: Feldheim, 1995), 306–19.
4. For example, see *Torat Moshe*, Rabbi Moshe Alshikh on Leviticus 19:9.
5. *The Ways of the Righteous*, 313.
6. *Babylonian Talmud, Sukkah* 41b.
7. Shlomo Wolbe, *Alei Shur*, vol. 2 (Jerusalem: Beit HaMussar, 1986), 320.

Tzav—Leviticus 6:1–8:36
Seder—Order as Response to Transgression

Rabbi Nicole Auerbach

OUR STORY OF CREATION is one of bringing order out of chaos. "When God began to create heaven and earth," Genesis tells us, the earth was *tohu vavohu* (תֹהוּ וָבֹהוּ—"a chaos, unformed") (Genesis 1:2). Out of this murky mess, God creates light and separates it from darkness. As the days of Creation pass, God continues to create by separating and sorting: light from dark, sky from water, water from land, every species of plant and animal from every other. God then assesses the orderly universe and declares it "good."

Almost immediately, human beings upend God's plan, their free will leading them to breach the boundaries God had set for them. Thus begins a tumultuous relationship between God and humankind, in which humans in general—and the nation of Israel in particular—vacillate between chaos and order, between sin and repentance. In the Book of Leviticus, ritual is employed as a way to create and maintain order within society, and also to reestablish order when we inevitably fall short of what God demands.

Take, for example, the *asham* (אָשָׁם, "reparation offering"): In *Tzav*, we are told:

> This is the ritual of the reparation offering: it is most holy. The reparation offering shall be slaughtered at the spot where the burnt offering is slaughtered, and the blood shall be dashed on all sides of the altar. All its fat shall be offered: the broad tail; the fat that covers the entrails; the two kidneys and the fat that is on them at the loins; and the protuberance on the liver, which

shall be removed with the kidneys. The priest shall turn them into smoke on the altar as an offering by fire to the Eternal; it is a reparation offering. Only the males in the priestly line may eat of it; it shall be eaten in the sacred precinct: it is most holy. (Leviticus 7:1–6)

God has learned something since encountering that first act of rebellion in the Garden of Eden. Rather than meet every transgression with permanent exile, God commands that Israelites who have strayed offer a sacrifice to make amends and to mark their intention to re-order their behavior. God gives them a detailed road map for repentance, down to what to do with the fat that covers the kidneys of the animal to be sacrificed.

The minutiae of this ritual, while perplexing to modern readers, are essential to the purpose it serves. This offering addresses a situation in which the person has in some way transgressed the boundaries that God has set, threatening the order that governs her relationship with society and with God. By requiring painstaking attention to detail, the guilt offering, like other sacrifices prescribed in Leviticus, calls individuals back from the inattention or lack of resolve that may have caused them to stray. It reasserts the importance of imposing scrupulous order in their behavior. Because the sacrifice is made publicly, the community comes to witness both the chaos that was created and the new commitment to re-ordering the penitent's behavior.

Mussar embraces the *middah* of *seder* (סֵדֶר, "order") both as a way to emulate God—who, from the moment of Creation, prefers order to chaos—and as a way to keep ourselves accountable to what God demands of us. Alan Morinis writes in *Everyday Holiness*:

> The rabbis who have drawn the commandments from the Torah have enumerated the ways to serve God and have given us the *seder* ("order") according to which each should be performed. For example, we are commanded to eat matzo and drink four cups of wine on Passover. At one point it is matzo, and a second later—beyond the eighteen minutes that it takes to leaven the matzo would be forbidden for Passover. There are

measurements for how much matzo is required to fulfill the commandment, and how much wine constitutes a "cup." And of course, all these acts are organized in a specific sequence, which takes place at the Passover Seder (the same word: "order").[1]

Nothing magic happens between minute eighteen and nineteen to render the matzah un-kosher. But by setting rules around the baking of the matzah, and being attentive to them, we heighten our attention to the particular moment we are celebrating. Likewise, we do not each pick the week we think most suitable for observing the holiday. We abide by the order of the Jewish calendar, which means to bring observance into line with that of our community.

In our everyday lives, we often employ the *middah* of *seder*, with its rules and rituals, to focus on the behaviors we want to cultivate. Through paper journals or applications on our phones, we can track our diet, the number of steps we take, or the amount of time we spend meditating each day. Through in-person or virtual communities, we connect to others who are seeking to build the same habits, increasing our sense of accountability. While there is no discernible difference between taking 9,850 steps and 10,000 on a particular day, using a tracking system makes us more aware of how much we are moving and therefore more likely to achieve our goal of becoming more active. Of course, like many *middot*, our aim with respect to *seder* is moderation. As Morinis writes, "Too little order gives birth to chaos, while at the other end of the range, too much order ties us up in obsessive rigidity."[2] If we find that the order we are imposing on our lives is causing us to be less present and aware, we may need to loosen the reins.

In *Tzav*, the Israelites use the *asham* sacrifice to acknowledge when their behavior has become disordered and to bring themselves back in line with the expectations of society. We can see a similar use of ritual today in twelve-step programs, like Alcoholics Anonymous. Just as *Parashat Tzav* prescribes a list of detailed steps that will bring individuals back into "right relationship" with God and society, AA and other such programs offer a very specific *seder*, namely those twelve steps, for achieving sobriety.[3]

According to the Hazelden Betty Ford Foundation, the purpose of these twelve steps is "to recover from compulsive, out-of-control behaviors and restore manageability and order to your life. It's a way of seeing that your behavior is only a symptom, a sort of 'check engine' light to discovering what's really going on under the hood."[4]

Much like the Israelites who brought an *asham* offering, members of twelve-step groups gather in community to reflect on how their disordered behavior has affected their lives and the lives of those they love, aiming to realign and reorder their behavior. And like the Israelites, each serves the others as a witness, encouraging them and holding them accountable.

From the beginning, God has a preference for order over chaos. And from the beginning, people struggle to order their own behavior in ways that align with God's commandments. *Tzav*'s description of the *asham* offering is at once an acknowledgment that human lives, unchecked, will tend toward chaos and an example of how we can use ritual to refocus our attention and to reorient and bring order to our behavior.

Questions to Ask

On the continuum from chaos on the one hand to "obsessive rigidity" on the other, where do you typically fall? What might you do to bring yourself more toward a "happy medium" when it comes to the role of order in your life?

What rituals or practices have you used to become more mindful of certain behaviors you want to cultivate? What role do other people play in keeping you accountable to your goals?

Practice for the *Middah* of *Seder*

Identify one area of your life that has become disordered, whether it is a bad habit or a messy desk. Spend ten minutes a day bringing more order to this area of your life. What other *middot* or behaviors are affected by your increased sense of order and control?

Another *Middah* to Consider

The priests are given great *kavod* (כָּבוֹד, "honor") in this portion; they wear special clothes and are the only ones allowed to eat from certain sacrifices brought by the Israelites. But the priests, including the High Priest, are also required to remove those special clothes and to clean up the ashes. How does this act of "humility" (*anavah*, עֲנָוָה) counterbalance the *kavod* that is given to the priests? How do humility and honor counterbalance one another in your own experience?

NOTES

1. Alan Morinis, *Everyday Holiness: The Jewish Spiritual Path of Mussar* (Boston: Trumpeter, 2007), 90–91.
2. Ibid., 86.
3. Hazelden Betty Ford Foundation, "The Twelve Steps of Alcoholics Anonymous," available at https://www.hazeldenbettyford.org/articles/twelve-steps-of-alcoholics-anonymous.
4. Ibid.

SH'MINI—LEVITICUS 9:1–11:47

Sh'tikah—What Kind of Silence?

RABBI JONATHAN KRAUS

WITH SPARE LANGUAGE, Leviticus 10:1–2 reports that God sent a consuming fire from the altar to kill Aaron's sons, the priests Nadab and Abihu, because they made an unauthorized offering of "alien fire." In the verse that follows, Moses explains to Aaron that this tragedy is consistent with God's declaration: *Bikrovai ekadeish v'al p'nei chol haam ekaveid* (בִּקְרֹבַי אֶקָּדֵשׁ וְעַל־פְּנֵי כָל־הָעָם אֶכָּבֵד), "Through those near to Me I show Myself holy, and gain glory before all the people" (Leviticus 10:3). Then, the verse concludes with this simple but stunning comment: *Vayidom Aharon* (וַיִּדֹּם אַהֲרֹן), "And Aaron was silent."

What is the nature of this silence? In what ways might Aaron's response deepen our understanding of the *middah* of *sh'tikah* (שְׁתִיקָה, "silence")?

The incomprehensible horror and anguish of being forced to watch as two of his children were burned alive could easily have rendered Aaron mute. It is not difficult to imagine such an overwhelming, traumatic moment leaving a parent completely paralyzed in heart, mind, and voice. In fact, Aaron's stupefaction would have been infinitely more profound and complex knowing that this terrible burning was sent by the same God he was in the process of being consecrated to serve. However, such a silence, though completely reasonable to our compassionate hearts, would not reflect the practice of *sh'tikah*—because it's not yet a choice. Instead, such a silence would simply be a symptom of a father's shattered and traumatized heart grown instantly numb with grief. Aaron would simply be unable to speak.

This interpretation is consistent with the Hebrew verb used here, *vayidom*, translated as "and he [Aaron] was silent." In its usage elsewhere in the *Tanach*, that verb often implies a passive cessation of action or speech, a simple stopping—for example, the sun standing still for Joshua (Joshua 10:13), the elders of Zion sitting silently on the ground in mourning (Lamentations 2:10), and the Psalmist praising God without stopping (Psalm 30:13).

By contrast, the *middah* of *sh'tikah* implies active restraint, a conscious decision not to speak, a choice not to give voice to one's thoughts or feelings. In its relatively few appearances in the *Tanach*, *sh'tikah* seems to imply an act of gaining control over tumultuous forces, such as God calming the raging waters of the sea (Jonah 1:11–12; Psalm 107:30) or fights being avoided with a quarrelsome individual (Proverbs 26:20).

Interestingly, this is how the Rabbis understand Aaron's silence: as a volitional recognition and acceptance of the justice of God's decision, however painful. In fact, the Talmud even suggests that Aaron is rewarded for his silence and the implicit acceptance of God's will.[1] *Orchot Tzadikim* (chapter 21) amplifies this idea further, explaining that Aaron's response exemplifies the ideal response to any experience of God's strict justice (*tziduk hadin*) and adds that we should respond with silence when we hear others insulting us, rather than acting on our understandable impulse to respond in kind.

The Rabbis lift up the practice of restraint—the capacity for self-awareness and control over one's verbal impulses—as a sign of strong character and the capacity for wisdom. They interpret Aaron's silence as an impressive sign of self-restraint. We could easily imagine him wanting to scream at Moses or even at God. At the very least, we could imagine Aaron demanding to know, in the manner of Job, how a compassionate God could possibly render such harsh, absolute, and even cruel punishment.

As understandable as such a reaction might have been, Aaron would have screamed at Moses or demanded an answer from God from a place of deep rage and hurt. We seldom speak with wisdom or humility, let alone holiness, when our words bubble out of the cauldron of heated, raw emotion. The heart boils over with intense feelings of anger, hurt, jealousy, insecurity, or worry, and we often spew out words we later regret, whether because of their content or their tone.

For that reason, we might stand in awe of the self-awareness and self-control required from Aaron at this terrible moment. Mindful of his inner state, even in this extreme situation, Aaron knows that he would not be capable of expressing himself in a way that would be worthy of his best self. And so Aaron chooses silence. He practices *sh'tikah*. Aware of the shattered condition of his spirit, and ever mindful of the tremendous power of words to be destructive or even dangerous, Aaron somehow finds the wisdom and the self-control to remain silent. In a similar way, *Cheshbon HaNefesh*[2] summarizes its teaching about *sh'tikah* by quoting both the words of the Psalmist, "My thought did not leave my mouth" (Psalm 17:3), and the simple teaching of the Rabbis, "Think before you speak."[3]

There is, however, another, less positive way to understand Aaron's silence. Perhaps Aaron's silence is a betrayal of his responsibility to speak out forcefully when he encounters injustice. It's possible that this silence, which our tradition frames as a virtuous act of restraint, humility, wisdom, and pious acceptance of God's will is, instead, a silence born of fear or even a lack of paternal feeling.

As with all of the *middot*, *sh'tikah* is not an absolute good. There is such a thing as too much silence, for example, remaining quiet when our responsibility would be to protest, even to God. Abraham does not hesitate to question God's plan, doing so famously regarding the impending destruction of Sodom and Gomorrah: "Will You indeed sweep away the innocent along with the wicked? . . . Must not the Judge of all the earth do justly?" (Genesis 18:23, 18:25). By contrast, in another, equally familiar incident, Abraham fails to protest at all when God calls him to sacrifice his own son. Moses protests when God threatens to destroy the people after they built the Golden Calf (see Exodus 32:11–13). Guiding us toward a balance between restraint and legitimate protest, *Orchot Tzadikim* (chapter 21) quotes Ecclesiastes: "There is a time to be silent, and a time to speak" (3:7).

Should Aaron have spoken out? Should he have questioned God? Should he have protested about an overly harsh punishment? Is the Rabbis' insistence that Aaron's silence was an expression of piety and acceptance of the divine judgment just a rationalization, disguising Aaron's true motivation—fear? Or is there an even worse explanation for Aaron's silence—a lack of feeling over the death of his two sons?

Shortly after this incident, when Moses chastises Aaron's remaining sons, Eleazar and Ithamar, for not eating their portion of the community's sin offering, Aaron finds his voice again. It is Aaron who responds calmly and rationally, reminding Moses that it could hardly have been appropriate for him and his remaining sons to partake of the sin offering at that moment when God was so obviously displeased with their service. And Moses concurs (Leviticus 10:19–20). If Aaron's previous silence really was a reflection of a broken heart, how does he so quickly find the capacity both to make a dispassionate analysis of what's ritually appropriate and to respond so calmly to his angry younger brother? And speaking of Eleazar and Ithamar: Might Aaron's remaining sons not need their father to voice some feeling, some sense of loss, some acknowledgment of the terrifying, shattering, possibly unjust loss of their two older brothers? Is Aaron's silence a sign of his pious virtue or a reflection of his limitations as a father?

There is yet another way to understand Aaron's silence. Instead of an act of incredible self-awareness, restraint, and public piety, of avoidance of the responsibility to speak out against injustice, or of a lack of fatherly feelings, Aaron's sh'tikah might have been a practice of mindfulness and an attempt at communion with God in the face of tragedy. Perhaps Aaron needs silence and stillness because he is desperate to find some way to reconnect with his own soul, with those around him, and even with God. Aaron takes refuge in his silence because it is the only spiritual tool with which he can meet the terrible anguish of his grief, the only way to honor the pain he feels for himself and his family. In silence, Aaron might find a way to hold that suffering while still remaining open to noticing that even if that overwhelming flood of sorrow is undeniably true at that moment, it is not his whole truth.

While intense sorrow, anger, and confusion are welling up inside him, a practice of silence and stillness might open Aaron's heart in a way that allows him to also experience his love for his surviving sons and even to begin reaching toward sorrowful acceptance of God's harsh decree. In silence, Aaron might begin to make room for the awful truth that the consequences of our most serious mistakes can be enormous and unalterable. And in silence, he might be held and comforted by the powerful truth that his own broken heart draws its feeling from the Heart of the Universe, which weeps along with him at the necessity of tragedy and which promises, even in such terrible moments, the continuing possibility of meaning, healing, and love. Sometimes, perhaps especially at times of tragedy, it is only in silence that we can quiet ourselves enough to hear the song of our own souls and the voice of its Author.

Questions to Ask

When you are silent, that is, practicing *sh'tikah*, is your silence the result of principled restraint and wisdom? Avoidance? A mindfulness tool for insight and healing?

When have you spoken and later wished you had kept silent? When have you kept silent and later wished you had spoken out?

Mussar calls us to be mindful of patterns of thought and feeling that give rise to problematic behaviors, including in our speech. Which techniques might you use to notice those inner patterns of thought and feeling unfolding? How might noticing these patterns enable you to choose more wisely whether to speak or be silent?

Mussar frequently connects the practice of silence with the development of wisdom. What are some of the ways in which silence helps to foster wisdom? What might we miss if we speak instead of remaining silent?

Practices for the *Middah* of *Sh'tikah*

The practice of *sh'tikah* begins with us getting more comfortable with silence:

> When you tend to speak a great deal, practice limiting your speech. Talk less and listen more, even when you feel that you have something to say. Notice what happens when you do not speak.

> If you struggle to speak up, challenge yourself to do so, even if only briefly. Notice your own voice in the room.

The work of *sh'tikah* continues as we bring a deepened awareness to the moments when we speak or choose to remain silent. Greater mindfulness of our physical sensations, emotions, or thoughts allows us to make more intentional, skillful, and holy choices. Our inner cues provide an "early warning system" that likely does not change how we feel, but enables us to respond to those challenging moments with wiser silences or words.

Other *Middot* to Consider:

> To what extent do Moses's words and actions in this *parashah* reflect the *middah* of *rachamim* (רַחֲמִים, "compassion") or suffer from its absence?

> Clearly, this incident tests Aaron's trust (*bitachon*, בִּטָחוֹן) in God. How do we reconcile tragedy and injustice in the world with our own trust in God?

> Is Aaron's silence an instance of exemplary humility (*anavah*, עֲנָוָה) or too much humility?

NOTES
1. *Babylonian Talmud, Z'vachim* 115b.
2. Menachem Mendel Levin of Satanov, *Cheshbon HaNefesh* (1812), trans. Dovid Landesman (New York: Feldheim, 1995), chapter 10.
3. *Tanna D'Vei Eliyahu* 3.

TAZRIA—LEVITICUS 12:1–13:59

Rachamim—Mercy:
Seeing the Whole Person

RABBI LISA J. GRUSHCOW, DPhil

ONCE, I WAS VISITING a congregant in the hospital when a resident came in. He looked at her briefly but spent most of his time looking at her chart. He summarized her symptoms, stated that the tests had not given any conclusive information, and suggested that her illness was in her head. He then moved on to the next room.

This was toward the beginning of a long journey; it would be years before my congregant would receive an accurate diagnosis of a painful and severe neurological disorder. But in that brief encounter, what was most striking to me was not the lack of diagnosis, but the lack of compassion. In a few short moments, the resident physician dismissed the woman lying in front of him: a young mother and wife, an intelligent and successful professional, a person with an extraordinary story of migration between countries and religions. The resident saw my congregant's file; he did not see her.

> The priest shall examine the affection on the skin of the body: if hair in the affected patch has turned white and the affection appears to be deeper than the skin of the body, it is a leprous affection; when the priest sees [the person], he shall pronounce the person impure. (Leviticus 13:3)

Tazria is all about identifying illness—*tzaraat*, a skin disease that, perhaps ironically, we are not entirely sure how to identify.[1] For our purposes here, we will call it "leprosy." The focus of the Torah portion is diagnosis and quarantine, and the eventual reintegration of the sufferer into the Israelite camp. The priest here is not a doctor or a healer; his role is to determine the presence or absence of the disease and the corresponding response.

It is a challenging *parashah*. Adding to a person's suffering by excluding them from the community is deeply problematic. When, as most traditional commentaries do,[2] we try to justify this approach by pointing to the sin at the root of the sickness (generally *lashon hara*, "evil speech" or "gossip," associated with leprosy because of the episode with Miriam, Aaron, and Moses in Numbers 12), we can find meaning—namely, that our actions have consequences—but at what cost? Both responses—exclusion and condemnation—seem at odds with the Jewish value of *rachamim*, "compassion."

However, just as the priest looks closely at the affliction, so, too, can we look closely at the text. In Leviticus 13:3, cited above, we notice that the verb "to see" is repeated twice. The first time, the priest sees the affliction. The second time, the priest sees the person. Rabbi Israel Joshua Trunk of Kutno (1820–1893) writes:

> It seems that there is a hint here, that when one checks a person, one must not see only what they lack, in the place of the affliction; rather, one must see them in their entirety, including their elevated qualities. And so Balak said [to Balaam]: "You will see only a portion of them [the Israelites]; you will not see all of them—and damn them for me from there" (Numbers 23:13). Therefore: "the priest will see the affliction"—and after that—"the priest will see the person"—he should see them in their entirety.[3]

It is striking that Balak understands that Balaam can only curse the Israelites if he sees them partially; if he sees them in their entirety, he will understand that they, like him, are three-dimensional human beings with their own stories and hopes and dreams. He will see that they, like him, want to live; that they, like him, want to be blessed. He will see that they are not so different.

When someone who is healthy encounters someone who is ill, the first instinct is often to distance oneself; to remind oneself of all the differentiating factors between ourselves and the person who is sick.

"She has lung cancer; she must have been a smoker." "I knew he'd end up in hospital; he's so out of shape." "It's so sad that she lost the pregnancy; I wonder what she did wrong." And the subtext is: "I am different. I'll be okay."

When it comes to illness, even as our human defenses motivate us to differentiate ourselves from the sick when we are well, our human condition should remind us how fine a line there is between these states. In her powerful essay "Illness as Metaphor," Susan Sontag begins with these profound words:

> Illness is the night side of life, a more onerous citizenship. Everyone who is born holds dual citizenship, in the kingdom of the well and in the kingdom of the sick. Although we all prefer to use the good passport, sooner or later each of us is obliged, at least for a spell, to identify ourselves as citizens of that other place.[4]

When we don't understand this, we risk seeing each other only partially; we see only the affliction, and not the human being. Mussar teacher Alan Morinis refers to this as seeing someone with the eyes of judgment rather than the eyes of compassion:

> What appears before us when we look at another in this way [with eyes of judgment] are that person's accumulated deeds and habits as they stand right now, which we judge from our own vantage point. When we lower or transcend the boundaries of self, however, and draw closer so that we can feel within us the truth of that other person's experience, and so see with eyes of compassion, we still ought to see that person as they are now, but something else will be added to that picture. We will also see more deeply to perceive the untainted soul that is the kernel of that being—the image of the divine that is reflected in ourselves as well.[5]

The key to the *middah* of *rachamim* is the understanding that we are all connected; in Morinis's words, that "the you and me are mingled in a oneness that transcends our perceptions of separate identities. . . . The soul-trait of compassion may be more accurately defined as the inner experience of touching another being so closely that you no longer perceive the other one as separate from you."[6]

Once we see this connection, we can no longer only see the person's illness. We are forced to see them as we ourselves would want to be seen: as whole human beings. After all, we too might find ourselves in need of being seen in such a light. *Orchot Tzadikim*, a fifteenth-century German Mussar text, states, "Just as one would want compassion in his time of need, so should one have compassion on others who are in need."[7]

It has often been noted that the Hebrew word *rachamim* is connected to *rechem*, "womb." The same is true in Arabic. In both Judaism and Islam, this quality is associated with God. Haroon Moghul, a scholar and commentator on Islam, wrote about this aspect of the Divine: "God is like a womb, within which creation is created, out of which life is issued, from which we emerge, but always [God] is the ultimate boundary, the shield and shell around us."[8]

What might it mean to cultivate this divine quality in ourselves? In some ways, it is the polar opposite of the *p'shat*, the plain meaning of the biblical text. In *Tazria*, the person who is afflicted with leprosy must be sent beyond the boundary of the camp. But when we look with the eyes of compassion, we see that in fact we are all within the boundary of Creation. The resident with the chart, who imagines he will never be a patient; the rabbi standing at graveside, who thinks she will live forever; the friend coming to comfort a friend on her divorce, reassuring herself of the stability of her own marriage—as much as we may try to separate ourselves, we are all in this world together. The more we see that, the more we cultivate compassion.

In Mussar, we endeavor to emulate the priest who saw not merely the skin disease but the whole person, striving for *rachamim* as among the most noble of the *middot*.

Questions to Ask

What are the situations in which you notice that you have the least compassion? Are there qualities in yourself from which you are trying to gain distance in these encounters? When have you experienced pity from others rather than compassion? How might you use this experiential knowledge to approach others with compassion rather than pity?

Practices for the *Middah* of *Rachamim*

Identify an encounter in which you saw someone with the eyes of judgment and distanced yourself from the person. Challenge yourself to identify how much you have in common with this person.

Try to use "people first" language: identify people as having an illness or disability, rather than being defined by it—for example, "a person with autism" rather than "an autistic person." (Note: there is some debate about "people first" versus "identity first" language; always ask someone how they would want to be referred to, and think this through for your own identity.)

Another *Middah* to Consider

Tazria also points to the need to cultivate *savlanut*, "patience." Sometimes, when we define others by their most obvious, external qualities, we do so because we are in a rush. We want to diagnose them, define them, and move on. Consider how having more patience with others can also increase our capacity for compassion.

NOTES

1. Baruch A. Levine, *The JPS Torah Commentary: Leviticus* (Philadelphia: Jewish Publication Society, 1989), 75.
2. See, for example, Rashi on Leviticus 14:4; *Vayikra Rabbah* 16:1-2, 16:4-7.
3. Aharon Yaakov Greenberg, *Iturei Torah*, 4:71 (Tel Aviv: Yavneh Press, 1996. Hebrew edition; translation mine).
4. Susan Sontag, "Illness as Metaphor," *New York Review of Books*, January 26, 1978.

5. Alan Morinis, *Everyday Holiness: The Jewish Spiritual Path of Mussar* (Boston: Trumpeter, 2007), 83–84.
6. Ibid., 79–80.
7. Cited in ibid., 75.
8. Haroon Moghul, Facebook post, May 6, 2019 (during Ramadan).

M'TZORA—LEVITICUS 14:1–15:33

Bushah—Shame:
The Soul-Trait of Shame

RABBI SAMUEL J. ROSE

ACCORDING TO THE TORAH, God created human beings without *bushah* (בּוּשָׁה), a "sense of embarrassment." At Creation, the Torah explains, "Now the two of them were naked, the man and his wife, and they were not ashamed (*lo yitboshashu*)" (Genesis 2:25). Rabbi Samson Raphael Hirsh explains in his commentary on the Book of Genesis that the word *bosh* literally means "to feel disappointment."[1] Up until the moment when they eat the forbidden fruit, Adam and Eve have no concept of morality, of good or evil; they had no reason to feel shame.

However, once Adam and Eve eat the fruit, "the eyes of both of them were opened" (Genesis 3:7) to the knowledge of good and evil and to the concept of disappointment, embarrassment, and shame. As the anonymous author of the medieval work of Mussar, *Orchot Tzadikim*, writes, "The sages have said: *Haseichel hu haboshet v'haboshet hu haseichel*—Intellect is shame, and shame is intellect."[2] When God calls out to Adam, "*Ayekah*—Where are you?" (Genesis 3:9), the question is not a matter of physical location. Rather, it is an investigation of Adam's new sense of morality. Adam is embarrassed.

The character trait, *middah*, of shame, according to Rabbi Hirsch, is "God's gift of grace [to humanity]. [God] instilled in [each person's] heart a sense of shame. God knew that a person would not always measure up to what [he/she/they were] meant to be. Therefore, God implanted within [each person] a sense of shame, which would always inform [that person] of [their] inadequacy. Thus [everyone] became [their] own monitor and guardian."³ However, just because human beings were granted this gift of shame, it should not be taken for granted. *Orchot Tzadikim* encourages human beings "to exert [themselves] to conduct [themselves] in accordance with this noble trait and employ wisdom in cultivating it until it is implanted in [their souls,]" because "the trait of shame is a great fence and an iron barrier against all transgressions."⁴

After those opening chapters of Genesis, we best see what happens when someone neglects their *middah* of *bushah* in the section of the Torah relating to the laws of the *m'tzora*. The Book of Leviticus lays out all the gory details. A *m'tzora* is the person afflicted with a condition that the Torah calls *nega tzaraat* (נֶגַע צָרָעַת). A priest declares the affected person impure, and the *m'tzora* must be isolated outside of the Israelite camp (Leviticus 13:46). The description of the various ailments affecting the skin have led some to translate *nega tzaraat* as leprosy, but Rabbi Hirsch insists that if we look deeper into the meaning of the words *nega* and *tzaraat*, we see that calling this particular collection of symptoms a disease in any sense is a misreading of the text. His definition also helps to explain why the person afflicted is exiled from the camp.

Rabbi Hirsch explains, "In the majority of cases where the word *nega* occurs, it clearly refers to a disease that comes as a result of a special Divine decree. A person afflicted with a *nega* is *nagu-a*, literally 'touched' by the finger of God."⁵ *Tzaraat*, he says, "denotes an inner rot that breaks out externally."⁶ The way that the *nega* serves God with respect to the *m'tzora* may be likened to the way the question "*Ayekah?*" serves God in relation to Adam. God knows the spiritual location of the individual; it's the spiritual state that is rotten. The *nega*, like the question "*Ayekah?*," forces the affected individual to acknowledge that there is a problem. Specifically, Rabbi Hirsch explains that "every *nega tzara-at* . . . is to be regarded as a punishment for social wrongdoing,"⁷ namely, having "haughty eyes, a lying tongue, hands that shed innocent blood, a heart that devises thoughts of violence, feet that are quick to run to evil, a false witness who spreads lies, and one who incites conflict between brothers."[8] Rabbi Hirsch explains that doing these things leads not only to the *nega tzaraat*, but also to the individual's confinement outside of the community. This period of exile has "no other purpose or reason than to instill in [the affected person] the awareness of [their] unworthiness,"[9] to recognize their guilt and to begin the process of restoring their character trait of shame.

The beginning of *Parashat M'tzora* contains "the ritual for the *m'tzora* at the time of being purified" (Leviticus 14:1), the rites of reintegration that the afflicted person must complete in order to rejoin Israelite society. The Torah sets forth three steps: (1) the taking of two pure birds, (2) the shaving off of all of the *m'tzora*'s hair, and (3) the offerings of two sheep and a yearling ewe (Leviticus 14:4–10). The first two of these rituals allow for the *m'tzora* to reenter the social realm of the community, while the third allows for renewed participation in religious life.

In the case of the ritual of the birds, Rabbi Hirsch, citing *Babylonian Talmud, Shabbat* 106b, explains that the Torah is referring to a specific variety of bird that cannot be tamed or domesticated.[10] For the purpose of this ritual, these two birds represent the most basic animal instinct. Through this ritual, the *m'tzora* is forced to reckon with their abandonment of shame, for allowing their basic animal instinct to be untamed. By killing one bird and sending one toward a field, the *m'tzora* commits to engage the *middah* of shame to "subordinate unbridled animality"[11] and reengage in the world of human morality.

The ritual of shaving off all the *m'tzora*'s hair occurs twice: on the first day and on the seventh day. Human hair "serves to protect the body and shield it from the outside world."[12] Hair is a natural insulator and represents the barriers that a person might construct in order to live a self-centered, antisocial life. Rabbi Hirsch posits that "stripping a body of all hair exposes it to the effects of the outside. For this reason, shaving is well suited to awaken the heart to turn away from isolating selfishness,"[13] to remind them of their sense of shame. After the first shave, the community allows the *m'tzora* to return, but they must remain outside of their tent for seven days, and they are still forbidden to engage in the religious life of the community. On the seventh day, the second round of shaving teaches the *m'tzora* "to appreciate the moral ideal . . . learned in the Sanctuary of the Torah . . . [which leads to] a practice of self-development."[14]

Finally, on the eighth day, the individual seeking reinstatement to religious life offers two male sheep and one yearling female sheep (Leviticus 14:10). Rabbi Hirsch explains that "in [their] arrogance they forgot God; [they] imagined that [their] fate was in [their] own hands."[15] Arrogance, which *Orchot Tzadikim* identifies as the opposite of shame,[16] "is the root of all social sin, and was the cause of [their] expulsion from God's community."[17] These sacrifices of three sheep atone for the person's arrogance and represent the individual's renewed commitment to being shepherded by God.[18]

We don't live in a world where God calls out to us, "*Ayekah*—Where are you?" for a spiritual checkup. We (thankfully) don't live in a world where individuals are struck with *nega tzaraat* in order to make them aware of their spiritual impropriety. And, also thankfully, we no longer rely on sacrificial ritual to make amends for our moral wrongdoing. But it is still vitally important to regularly cultivate our sense of shame. Rabbi Abraham Joshua Heschel wrote, "Let not the wise glory in his wisdom, let not the mighty man glory in his might; but let him who glories glory in this; that he has a sense of ultimate embarrassment."[19]

We would all do well to learn from Heschel's words. A properly developed sense of *bushah* acts as a mechanism to prevent us from individual wrongdoing. In our personal lives, when we exercise our power over others unjustly, when we are unfaithful in our relationships both personal and professional, when we succumb to peer pressure, when we act in a demeaning or dehumanizing way toward others, when we act violently, we should feel *bushah*.

As members of society, when we see the devastation we are causing to our planet—through the overutilization of natural resources, the overbearing levels of pollution, and the destruction of our fragile ecosystems—we should feel shame. When we when we see but refuse to respond to the many faces of injustice, we should be ashamed.

In both cases, shame must not be an end to itself. With respect to our individual actions, *bushah* should turn us to *t'shuvah*, not to the slaughtering of sheep or birds, but to repairing our behavior and our relationships. With respect to world at large, our shame should fuel our drive to confronting our society's ills, to pursue justice, safety, sustainability, and peace. Then, our *bushah* may be called a blessing.

Questions to Ask

Have there been times in your life when you justified your wrongdoing by looking at the behavior of someone else? Or excused your own immoral behavior because someone else was doing it? How should we respond to those who respond to criticism of immorality not by confronting the wrongdoing, but by pointing to another person's misconduct, a deflection we have come to know as "whataboutism"?

In many of our sanctuaries we find the words *Da lifnei mi atah omeid* (דַּע לִפְנֵי מִי אַתָּה עוֹמֵד, "Know before whom you stand"). How has your audience influenced your moral behavior?

Practices for the *Middah* of *Bushah*

Orchot Tzadikim suggests that a person "who wishes to habituate himself to the sense of shame always should sit before one in whose presence [one] is ashamed."[20] Consider how you might "sit before the one in whose presence" you are "ashamed." Do it.

Other *Middot* to Consider

Chesed (חֶסֶד, "loving-kindness"): Rabbi Isaiah Halevi Horowitz, in his book *Sh'nei Luchot HaB'rit*, suggests that the priest's role in diagnoses and purification of the *m'tzora* comes from a place of *chesed*, "loving-kindness."[21] In what ways do you see *chesed* in the performance of these rituals of purification?

N'*divut* (נְדִיבוּת—"generosity"): The Gemara reveals why a house might contract *nega tzaraat*: "The house belongs to one who dedicates his house to himself alone, who refuses to lend vessels to others and says that he does not have them."[22] This should cause us to look at the *middah* of n'*divut*, "generosity."

NOTES

1. Samson Raphael Hirsch, *The Hirsch Chumash, The Five Books of the Torah: Sefer Bereshis*. Translated by Daniel Haberman (Jerusalem-New York: Feldheim Publishers and Judaica Press, 2016), 93.
2. *Orchot Tzaddikim: The Ways of the Tzaddikim*. Edited by Rabbi Gavriel Zaloshinsky. Translated by Rabbi Shraga Silverstein (Jerusalem-New York: Feldheim Publishers, 1995), 81.
3. Samson Raphael Hirsch, *The Hirsch Chumash, Sefer Bereishis*, 93.
4. *Orchot Tzaddikim*, 81–83.
5. Samson Raphael Hirsch, *The Hirsch Chumash, Sefer Vayikra*, 385–86.
6. Ibid.
7. Ibid., 420–21.
8. *Vayikra Rabbah* on *Parashat M'tzora*. *Babylonian Talmud, Arachin* 16a explains the seven sins differently, but the conclusion is the same; that these are essentially social sins. "N'*gaim* result from seven things: slander, the shedding of blood, perjury, sexual immorality, arrogance, robbery, and stinginess."
9. Samson Raphael Hirsch, *The Hirsch Chumash, Sefer Vayikra*, 421.
10. Ibid., 432.
11. Ibid., 437.
12. Ibid., 439.
13. Ibid.
14. Ibid., 440.
15. Ibid., 441.
16. *Orchot Tzaddikim: The Ways of the Tzaddikim*, 97.
17. Samson Raphael Hirsch, *The Hirsch Chumash, Sefer Vayikra*, 441.
18. Ibid.
19. Rabbi Abraham Joshua Heschel, *Who Is Man?* (Stanford, CA: Stanford University Press, 1965), 112–13.
20. *Orchot Tzadikim*, "Third Gate: Gate of Shame," 87.
21. *Sh'nei Luchot HaB'rit, Torah Shebichtav, Ki Teitzei, Torah Or*, 47.
22. *Babylonian Talmud, Yoma* 11b.

ACHAREI MOT—LEVITICUS 16:1–18:30
Acharayut—Responsibility:
The Personal and the Communal

RABBI PETER B. SCHAKTMAN

"This is your life. You are responsible for it. You will not live
forever. Don't wait."   —*Natalie Goldberg*

IN *PARASHAT ACHAREI MOT*, we find important insights about
the nature of responsibility and accountability—insights that can
inform our own understanding and practice of Mussar.

The *parashah* begins by evoking an episode of dramatic irrespon-
sibility described earlier in Leviticus: the offering of "alien fire" by
Aaron's sons Nadab and Abihu, an act that resulted in both priests
being consumed by a divine fire (Leviticus 10:2). It continues by
delineating the specific role of the High Priest in purifying the sacred
shrine of the Israelites, by making expiation first for himself and his
household and then on behalf of the entire community. Once the
shrine has been purified, the High Priest symbolically transfers his
own transgressions and the sins of others onto the scapegoat (*azazel*), which is then sent into the wilderness, carrying the people's sins
away. Later in the *parashah*, we read a long list of tersely rendered
mitzvot regarding sexual boundaries, ostensibly aimed at preserving
the *k'dushah* ("holiness") of the entire Israelite community.

Hidden in the name of the *parashah* is a key to understanding the
middah of *acharayut* (אַחֲרָיוּת, "responsibility"). The root of the first
word, *acharei* (אַחֲרֵי, "after"), is the same as that of the *middah, acharayut*. Our Mussar teachers have taught us that this single root can be
understood in two different ways, both of which help us discern the

essence of the *middah*.[1] When we connect *acharayut* to *achar*, to "after," we understand responsibility as measuring the consequences of our actions or words. The Rabbinic tradition considers us "forewarned," so that—as long as we possess free will—we are always responsible for the consequences of our words or actions, whether deliberate or inadvertent.[2] When, on the other hand, we connect *acharayut* to *acheir* (אַחֵר, "other"), our focus is on our duties to those around us and our realization that we are, in fact, "our brother's keeper" (Genesis 4:9).

As the *parashah* opens, the momentous responsibility of the High Priest is established by God's directive to Moses in the context of Aaron's loss of his sons: "Tell your brother Aaron that he is not to come at will into the Shrine behind the curtain, in front of the cover that is upon the ark, lest he die" (Leviticus 16:2). Here, the rationale for compliant behavior is the avoidance of dire consequences—*acharayut* in its sense of after-effects—in this case, death. Once Aaron understands the basic rules, he can begin the process of purgation of the sacred space. This process begins with the High Priest's offering on behalf of himself and his household.

Once that sacrifice has been completed, "he shall then slaughter the people's goat of sin offering, bring its blood behind the curtain, and do with its blood as he has done with the blood of the bull: he shall sprinkle it over the cover and in front of the cover" (Leviticus 16:15). This ritual has now become fully inclusive of the camp as a whole: "All assume some responsibility for tainting the shrine and the community, and they release themselves from the consequences through the chief priest's confessions and the symbolic rites of sacrifice."[3] Note that the word *acharayut*, begins, as does the Hebrew alphabet, with *alef* and ends with *tav* (the last letter of the alphabet), which may suggest that responsibility must be all-inclusive. We are accountable not only for our own actions but also for those of our families and the wider community. "We have an ethical responsibility to care for one another, our community, our world, and ourselves."[4]

This emphasis on collective responsibility is extended in the description of the scapegoat ritual:

When he has finished purging the Shrine, the Tent of Meeting, and the altar, the live goat shall be brought forward. Aaron shall lay both his hands upon the head of the live goat and confess over it all the iniquities and transgressions of the Israelites, whatever their sins, putting them on the head of the goat; and it shall be sent off to the wilderness through a designated individual. Thus the goat shall carry on it all their iniquities to an inaccessible region; and the goat shall be set free in the wilderness. (Leviticus 16:20–22)

This ritual represents both of the Mussar approaches to *acharayut*. The *achar* ("after") element: the sacred protocol is meant to protect the community from the consequences of divine displeasure at their transgressions. Additionally, the scapegoat ritual also requires the entire community to seek each individual's release from a transgressive state. Here, we see the *acheir* ("other") element in *acharayut*, since everybody must do their best to support their neighbors in purging themselves of sin.

The *azazel* narrative also helps understand the potential for *acharayut*, like all *middot*, to be taken to an extreme, by calling to mind the important distinction between responsibility and guilt. While responsibility leads to greater wholeness, guilt—neurotic, and often narcissistic—instead engenders anxiety. Guilt is a source of spiritual negativity, a potentially debilitating state of being. No such angst is associated with the scapegoat. The ritual is prescribed, the High Priest and people enact it, and what results is a cleansed, confident community that has acted responsibly.

One could, however, argue that forgiveness-by-goats replaces actual repentance with empty ritual and therefore short-circuits real *acharayut*, "responsibilty." A story is told of Rabbi Shlomo Rabinowicz, who excoriated leaders of the Jewish community for not being attuned to the economic state of the people they led. "Indeed," he taught, "the sin of Nadab and Abihu was that they were content to draw near to God, but did nothing to help the people. They died because they didn't deserve to be leaders of Israel. . . . Do you think you were appointed to make decisions about the kashrut of a pot or spoon?"[5] *Acharayut*, from this perspective, is never about "checking items off a list," like sacrificing one goat and sending another into the wilderness; it is, instead, about being wholly responsible for one's actions.

The last chapter of the *parashah*, Leviticus 18, confronts liberal Jews with a particularly difficult challenge regarding *acharayut* on a communal and institutional level. In this section, the command to be responsible for one's actions is framed in terms of maintaining specific sexual boundaries. Here, the focal point is the sacred expectation that Israelite men (women are addressed in only part of one verse) will fulfill their covenantal responsibilities and preserve the *k'dushah* ("holiness") of the entire polity. Often misunderstood and weaponized as a source for moral judgment and excoriation, it is also the text that the Sages determined should be read on Yom Kippur afternoon.[6] Since the mid-nineteenth century, however, this passage has been replaced in most Reform services by other readings deemed more appropriate by Reform liturgists, most often drawn from Leviticus 19.

Rabbi Jeffrey Brown takes issue with this historical Reform substitution of Leviticus 18 with other, less provocative, readings.[7] He acknowledges that we can only speculate on the specific objections that motivated the early Reformers but notes that, in our contemporary context, the continued absence of this chapter on Yom Kippur afternoon is frequently supported by those who ostensibly seek to spare members of the LGBTQ community pain at its characterization of homosexuality as *to-eivah*, "abhorrent" (Leviticus 18:22).

Brown argues that reading this text on Yom Kippur in fact demonstrates an important and necessary expression of communal *acharayut*, insofar as it allows the text to be faced head-on and for the moral judgment it renders on what is now understood to be sacred expressions of sexuality to be rejected. "But we can, and must, speak about Leviticus 18," he asserts. "We must speak the truth and call the Torah what [it] is: a holy but imperfect document."[8]

In making his case, Brown cites (among others) Jewish feminist scholar Judith Plaskow, who describes her own change of heart regarding the inclusion of Leviticus 18 on Yom Kippur after talking to a woman who had attended one of her lectures: "She belonged to a Conservative synagogue that had abandoned the practice of reading Leviticus 18 on Yom Kippur, and as a victim of childhood sexual abuse by her grandfather, she felt betrayed by that decision." Plaskow notes that despite the woman's ambivalence regarding the specific moral mandates of the chapter, "she felt that in quietly changing the reading without communal discussion, her congregation had avoided issues of sexual responsibility altogether"[9] and, in so doing, demonstrated a lack of *acharayut* toward those impacted by acts of *gilui arayot* (sexual transgressions).

Notable is that both Brown's position and the position he challenges emanate from a commitment to manifest *acharayut* in communal worship. Both seek to demonstrate sensitivity and inclusivity. Reading the objectionable text publicly and preaching against it discharge the Mussar charge "to diligently seek the benefit of the other in every possible way."[10] In this sense, it might be argued that the *middah* of *acharayut* is the foundation upon which all the other *middot* rest and that living a life of responsibility is the ultimate objective of Torah, such that every decision we confront challenges us to respond by acting with *acharayut*.

Questions to Ask

Does your intuitive approach to *acharayut* emanate more from a focus on the consequences of your behavior or from identifying with others around you?

Do you think about responsibility as the successful execution of specific tasks (and/or the avoidance of certain behaviors) or as a general approach to life?

How do others, like the ancient High Priest, contribute to your understanding of *acharayut*?

Practice for the *Middah* of *Acharayut*

Most of us are implicitly engaged in the practice of *acharayut*; most of us demonstrate a sense of responsibility toward certain people and tasks. The Mussar tradition, however, asks us to examine whether our practice of responsibility is in fact consistent with our goals, our values, and the image of God we strive to embody.

Begin by reviewing your calendar—or, if you do not keep a detailed calendar, do so for a week. Note what and whom you prioritize. Do not look for greater efficiency. Rather, seek to discern the values reflected in your allocation of time and energy. In what ways does this allocation reflect your responsibility as "being your brother's/ sister's keeper"? Reflect on the extent you wish to more mindfully focus on the needs of others and on the ways in which your sense of *acharayut* toward others is inspired by a needless sense of guilt. Further, consider the consequences of the allotment of your time and attention. Is your calendar reflecting the values you seek to manifest in your moral and spiritual life?

Other *Middot* to Consider

In addition to *acharayut*, the priestly material in this *parashah* offers examples of the *middot* of both *kavod* (כָּבוֹד, "honor") and seder (סֵדֶר, "order"). The special role of the High Priest begs the question who today is deserving of such deference. The text reflects the desire to establish a system of orderly service to God.

NOTES

1. Alan Morinis, *Everyday Holiness: The Jewish Spiritual Path of Mussar* (Boston: Trumpeter, 2007), 198.
2. *Babylonian Talmud, Bava Kama* 26a.
3. Rachel Havrelock, in *The Torah: A Women's Commentary*, ed. Tamara Cohn Eskenazi and Andrea L. Weiss (New York: Reform Judaism Publishing, an imprint of CCAR Press, and Women of Reform Judaism, 2008), 686.
4. Dr. Erica Brown, "A Pedagogy of Achrayut/Responsibility," essay in the program for Jewish Early Childhood Education Conference, Jewish Federation of Greater Washington, 2017).
5. From "*Mei-Otzar Ha-Mahashavah shel Ha-Hasidut*," found in *Torah Gems*

by Aharon Yaakov Greenberg (Tel Aviv: Yavneh Publishing House Ltd.),
2:300.

6. *Babylonian Talmud, M'gilah* 31a.
7. Jeffrey Brown, "Preaching Against the Text: An Argument for Restoring Leviticus 18 to Yom Kippur Afternoon," in *The Sacred Encounter: Jewish Perspectives on Sexuality*, ed. Lisa J. Grushcow (New York: CCAR Press, 2014), 65–85.
8. Ibid., 73.
9. Ibid., 75, citing Judith Plaskow, "Sexuality," in *The Coming of Lilith: Essays on Feminism, Judaism and Sexual Ethics, 1972–2003*, ed. Judith Plaskow and Donna Berman (Boston: Beacon Press, 2005), 166.
10. Rabbi Simcha Zissel Ziv, *Chochmah u'Mussar*, cited in Alan Morinis, *Everyday Holiness: The Jewish Spiritual Path of Mussar* (Boston: Trumpeter, 2007), 204.

K'DOSHIM—LEVITICUS 19:1–20:27

Hakarut HaTov—Gratitude: Our Daily Struggle for K'dushah

RABBI ERIC S. GURVIS

PARASHAT K'DOSHIM sits at the center of the Torah scroll. This has always seemed significant to me, as "the Holiness Code" is at the heart of Torah's teachings on leading an ethical life. Even more than ethics, this portion calls us to reach for *k'dushah*, for holiness through which we animate the spark of divinity within each of us.

The study and practice of Mussar can be beneficial in navigating life's challenges, as we strive to be and do the best of which we are each capable. Seeing life and our world through the lenses of various *middot*, we gain additional perspectives on the many aspects and dimensions of our relationships, our challenges, and—more broadly—our lives.

Mussar teaches us to develop and live by the soul-trait known as *hakarat hatov*. Most often *hakarat hatov* is translated as "gratitude." I suggest a more expansive and nuanced view of this concept. My teacher Alan Morinis writes, "The Hebrew term for gratitude is *hakarat hatov*, which means, literally, 'recognizing the good.' The good is already there. Practicing gratitude means being fully aware of the good that is already yours."[1] This second (and to my mind, more expansive) view of *hakarat hatov* provides us with an additional lens through which to read and understand *Parashat K'doshim*.

Again and again, Jewish tradition teaches us to give thanks for the myriad blessings of our lives. As Psalm 92 reminds us, "It is good to praise the Eternal, to sing hymns to Your name, O Most High" (Psalm 92:2). And, in Psalm 100 we read, "Enter God's gates with thanksgiving, God's courts with praise" (Psalm 100:4). Giving thanks is central to Jewish tradition's view of how we interact with our world, with our fellow human beings, and with God. I believe we should look beyond *hakarat hatov* as simply "giving thanks for the good," and in so doing we can acquire an additional quality with which we can navigate our lives and relationships.

If we read *Parashat K'doshim* beyond the simple understanding of *hakarat hatov* as "gratitude," we can open ourselves to being more mindful of the good that is both present and possible in our lives. With this additional layer, *Parashat K'doshim* can become more than a checklist of behaviors and attitudes by which we are called to live. Read through the lens of *hakarat hatov*, seeing the good that is present, seeing our strengths even in the midst of our struggles and imperfections, *Parashat K'doshim* can help us to summon the courage and strength, not to mention the will, to reach higher, toward the good and the holy.

We live our lives in the context of a world and relationships that challenge our striving to do good and be holy. Alan Morinis writes:

> In the Mussar classic *Duties of the Heart*, Rabbi Bachya ibn Pakuda[2] tells us that there is not a person alive who has not been given gifts, if only the gifts of life and hope. But we tend to suffer a kind of blindness that keeps us from seeing and appreciating what we have. . . . First, he says we tend not to feel appreciative because we are too absorbed in worldly things and in the enjoyment of them. He points out that physical pleasures can never be fully gratified and so we pursue them endlessly, which keeps us from gratitude for what we have. Second, we are so used to our gifts that we don't even really see them any more.[3]

In Leviticus 19:9 we read, "When you reap the harvest of your land, you shall not reap all the way to the edges of your field, or gather the gleanings of your harvest." We know this principle of *pei-ah* (פֵּאָה)[4] as a cornerstone of our tradition's expansive teachings on *tzedakah* (צְדָקָה, "righteous acts of providing for those in need"). Might we also view our acts of *tzedakah* through the lens of *hakarat hatov*? In my fulfillment of the sacred responsibility of *tzedakah*, can I see not only an extension of myself to others, but also an aspect of recognizing and acknowledging the good that I enjoy?

The same could be said of the instruction in Leviticus 19:10, "You shall not pick your vineyard bare, or gather the fallen fruit of your vineyard; you shall leave them for the poor and the stranger: I the Eternal am your God." Again, the significance of our *tzedakah* may be deepened when we connect it with the *middah* of *hakarat hatov*: we may be best show our *hakarat hatov* for our blessings when we share them with others.

In Leviticus 19:18, we read, "Love your neighbor as yourself." This verse is well-known, not only in the context of Jewish tradition but has been embraced far beyond the boundaries of our people and our communities. Yet, in the real world, we know that "loving" our neighbor is not always a simple matter. Still, hearing this call through the lens of *hakarat hatov*, we may better be able to fulfill this commandment. I may not love everything about my neighbor, but can I recognize what is good in her? Can I use *hakarat hatov* to appreciate and honor the ways in which she adds to our world?

In Leviticus 19:32, we read, "You shall rise before the aged and show deference to the old." Many of us experience the treatment of the elders among us as deficient, a personal and communal failure to fulfill this mitzvah. As a society, we can do better. How might our engagement with our elders change if we viewed them not only through the lens of the *kavod* ("honor") to which this verse calls us, but also through *hakarat hatov*? Might we do better if we contemplate the good that our elders have contributed over the course of their lives? I cannot help but think of the stories of Choni HaMaagalin Tractate *Taanit* of the Babylonian Talmud, wherein he is taught to appreciate his forebearers who planted trees that he might enjoy their fruit and their shade.[5]

As he closes his commentary on *Parashat K'doshim* in his seminal work *Lev Eliyahu*, Rabbi Eliyahu Lopian (1876–1970), a prominent disciple of the Kelm school of Mussar,[6] directs our attention to the poem in Deuteronomy 32 wherein we read, "The Rock!—whose deeds are perfect, / Yea, all God ways are just; / A faithful God, never false, / True and upright indeed" (Deuteronomy 32:4–6). In its context in the Book of Deuteronomy, this poem is Moses's review of Israel's experience since Egypt. It describes the good God has bestowed on Israel in its journey, as well as Israel's faithlessness and ingratitude along the way. Rav Lopian reads these verses as declaring, "Our Torah is demanding, 'Where is your *hakarat hatov*? Is this how you repay God for all that God has conferred upon you?'"[7] As he closes his commentary on *K'doshim*, Rav Lopian reminds his students that "our main service to God, and our purpose in this world, is to improve ourselves, through working on our dispositions, and on the *middot* which reside in our soul."[8]

We can read *Parashat K'doshim* and find many of the *middot* of the tradition of Mussar embedded herein. As we strive to perfect ourselves, we know that we will inevitably fall short. Along our journey and through our striving, we will return to the sacred moral principles of our tradition.

> On the way, let us not lose the *tov*—
> the good within us and that which arises from us.
> Rather, let us shine light, with *hakarat hatov*,
> in recognition of the good that is in us.
> Let us utilize that light as a foundation
> on which to reach higher and higher
> in our pursuit of living
> the ideals of our tradition.

Questions to Ask

As you read through *Parashat K'doshim*, which of the mitzvot in the portion offer you an opportunity to practice *hakarat hatov* (e.g., Leviticus 19:32, "You shall rise before the aged and show deference to the old; you shall fear your God: I am the Eternal")?

How might you extend *hakarat hatov* to the fulfillment of Leviticus 19:30, "You shall keep My sabbaths and venerate

My sanctuary"?

In Leviticus 20:26 we read, "You shall be holy to Me, for I the Eternal am holy." How might one bring the practice of *hakarat hatov* to this penultimate verse of our portion?

Practice for the *Middah* of *Hakarat Hatov*

In his commentary on this portion, Rav Eliyahu Lopian spends a good deal of time emphasizing the important of *hakarat hatov* specifically with one's parents (Leviticus 19:3). In fulfillment of one or more of the mitzvot in *Parashat K'doshim*, focus on those in your family, immediate or extended, to whom you might extend the practice of *hakarat hatov*.

Other *Middot* to Consider

The most common phrase in the two chapters of *K'doshim* is *Ani Adonai*, "I am Adonai." How might the recurrence of this phrase throughout our portion lift up the *middah* of *anavah* (עֲנָוָה, "humility")?

Another *middah* that virtually leaps out of the words of *K'doshim* is *kavod* (כָּבוֹד, "honor"). This *middah* may be seen, for example, in the commandments to honor parents, to observe Shabbat, and to rise before the elderly and in the method by which food is left for the needy.

NOTES

1. Alan Morinis, *Everyday Holiness: The Jewish Spiritual Path of Mussar* (Boston: Trumpeter, 2007), 69.
2. Bachya ben Joseph ibn Pakuda (1050–1120) was a Jewish philosopher and rabbi who lived at Zaragoza, Al-Andalus, in the first half of the eleventh century. He is often referred to as Rabbeinu Bachya.
3. Morinis, *Everyday Holiness*, 72.
4. The Bible's model of *tzedakah* (social justice and support) included a variety of agricultural gifts. Grain and produce that were left or forgotten during the harvest were available for the poor to glean. The corners of the fields (*pei-ah*) were also designated for the poor. A biblical source for these laws comes from Leviticus 19:9–1.
5. *Babylonian Talmud*, *Taanit* 23a: "One day, he was walking along the road

when he saw a certain man planting a carob tree. Choni said to him: 'This tree, after how many years will it bear fruit?' The man said to him: 'It will not produce fruit until seventy years have passed.' Choni said to him: 'Is it obvious to you that you will live seventy years, that you expect to benefit from this tree?' He said to him: 'That man himself found a world full of carob trees. Just as my ancestors planted for me, I too am planting for my descendants.'"

6. The Kelm school of Mussar was established by Rabbi Simcha Zissel Ziv, known fondly as the Alter (Elder) of Kelm (1824–98). The Alter founded a yeshiva in the Lithuanian town of Kelm.

7. Eliyahu Lopian, *Lev Eliyahu: A Collection of Talks*, 58. (Goldberg Press, 1975).

8. Ibid.

EMOR—LEVITICUS 21:1–24:23

Sh'vil HaZahav—Moderation: Affliction, Elevation, and Celebration

RABBI MARC KATZ

JUDAISM LIVES ON A CONTINUUM between hedonism and asceticism, and it fears both. This tension between self-indulgence and self-denial is seen, perhaps in its most salient form, in the way that we are commanded to celebrate our holidays in *Parashat Emor*.

Our Torah, and especially our later commentaries, understood the temptations of both extremes. For our ancestors, hedonism meant turning to gluttony, drunkenness, avarice, and debauchery. In abusing our bodies and ignoring the consequences of our actions, we engage in an act of idolatry, promoting our own desires above everything else. Not only do the people in our lives become secondary, but even God, who frowns on these acts, must take a back seat.

Asceticism likewise was seen as a form of idolatry, specifically making abstinence a false spiritual practice. When we fast excessively, pull away from society, or inflict injury on our bodies, we create a false and shallow religious experience under the guise of true faith, because God commands no such excessive practice. We worship an agent of harm and call it Judaism.

The goal, therefore, is to follow a middle path. Maimonides explains in his ethical tract *Hilchot Dei-ot* (part of his magnum opus, the *Mishneh Torah*) that we must avoid the extremes of behavior:

> A person might say, "Since envy, desire, [the pursuit] of honor, and the like, are a wrong path and drive a person from the world, I shall separate from them to a very great degree and move away

from them to the opposite extreme." For example, he will not
eat meat, nor drink wine, nor live in a pleasant home, nor wear
fine clothing, but, rather, [wear] sackcloth and coarse wool and
the like—just as the pagan priests do. This, too, is a bad path
and it is forbidden to walk upon it.[1]

Since our tradition only spills ink to prohibit practices that might be
problematic, we may assume that human nature does indeed lead us
toward extremes. Thus, one of the great fears of our ancient Rabbis
was that one might become either too zealous or too lax in observance, especially around holiday celebrations, and gravitate away
from the *middah* of the *sh'vil hazahav* (שְׁבִיל הַזָּהָב), "the golden path"
of moderation. There are numerous examples of the ways our Rabbis legislate for moderation, and we will look at two cases in depth:
Yom Kippur and Sukkot.

Though we have become accustomed to the practice of fasting
on Yom Kippur in order to atone for our sins, *Parashat Emor* gives
no indication that this practice is indeed the correct way to observe
the day. Instead, we are commanded, *V'initem et nafshoteichem*, "You
shall practice self-denial" (Leviticus 23:27). Over the course of time,
"self-denial"—or in some translations, "affliction"—has come to
mean five distinct categories of behavior we should avoid on Yom
Kippur: we should not (1) imbibe food or drink, (2) bathe, (3) anoint
[or wear perfumes], (4) wear [leather] shoes, or (5) have sexual
relations.[2]

Because they are so ingrained in Jewish practice, refraining from
these behaviors might seems like self-evident fulfillments of the
biblical command. However, the Jewish tradition could have chosen any number of other activities that equally fulfill the mandate to
afflict ourselves—for example, sleep deprivation, ice baths, or self-
flagellation. In fact, our Rabbis even consider briefly the possibility
of sitting for prolonged times in the sun or shade on Yom Kippur.[3]
However, what separates these options from the five adopted categories of afflictions is that the latter form a sort of middle ground.
They serve the purpose, set out by our Torah, to practice self-denial,
while remaining firmly planted in the everyday events of our world.

Practiced only for one day, they do not go so far as to cross into the ascetic.

There is little question that many acts of asceticism can be addictive. Thus, even those practices that were rejected as dangerous have crept into Jewish practice. In his work *HaRokei-ach*,[4] the famous Ashkenazi pietist Rabbi Elazar of Worms even prescribes the kabbalistic practice known as *t'shuvat hamishkal*, whereby people would fast excessively, as well as beat themselves with whips, in an attempt to enter into a spiritual communion with God. If those behaviors are tempting enough to lead someone to look outside of mainstream Jewish practice for religious fulfillment, then we should not be surprised that acceptable practices like fasting on Yom Kippur have a tremendous spiritual pull.

The *Kuzari*, the premier twelfth-century philosophical tract of medieval Spain by Yehudah Halevi, explains:

> And they fast on this day *to approach a resemblance to the angels*, inasmuch as the fast is consummated by humbling themselves, lowering their heads, standing, bending their knees, and singing hymns of praise. Then all the physical powers abandon their natural functions and engage in spiritual functions, as though having no animal nature.[5]

Here, fasting is not merely a form of self-denial. Rather, the act of restraint is meant to elevate the one who fasts to unknown spiritual heights, to the level of angels. The Rabbis feared that one who stands in the place of angels may never want to leave again. Thus, many medieval commentators advocate vigorously for the restriction of Yom Kippur observances to one day in the Diaspora—different from the rest of the holidays, which are celebrated for two days. They know that, if left to their own devices, many would put their bodies in danger by reaching for the spiritual release that comes with starvation. As Moshe Isserles writes in his gloss to the *Shulchan Aruch*, "There are those who are strict and seek to observe two days of Yom Kippur. . . . But they shouldn't behave so stringently because of the fear that they might fall into danger."[6] Keep Yom Kippur, he says, but do not make it a habit. Observing fast days with our Torah's prescribed moderation permits us to engage our ascetic impulses without neglecting our "this-worldly" existence.

If Yom Kippur draws dangerously close to asceticism, Sukkot tempts us with hedonism. Therefore, it, too, needs strictures to keep our extremist tendencies in check. Our Torah commands us to be happy on Sukkot: "You shall rejoice (*us'machtem*) before the Eternal your God seven days" (Leviticus 23:40). However, like with Yom Kippur, the Torah does not legislate the specifics of fulfilling this principle.

Though there are certainly cases in which commentators see the mandate to rejoice as obligating us to study and prayer,[7] the majority of commentators see the command as fundamentally carnal. There are numerous instances in which the avenues to happiness imply drinking wine,[8] eating meat,[9] or sexual relations.[10] Maimonides writes that in an effort to gladden those in our house, we must provide our children with "roasted seeds, nuts, and sweets" and our wives with "attractive clothes and jewelry according to one's financial capacity."[11] These behaviors can easily be taken too far. People can become gluttonous and drunk. Healthy sexuality can become hypersexuality. In an effort to entice our children, we might spoil them. A healthy enjoyment of fashion can quickly turn into materialism.

With this in mind, our Rabbis took two approaches to limiting our hedonistic tendencies. We are taught in the Book of Proverbs that "a righteous person eats until they are sated" (Proverbs 13:25). The Rabbis came out strongly against excessive behavior. They liken a drunk to a "pig" and a "monkey."[12] Anyone who overeats may be considered "wicked." The Talmud teaches:

> Every scholar who feasts much in every place eventually destroys his home, widows his wife, orphans his young, forgets his learning, and becomes involved in many quarrels; his words are unheeded, and he desecrates the Name of Heaven and the name of his teacher and the name of his father and causes an evil name for himself, his children, and his children's' children until the end of time.[13]

If those texts do not scare you into acting with moderation, our tradition still has an additional tool to employ. Built into the fabric of the Sukkot celebration is the command to be generous. As Maimonides explains:

> When a person eats and drinks [in celebration of a holiday], he is obligated to feed converts, orphans, widows, and others who are destitute and poor. In contrast, a person who locks the gates of his courtyard and eats and drinks with his children and his wife, without feeding the poor and the embittered, is [not indulging in] rejoicing associated with a mitzvah, but rather the rejoicing of his gut.[14]

Thus, when our inclination is toward hedonism, we are commanded to provide hospitality. The antidote to overeating and drinking is not to abstain from them altogether, but rather to share them. True happiness means gladdening the hearts of others, even when we enliven our own.

Both Yom Kippur and Sukkot are powerful lessons on the subject of the *sh'vil hazahav*, the golden path of moderation. The Rabbinic limitations placed on observing each of these holidays acknowledge that people can take their ritual observances too far. Thus, our Rabbis mindfully limit us in our religious behavior. If we mark our holy days properly, our Jewish festival calendar grounds us, guiding us toward restraint and allowing us to control our impulses, rather than letting them rule us.

Questions to Ask

In what ways do you experience challenges in your holiday celebrations? When are you excessively zealous? When do you struggle with too much self-indulgence?

What does *sh'vil hazahav* look like for you in your observance of Yom Kippur and Sukkot?

Practice for the *Middah* of *Sh'vil Hazahav*

Write down a list of behaviors that border either on hedonism or on asceticism for you. Then, think back to times in your life when you engaged in them. What was going on in your life? What made you change your behavior? Identifying these moments will keep you from slipping back into these behaviors again.

Another *Middah* to Consider

The holidays include a number of practices meant to instill within us the *middah* of *seder* (סֵדֶר, "order"). How does following the laws of our holiday cycle help us appreciate order, and how can our calendar become a training ground for appreciating order in other parts of our religious and secular lives?

NOTES

1. Maimonides, *Mishneh Torah, Hilchot Dei-ot* 3:1.
2. See *Mishnah Yoma* 8:1.
3. *Babylonian Talmud, Yoma* 74b.
4. *Sefer HaRokei-ach HaGadol*, ed. B. S. Shneurson (Jerusalem: 1967), 27.
5. *Kuzari* 3:5.
6. *Shulchan Aruch, Orach Chayim* 624:5.
7. *Babylonian Talmud, Beitzah* 15b.
8. *Babylonian Talmud, P'sachim* 109a.
9. Ibid.
10. *Mishneh Torah, Hilchot Shabbat* 30:14.
11. *Mishneh Torah, Hilchot Yom Tov* 6:18.
12. *Tanchuma, Noach* 14.
13. *Babylonian Talmud, P'sachim* 49a.
14. *Mishneh Torah, Hilchot Yom Tov* 6:18.

B'HAR—LEVITICUS 25:1–26:2

Bitachon—Trust:
Trusting the Process

RABBI MARC MARGOLIUS

PARASHAT B'HAR POWERFULLY DESCRIBES two important mitz-vot: giving the land a Sabbatical every seventh year, and declaring a *Yoveil* ("Jubilee") every fifty years. Each of these commandments calls upon us to engage in what we might call "Shabbat practice": to stop engaging in creation and productivity by cultivating the *middah* of *bitachon* (בִּטָּחוֹן), "learning to trust in God" or, as many may prefer, "trust in a force greater than ourselves."

The Sabbatical and Jubilee years invite us to set down the tools by which we "work the land," to relinquish what others may owe us, and surrender our inclination to control. To the extent that we can learn to "trust the process" or "go with the flow" of life, we may learn that the current carries us where we need to go. In practicing *bitachon*, we learn (in the terminology of twelve-step programs) to "let go and let God."

The first of *B'har*'s Shabbat-based mitzvot is the "Sabbatical year of rest for the land" (described elsewhere in Torah as the *Sh'mitah*[1]):

> Speak to the Israelite people and say to them: When you enter the land that I assign to you, the land shall observe a sabbath of the Eternal. Six years you may sow your field, and six years you may prune your vineyard and gather in the yield. But the seventh year the land shall have a sabbath of complete rest a sabbath of the Eternal: you shall not sow your field or prune your vineyard. (Leviticus 25:2–4)

The second Shabbat-based mitzvah is the *Yoveil* or "Jubilee" year, which takes place in the fiftieth year, the year after seven Sabbatical year cycles. In the Jubilee year, slaves must be emancipated, and Israelites who have had to sell their ancestral homestead as a result of financial hardship are entitled to return home.

> You shall hallow the fiftieth year. You shall proclaim release throughout the land for all its inhabitants. It shall be a jubilee to you: each of you shall return to your holding and each of you shall return each to your family. (Leviticus 25:10)

Unlike most mitzvot, which can be performed in the moment, the *Sh'mitah* and *Yoveil* mitzvot are enacted over a period of a full year. In a midrash on Psalm 103:20 ("Bless the Eternal, O the Eternal's angels, mighty creatures who do God's bidding, ever obedient to the Eternal's bidding"), Rabbi Yitzchak Nafcha comments:

> This refers to those who observe *Sh'mitah*. It is customary for a person to perform a mitzvah for a day, a week, or a month. Does one usually observe a mitzvah for an entire year? Yet the farmer lets the field lie fallow for a year, the vineyard for a year, and remains silent. Is there greater strength of character than this?[2]

Leviticus 25:23 clearly expresses the rationale for the Jubilee: "The land must not be sold beyond reclaim, for the land is Mine; you are but strangers resident with Me." Nachmanides views this verse as exhorting Israelites "to practice the Jubilee year and not feel bad about it—for the land is Mine and I do not want you selling it outright as you do with other things. That is the *Sifra*'s [midrash]'s point in saying: 'You are but strangers resident with Me'—do not imagine that you are the point of it all."

We are not the point of it all. For the medieval Spanish Jewish philosopher Bachya ibn Pakuda, *B'har* teaches that each of us must be "ready to move on and relocate, and not feel settled and secure,"[3] noting that "the soul is also a stranger in this world; all people are like strangers here, as the verse says: 'because you are strangers and temporary residents with Me.'"[4]

The mitzvot of the Sabbatical and Jubilee years therefore teach us to notice our natural human inclination toward attachment and to strive, over and over, to surrender that predilection. In a sermon entitled "To Hold with Open Arms," Rabbi Milton Steinberg captured this paradox after he recovered from a near-fatal heart attack. Steinberg stressed the need to live fully and joyfully with the awareness of our impermanence, learning to "clasp the world, but with relaxed hands; to embrace it, but with open arms."⁵ Practicing *bitachon* means, as Steinberg taught, to care for ourselves, others, and our world, without succumbing to the illusion that we "possess" anything.

We can understand our inclination to "cling" or "grasp" for control as symptomatic of anxiety induced by our sense of separation and disconnection from self, others, and God. We can notice the impulse to attach but allow that urge to pass through us, instead of expressing itself in futile attempts to seize control. By opening our mind, heart, and hands, we may settle into an awareness of the underlying interconnectedness of all.

Honestly facing our ultimate surrender can open our eyes to a deeper truth, as my friend and Mussar teacher Miki Young, *z"l*, expressed in a blog post while struggling with what proved to be terminal illness:

> I think that there's a comfort to mortality. I think some day, when the timing is right, I will simply fall back into a large white parachute, letting go of worry, letting go of fear and just relaxing into the silkiness. Until that time, I find it comforting to think that the reason for my mortality is to drive my living. We are all here for such a short time that it is important to discern what we really want our lives to be about.

We can practice *bitachon* by remembering that "large white parachute" and experiencing it as an ever-present source of comfort and support. We must pause and notice, without judging, our propensity to grasp for control. Then, at the *n'kudat b'chirah* (נְקֻדַּת בְּחִירָה), the "choice point" or "awareness point," we must remember the truth that "we are not the point." It is more than enough for us to understand that we are always *gerim v'toshavim* (גֵּרִים וְתוֹשָׁבִים—"strangers and temporary residents") with God, just passing through.

We can be ready, at any moment, to emulate our ancestors Abraham and Sarah by "going forth," uprooting and relocating ourselves to the next moment, the next place. We access our innate capacity for *bitachon* by opening our minds, bodies, and spirits, holding all that is precious with open hands, treading lightly on this world, treasuring and releasing each breath, each moment.

Bitachon is a particularly challenging *middah*, especially for those of us whose trust has been undermined by small and large personal traumas and challenges, natural disasters, or unspeakable tragedies. There seems to be ample reason to mistrust the ever-changing flow of life, since it often leads us onto rocky shores. But practicing *bitachon* does not require passive reliance on that flow; Rabbinic tradition calls upon us not to trust in supernatural intervention, but rather to exert our own efforts to make manifest the divinity latent in the world. Practicing *bitachon* involves active, intentional engagement with an underlying, often unnoticed and supportive process that we perceive, trust, and reveal through our words and actions.

Questions to Ask

What is your basic level of trust in yourself? In others? In God? In life in general?

What, if anything, reminds you of your capacity to trust in that which you cannot see, feel, touch, taste, or hear?

At times in your life when things have seemed bleak, have you been able to perceive within or beneath the bleakness a spark of light and hope?

Do you have a sense of trusting the "unfolding process of life"?

Practices for the *Middah* of *Bitachon*

Notice the presence of *bitachon* in your mind and body:
When we attend to the process of breathing, we notice
how we automatically trust that the next breath will
arise, even when we are not making a conscious effort to
breathe. When we bring awareness to the sensations of
sitting in a chair or feeling the ground beneath us as we
walk, we notice how we habitually trust in underlying
supportive structures even in our less conscious moments.
When we manifest confidence even while experiencing
insecurity and anxiety, we manifest and build trust in
ourselves. When we delegate a task to others, we notice
our capacity to trust in someone or something beyond
ourselves. When we get out of bed each morning, we
notice how we trust the life process itself.

Befriend worry: "If worry comes to your heart," teaches the
Mussar master Rabbi Menachem Mendel of Satanov in
his *Cheshbon HaNefesh*, "take it as a warning from God who
loves you."[7] Rather than an impediment to practicing *bitachon*, worry can be an effective reminder of our capacity for
feeling held and supported. When you notice anxiety or
worry arising, greet and welcome it by placing a hand on
your heart, taking a breath, and experiencing what it feels
like to accept love from yourself and the universe.

Meet fear with *bitachon*: We are called to balance healthy
fear with *bitachon*, which enables us to step outside our
comfort zone, not knowing the outcome in advance.
Practice *bitachon* by noticing a recurrent situation that
provokes anxiety in you. See if you can discern if that fear
is exaggerated and whether fostering a sense of trust in
yourself or another person may ease the constriction.

Cultivate *bitachon* in others: Investigate moments when you
feel alone, unsupported, or helpless in meeting a challenge. Identify potential sources of assistance, and ask for

help. Delegate a task that feels like more than you can or should handle right now. Trust others, and trust yourself to ask for help.

Other *Middot* to Consider

The process of intentionally "letting go" of control by engaging in *bitachon*, trust, implicates several other related *middot*:

Savlanut (סַבְלָנוּת, "patience, forbearance"), our innate capacity to "bear the burden" of waiting. How would *savlanut* come up for bonded servants awaiting the *Yoveil*?

G'vurah (גְּבוּרָה, "strength"), engaging our inner strength to maintain our boundary by restraining our impulse to "retake the wheel" and exert control. Imagine the *g'vurah* required of farmers observing the *Sh'mitah*.

NOTES

1. The Sabbatical year is referred to by the term *Sh'mitah* ("release") in the Book of Deuteronomy: "Every seventh year you shall practice remission [*sh'mitah*] of debts. This shall be the nature of the remission: all creditors shall remit the due that they claim from their fellow [Israelites]; they shall not dun their fellow [Israelites] or kin, for the remission proclaimed is of the Eternal" (Deuteronomy 15:1–2).
2. *Yalkut T'hillim* 860.
3. Bachya ibn Pakuda, "Gate of Self-Accounting," in *Duties of the Heart*, vol. 2, trans. Daniel Haberman (New York: Feldheim, 1996), 767.
4. Ibid., 419.
5. Milton Steinberg, *A Believing Jew: The Writings of Rabbi Milton Steinberg* (New York: Harcourt Brace, 1951), 318.
6. Menachem Mendel Levin of Satanov, *Cheshbon HaNefesh* (1812), trans. Dovid Landesman (New York: Feldheim, 1995), 182–83.
7. Menachem Mendel Levin of Satanov, *Cheshbon HaNefesh* (1812), trans. Dovid Landesman (New York: Feldheim, 1995).

B'CHUKOTAI—LEVITICUS 26:3–27:34

Histapkut—Simplicity: Recognizing Our Blessings

RABBI MARLA JOY SUBECK SPANJER, DD

MAHATMA GANDHI TAUGHT, "Earth . . . provides enough to satisfy everyone's needs, but not for everyone's greed."[1] *Histapkut*, from the Hebrew word for "enough," is the antithesis of greed. Where greed breeds insatiable desires, *histapkut* (הִסְתַּפְּקוּת, "simplicity") enables a person to experience satisfaction from having even the most basic needs met. It is contentment without complacency.

The paradox of *histapkut* is that when we give up things, we feel greater joy rather than increased yearning. Alan Morinis writes, "The primary target in sight here is to liberate yourself from the bondage of insatiable desire. And you are satisfied."[2] This kind of satisfaction does not depend on accumulating objects or accolades.

Parashat B'chukotai begins with a promise and a threat. The promise assures us that we will derive satisfaction in major areas of our lives, should we walk faithfully in the ways of Torah. The threat details the countless forms of discontent we will experience, should we turn away from a life of Torah. The language of blessings and curses is hyperbolic and vivid.

Such lists of blessings and curses, presented as divine responses to human behavior here and elsewhere[3] in the Torah, tend to disturb us. In our lives, we regularly experience blessings that we know we could not have earned by the merit of our efforts alone, and we witness curses grievously disproportional to anyone's misdeeds. If the opening verses of *B'chukotai* are to serve as more than mere scare tactics, we need to reconsider the nature of what it means to be blessed or cursed.

Whether we perceive the circumstances of our lives to come from God, fate, chance, or other people, we often experience them as something thrust upon us without our doing. However, the ability to perceive a circumstance as a blessing is, in and of itself, a tremendous blessing, and Mussar calls that perception *histapkut*. By contrast, the perception of a circumstance as a curse is itself a torturous curse.

Specifically, the ability to find satisfaction when our basic needs are fulfilled can bring us calm and even joy, while the compulsion to chase endlessly after all that we desire may cause more suffering and damage than the deprivation we fear so much. Moreover, the compulsive hoarding of resources stemming from such unfounded fear often leads to actual deprivation for others, making *histapkut* a crucial *middah* for us to cultivate.

Let us consider the impact of a well-developed *middah* of *histapkut* on the blessings and curses described in our *parashah*. To what extent is the content of a given blessing or curse a matter of perception or state of mind?

When we read, "You shall eat your fill of bread and dwell securely in your land" (Leviticus 26:5), a reasonable understanding is that we are being assured of sufficient food and a lack of violent enemies—or, at least, strong protection from such enemies should they exist. Similarly, "I will grant peace in the land, and you shall lie down untroubled by anyone" (Leviticus 26:6) might indicate that no one will seek to threaten or harm us or that no one will succeed in doing so, especially since this blessing is followed by examples of military victory.

Yet, what physical circumstances could be described by the curse "I will wreak misery upon you" (Leviticus 26:16; also translated "I will direct panic against you"[4]) or the threats of despair (*m'chalot einayim*) and despondency (*m'divot nafesh*) in the same verse?

Some verses even state explicitly that a given curse refers exclusively to a state of mind. Examples include "You shall flee though none pursues" (Leviticus 26:17) and "As for those of you who survive,

I will cast a faintness into their hearts. . . . The sound of a driven leaf shall put them to flight. Fleeing as though from the sword, they shall fall though none pursues. With no one pursuing, they shall stumble over one another as before the sword" (Leviticus 26:36–37).

The impact of these curses is entirely on attitude or mental health. Nothing physical has been taken, nor has any external situation changed; yet these are among the most painful and debilitating of the curses described in this *parashah*. Furthermore, these curses of the mind rather than the body invite us to reexamine some of the blessings that may otherwise have seemed to focus only on the body.

The blessing "You shall eat your fill of bread" (Leviticus 26:5) takes on a new layer of meaning when juxtaposed against the curse "And though you eat, you shall not be satisfied" (Leviticus 26:26). Apparently, one's "fill of bread" refers to more than just the quantity of food available or consumed. Indeed, Rashi taught that "a single grain would become blessed [when consumed]."[5] In other words, the amount of food would not change, but rather its effect on the person eating it.

Similarly, it would seem redundant to state, "I will grant peace in the land, and you shall lie down untroubled by anyone" (Leviticus 16:6) immediately after promising that "you shall . . . dwell securely in your land" (Leviticus 16:5), unless the second blessing added something new, such as the ability not only to be safe but to feel safe as well.

We cannot determine how much bread leads to satisfaction, nor what fortifications lead a people to dwell securely in their land, because satisfaction and security result from the interaction of physical realities with a mental and spiritual state of mind. To what extent can we control these states of mind through Mussar practice? What can we do if this trait is particularly weak in us?

In response, I share with you this memory. After leading a weekly discussion group based on Alan Morinis's book *Everyday Holiness*, I invited Dr. Morinis as scholar-in-residence. During the visit, I had the opportunity to ask him a personal question. I was concerned that my struggles with the *middah* of *seder* (סֵדֶר, "order") could prevent me from undertaking the disciplined process of Mussar practice.

Dr. Morinis glanced at the tallit I had thoughtlessly tossed onto my desk after services. "Why not start simply by taking care to neatly fold or hang up your tallis after every service?" he suggested. Then, he asked me if I knew why he had chosen that particular practice as a way to begin. "Yes," I replied. "You know that I already have *kavod* [כָּבוֹד, "honor"] for the tallit, and the best way for me to strengthen a weak *middah* is to link it to one in which I am already strong." I knew this lesson because it was one of the many I had learned from Dr. Morinis himself.

Although this technique depends upon the relative strength of each individual's *middot*, let us consider the impact of linking *histapkut* with gratitude, for example. *Dayeinu*, we say at the Passover seder—"It would have been enough." We say this about each one of the things God did for us as part of our redemption from Egypt, even though none of them alone would have been enough to make us a people free to live a life of Torah.

Saying that each of those gifts was enough means that any one of the miracles would have been reason enough for us to be grateful. Blessings do not lose their value when they are only part of a larger story. Even Moses does not get the full experience, and yet what he does get is sufficient.

From this perspective, any one of the blessings in *B'chukotai* would have been enough. We could feel satisfaction from rain coming down at the proper season so that the earth yields its produce and the trees of the field their fruit. Every one of the blessings listed in our *parashah*, like every one of the blessings we experience today, could lead us to say, *Dayeinu*, "It would have been enough," and yet we yearn for so much more.

Our lives, we tell ourselves, will not be livable unless we get into the right college (or any college), unless we get the perfect job (or the one we want right now), unless we live where we want to live, unless other people do what we want them to do. The real blessing is to be able to live with what we have right now and to live with what we are right now. Our imperfect bodies, our imperfect minds, our imperfect lives can be enough, and when we know this, we are blessed beyond compare.

Questions to Ask

What can we learn from the progression of blessings—from climate to agriculture to nourishment, from safety and peace in the land to restfulness and confidence in the body and mind, from a strengthened covenantal relationship to abundance and freedom?

Why might the conditional promise of blessings and threat of curses in B'chukotai be presented to us in the plural form? On what level of family or community does it ring truest to our experience of natural consequences? What enduring impact can an individual's words and actions have on the earth and its inhabitants, and how formative can a society's messages and actions be on an individual?

Practice for the *Middah* of *Histapkut*

Set an intention to live without a product or service that enhances comfort or convenience in your life and to do without whatever that may be for a period of at least one month. Pay attention to the discomfort or inconvenience you experience. Are you missing the product or service itself, or is your affliction "all in your head"? Could you live in contentment without this product or service long-term?

Other *Middot* to Consider

The concept of reward and punishment presented in B'chukotai challenges us to find a healthy balance in the trait of *anavah*, "humility." On the one hand, it requires us to acknowledge the limited extent of our direct control over some of the most essential aspects of our existence. On the other hand, it opens our eyes to the vast power we yield over nature and the weight of our responsibility to both current and future generations.

NOTES

1. Adapted from Y. P. Anand and Mark Lindley, *Gandhi on Providence and Greed*, https://www.academia.edu/303042/Gandhi_on_providence_and_greed.
2. Alan Morinis, *Everyday Holiness: The Jewish Spiritual Path of Mussar* (Boston: Trumpeter, 2007), 122.
3. For example, in *Parashat Ki Tavo*, parallel lists of blessings and curses are contained in Deuteronomy 28:1–19, part of a longer list from Deuteronomy 27:15–28:68.
4. Robert Alter, *The Hebrew Bible: A Translation with Commentary*, vol. 1, *The Five Books of Moses* (New York: Norton, 2019), 458.
5. Rashi on Leviticus 26:5.

NUMBERS

Seder—Order:
The Measure and Ideal of Middot

RABBI AVI FERTIG

PARASHAT B'MIDBAR BEGINS the fourth book of Torah, also called B'midbar, which means "in the desert," though the familiar English name is "Numbers." This name is based on the Gemara, which refers to the fourth book as *Chumash HaP'kudim*, "The Book of Counting."[1] Indeed, the *parashah* starts with God instructing Moses and Aaron to "take a census of the whole Israelite company" (Numbers 1:2). Is counting and accounting such a central theme as to merit the naming of an entire book of the Torah?

The *middah* of *seder* (סֵדֶר, "order") permeates the entire *parashah*. After the taking of the census, the Torah describes the formation of the Israelites into encampments and marching formations. We then get more counting and the organization of Levitical duties to be carried out in the Tabernacle.

The Torah is God's instruction to humanity for living a spiritually elevated life, and *seder* is clearly being stressed as a core spiritual value. We receive this very message from Rabbi Simcha Zissel Broide (1824–98), the famed Alter ("elder") of Kelm,[2] who said:

> A person is like a strand of precious pearls, with many natural abilities, intellect, *middot* ("character traits"), and exalted qualities. Order is like the clasp that holds the strand of pearls together. Without order, all of a person's exalted qualities will be wasted and the person will be left empty.[3]

In the Yeshiva of Kelm, the *middah* of *seder* was not seen as simply an external matter, but rather a vital aspect of our personality and a mir-

ror to our innermost self. If something is out of order in our external
life, it is a sign that something is wrong within our inner world. If
things are messy, then our mind will be confused as well. The Alter of
Kelm summed up his primary educational focus by saying, "External
order brings us to think clearly and act with restraint."

Reb Simcha Zissel once traveled to visit his only son, Reb Nachum
Zeev, who was studying in another city. Upon arriving, the Alter first
went to the room in which his son had been sleeping and checked to
see that his son's clothing and things were in order. Only after that
did he go and actually visit with his son.[4]

I am privileged to live in Israel. When you ask how someone is
doing and they are well, the response is usually *Hakol b'seder*, "Everything is in order." The Hebrew language appreciates the centrality of
order to a life well lived.

I consider myself a fairly organized person. My computer has
thousands of files neatly organized into folders and subfolders. Yet
the level of organization required in today's modern world seems
to be ever elusive. How often do I forget where I put the password
to that site or account? One wrong character and my e-mail is not
received. Living in Israel, I find myself having to schedule meetings
in three different time zones. How often do I make a wrong calcula-
tion and miss my meeting? And what happens if, God forbid, my hard
drive crashes, as it has done twice in the span of just three months?!

I get it. We need the *middah* of order to get us through our days in
one piece, to remind us to *back up our computer files*! But the Alter is
clearly saying more. Rabbi Broide is teaching us that an ordered life
allows all of one's abilities to be properly expressed.

Seder is not simply a practical safeguard; it is a central feature of
our spiritual lives. However, returning to our *parashah*, we are struck
by the following question: Is counting good or bad? Is order a primary value? After all, the Talmud makes a radical statement: "Rabbi
Yitzchak said, 'It is forbidden to count Israel, even for the purpose of
a mitzvah.'"[5] Is there a potential danger in acting with *seder*?

While tempted to oversimplify *seder* as an absolute virtue, we all
know that it is not. Excessive obsession with order is not healthy. We

know people who need things to be so precisely neat in their environment that the tiniest bit of the disorder that inevitably creeps into every life brings them great distress.

The way we act with *seder* determines if it is a virtue. The danger of counting people is that people become just numbers. I remember the visceral reaction I experienced as a child upon seeing an elderly Jew with a number stamped on his arm. The Nazis (may their names be erased) were extremely orderly. Every diabolical step was carefully planned and precisely executed. Clearly, this order was not a virtue. When they stamped a number on the arm of a prisoner, they tattooed those numbers to remove all sense of individuality and to rob human beings of their intrinsic worth.

In contrast, the counting and division of the camps in our *parashah* is carefully orchestrated to balance the individual with the greater community: "The Israelites shall camp each man with his standard, under the banners of their ancestral house; they shall camp around the Tent of Meeting at a distance" (Numbers 2:2).

Rabbi Eliyahu Dessler identifies the highest level of order as *seder l'shem hitachdut hap'ulah*, "order for the sake of unity of function." At this level of order, separate components are organized and connected in such a way that they blend into a unified whole. The order of the Israelite camps described in the Torah is an illustration of this highest form of order:

> The separation of individuals and the separation of different groups prevents the reaching of goals. However, mixing them all together [into one unified mass] is also not good. Rather, the optimal system is when each individual uses their unique *middot* and abilities . . . directing these abilities to one purpose, to the whole . . . to reach spiritual wholeness each individual learns from one another.[6]

The camp of Israel had a clearly defined inner structure in which everyone knew their place and purpose. Each tribe, and every individual within the tribe, possessed a unique identity and unique qualities. As Rashi comments on the verse above: "Each banner had an insignia, a covered flag hung upon it, the color of one was not like the color of the other." At the same time, each individual Jew blended into the whole of Israel to be part of the purpose for which the entire Jewish nation has been called into covenant.

The Torah's unique description of the ordered encampments teaches us that while each of us is unique, we acquire and express our unique abilities precisely when we function as parts of a larger order. One's unique abilities and strengths are to be valued especially as they are given toward the greater community.

The deep lesson to learn from the Torah's *seder* is that every *middah* requires a careful balance. At times rigid attention to order is demanded, and at times we need the flexibility to allow for a break in that order. Be willing to be part of a larger order, but retain your sense as a separate individual. Know when to follow the "orders" of a system, and know when to take a stand against that system. Character traits are referred to as *middot*, which literally means a "measure," because in every *middah* we are charged to determine the correct measure.

Moreover, being a virtue depends on the purpose for which *seder* is used. Mussar teaches that *middot* are only virtues when they are aligned with the greater ideals of Torah. Organizing the Jewish people into a unified whole is not a virtue if it comes at the expense of losing individual identity. Counting is good when each individual does not become just a number. When we use order to be generous, to be kind, to do good in the world, to accomplish the mitzvot as directed by Torah, it is then a virtue and it is then that we emulate God.

Each of our *middot* can be used in a positive or negative way; it depends upon the measure and the ideal for which we use them.

The Torah instructs us by illustrating where and how being orderly is a virtue, giving us even greater insight into the lesson from the Alter of Kelm. Order is like the clasp that holds the strand of pearls together. *Seder* teaches us a universal truth about all *middot*. Just as it is apparent how easily order can be misused and misdirected, so too must we appreciate this truth regarding all *middot*, even those that we naturally assume to be positive. The clasp on the pearls, symbolizing *seder*, reminds us to bring balance to all our *middot* as we direct them toward the Torah's ideal.

When we observe the Israelites encamped in an orderly way in the desert, both unified into one community and maintaining their distinct individuality, we may find deeper meaning in the Israeli expression of *hakol b'seder*, and that is "all is contained in the *middah* of *seder*."

Questions to Ask

Which of your life goals become unreachable without *seder*?
In what ways does *seder* allow you to live by your core values?
When is it good to observe uniform order, and when should individual expression be the greater value? Do you think schools should have a dress code? Why or why not?
What might be a circumstance in your life in which *seder* might prevent you from living by your core values?

Practice for the *Middah* of *Seder*

Identify a situation in your life where an excessive regard for *seder* is not contributing to furthering your values. Resolve to be more flexible in this situation in the coming week(s). Then, identify a circumstance where acting with greater *seder* would help you achieve your values. Commit to acting with greater *seder* in this area in the coming week(s).

Other *Middot* to Consider

In Numbers 2, the Torah describes the formation of the Israelite encampments into clear divisions that were to be strictly maintained even when journeying through the desert. This detailed account illustrates the Torah's regard for *g'vurah* (גְּבוּרָה, "strength, discipline"). Similarly, we find in Exodus 19:12, at the giving of the Torah at Mount Sinai, that God instructs Moses to "set boundaries for the people."

The organization of the Levites into various services to be performed in the Tabernacle is a prime example of the

middah of *acharayut* (אַחֲרָיוּת, responsibility"). The Levites
replace the firstborn as the most elevated and honored
faction of the Israelites (Numbers 3:12). They are then
given jobs serving the community, teaching us that the
highest honor is to serve others and the community.

NOTES

1. *Babylonian Talmud, M'nachot* 45b. In Hebrew, חומש הפיקודים.
2. The Alter of Kelm was the primary student of Rabbi Yisrael Salanter, founder
   of the modern-day Mussar movement.
3. See Shlomo Wolbe, *Alei Shur*, vol. 2 (Jerusalem: Beit HaMussar, 1986), 320,
   who quotes this teaching in the name of Rabbi Simcha Zissel.
4. Katz, *Tenuat HaMussar / The Mussar Movement*, vol. 2 (New York: Feldheim,
   1966), 155.
5. *Babylonian Talmud, Yoma* 22b.
6. *Michtav M'Eliyahu*, vol. 1, 92. The first two levels Rabbi Dessler describes are
   as follows: (1) *Seder l'shem seder*, "order for the sake of order"—this is aesthetic
   order, or the symmetry and harmony apparent in the world. It is order that
   brings pleasure to the one who experiences it. (2) *Seder l'shem totz'otav*, "order
   for the sake of its results"—this is the order that allows systems to function
   optimally, such as the index of a library. The index is the key to the successful
   functioning of the library; without it the books may be useless and every
   additional book makes the library less useful. Each book maintains its own
   completely separate identity, but without the index one cannot make use of
   the book.

NASO—NUMBERS 4:21–7:89
Z'rizut—Alacrity:
Doing What Ought to Be Done

RABBI MARCIA R. PLUMB

Speak to the Israelites and say to them: If any men or women explicitly utter a Nazirite's vow, to set themselves apart for the Eternal, they shall abstain from wine and any other intoxicant. . . . Throughout their term as Nazirite, no razor shall touch their head; it shall remain consecrated until the completion of their term as Nazirite of the Eternal, the hair of their head being left to grow untrimmed. Throughout the term that they have set apart for the Eternal, they shall not go in where there is a dead person. Even if their father or mother, or their brother or sister should die, they must not become defiled for any of them, since hair set apart for their God is upon their head. . . .

This is the ritual for the Nazirite: On the day that the term as Nazirite is completed, the person shall be brought to the entrance of the Tent of Meeting. . . .

Such is the obligation of a Nazirite; except that those who vow an offering to the Eternal of what they can afford, beyond their Nazirite requirements, must do exactly according to the vow that they have made beyond his obligation as Nazirites.

—*Numbers 6:2–3, 5–8, 13, 21*

THE WORD *NAZIR* ("Nazirite") derives from the same root as the word *z'rizut* (זְרִיזוּת). As a *middah*, the word *z'rizut* refers to "alacrity," "enthusiasm," and "persistence." It is often seen as a trait to help motivate us to achieve our goals. It is a great *middah* for procrastinators. When we feel overwhelmed by our to-do lists or want to achieve a goal but find ourselves avoiding it, we need *z'rizut*. *Z'rizut* helps us make progress because it reminds us to embrace our dreams and bring them to reality. *Z'rizut* helps us clear obstacles that keep us from moving forward.

Alan Morinis suggests that "*zerizut* means you get out of bed as soon as you get up. It means you don't delay to do what needs to be done, what ought to be done, and what can be done."[1] Rav Shlomo Wolbe defines it as "efficiency."[2]

In the case of this *parashah*, there are three ways to understand *z'rizut*. One is being quick off the mark to take action. *Z'rizut* is the joyful and efficient energy that gets us going and enables us to fire up new endeavors. Morinis explains this kind of *z'rizut* by reference to *Akeidat Yitzchak*, the Binding of Isaac. In Genesis 22:3, we read, "Abraham rose early." In the story of the Binding of Isaac, God gave Abraham a task. Regardless of what we may think of that task (to sacrifice Isaac), Abraham embraced it with joyful energy and love for God. His passion, his *z'rizut*, drove him not to delay and to do, as Morinis says, "what needed to be done."[3]

Parashat Naso gives us another example of doing what needs to be done. At the beginning of the *sidrah*, God gives each of the tribes a to-do list that will contribute to building the *Mishkan*. No tribe has to take full responsibility for it, but all have to play a role for it to be built. At the end of the long list of tasks (Numbers 4:21–49), we read, "Each one was given responsibility for his service and porterage at the command of the Eternal through Moses, and each was recorded as the Eternal had commanded Moses" (Numbers 4:49). In other words, each tribe practiced *z'rizut* by stepping up, embracing its role in the sacred work, and accomplishing it. God rewarded them by recording it.

The second possible understanding of *z'rizut* is "having the persistence to stay with the task through to completion." It is common to have great new ideas, begin to act on them, and then not to follow through. Maybe we lost our enthusiasm or became afraid of the work needed to bring our ideas to fruition. *Z'rizut* is the *middah* we cultivate to keep putting one foot in front of the other, slowly but surely overcoming all obstacles.

I once watched the winner of the wheelchair race of the Boston Marathon cross the finish line. He was a senior in college but had trained hard enough to win the marathon. He managed to do his work on time to graduate, while training to strengthen his disabled body enough not only to race in the marathon, but win it, all at the same time. This young man was a master of *z'rizut*. Day by day, little by little, exercise by exercise, he maintained his dedication and kept his passion alive until he reached his goal. The winner knew "what ought to be done," and he did it.

Similarly, Nazirites are not distracted by temptations. They keep their eyes on their goals, and they adhere to their paths of self-discipline. Nazirites have the dedication to live by their principles, and they know that they must maintain continuous discipline, not hot passion or quick enthusiasm. They know that they must steadily put one foot in front of the other, being gentle and compassionate with themselves and others, while attempting to walk their paths. They may not always get it right, but they use *z'rizut*—"determination," "persistence," and "endurance"—to live the spiritual lives they seek.

A third way to understand *z'rizut* is "having the determination to restrain oneself from acting." Just as we need *z'rizut* to help us act, *z'rizut* can help us have the discipline not to act. *Z'rizut* helps us refrain from overeating, over-drinking, or indulging in other self-destructive behaviour.

The Nazirites in our *parashah* practice this third definition of *z'rizut*. Nazirites decide to follow a spiritual path built on strict discipline. They must abstain from drinking alcohol and from cutting their hair. They take on obligations that enable them to find holiness and closeness to God. For them, reaching this spiritual closeness is paramount, pursued with passion.

Orchot Tzadikim says, "Those who act with zeal demonstrate clearly that they love their Creator, as servants who loves their master and spur themselves to render service and to do God's will. For zeal depends upon the state of one's heart. When people free their hearts of all other thoughts that reside in it and seize upon one thought, then they will undoubtedly be zealous in its execution."[4]

The Boston Marathon winner had the love of his sport in his heart, and his mind focused on his goal. His dedication to his dreams kept him practicing and working. Like a *Nazir*, he had to refrain from unhealthy behavior, the temptation to give up, and the distractions of self-doubt. His *z'rizut* paid off. He found out, as Fertig says, "what can be done"[6] when *z'rizut* is in our toolbox.

Z'rizut gives us the enthusiasm we need to embrace our goals. We draw on it to maintain our determination and persistence when our goals feel overwhelmingly far away and beyond our reach. *Z'rizut* enables us to keep our focus on what we are trying to achieve, and refrain from that which draws us away from it. *Z'rizut* is the joyful and efficient energy that gets us going and lifts us over our challenges.

Questions to Ask

Everyone tends to be lazy in situations in which they feel they have no obligation to act. What then creates a sense of obligation that motivates us to act?

Identify situation where you lacked enthusiasm or were lazy. Identify situations where you sprung to action enthusiastically.

Try to uncover the source of your laziness, inaction, or lack of enthusiasm.

Identify situations where you sprung to action enthusiastically. What was the source of the enthusiasm?

Practices for the *Middah* of *Z'rizut*

A spiritual source of laziness arises in a person who has not fully (or at all!) internalized the notion that life is a gift and we are indebted by it. The awareness of our strengths, which are also gifts from God, is also often hard to acquire and believe in.

If you spend time every day consciously considering and meditating on the astounding gifts you have received in your life and the ensuing obligation to put them to work, both in your personal life and in your professional capacity, then laziness will begin to lose its appeal and will seem instead to be an abomination. We can train ourselves to develop *z'rizut* by understanding that the traits we are given are not to remain dormant. Our strengths and blessings in our lives were given to us to be cultivated and used. In effect, we are obligated to fulfill our potential.

As a start, take five minutes to make a list of some of the gifts you have received in your life. Keep that list with you. If you haven't included your strengths in that list, take another five minutes and add those.

A second spiritual root of laziness is fear. Here the practice is to peer down into the wellsprings from which laziness springs (if so active a metaphor applies) to seek out a fear that is an impediment to energetic action. This introspection is likely to reveal a fear of one kind or another, such as a fear of loss ("If I put myself out like that, I'll be sacrificing my personal time"), commitment ("If I speak up, they'll make me head of the committee"), shame ("They'll think I'm a geek for being so enthusiastic"), and so on. These fears are just thoughts, nothing substantial—but they can still put up walls against our success if we give them too much reality.

Add to your list at least one fear that affects you.

Other *Middot* to Consider

T'shuvah (תְּשׁוּבָה, "forgiveness"): "Speak to the Israelites: When men or women individually commit any wrong toward a fellow human being, thus breaking faith with the Eternal, and they realize their guilt, they shall confess the wrong that they have done. They shall make restitution in the principal amount and add one-fifth to it, giving it to the one who was wronged" (Numbers 5:6–7). It is clear from Numbers 5:6–7 that *t'shuvah* is a central *middah* in the *parashah.* We are to follow three steps to practice *t'shuvah*: (1) gain awareness of our misdeed; (2) apologize to the person we wronged; and (3) make restitution as best we can. The children's book *The Hardest Word* suggests that "sorry" is the hardest word to say. Practicing the *middah* of *t'shuvah* enables us to use the trait easily to rebuild broken relationships and heal hurts.

N'divut lev (נְדִיבוּת לֵב, "giving from the heart"): In Numbers 7, we watch the Israelites bring offerings to the *Mishkan*, as gifts from their hearts. They did this even though they had done all the work to build it. It would be understandable if the tribes decided that they had done and given enough. But the *middah* of *n'divut lev* inspired them to continue giving, simply for the sake of giving.

NOTES

1. Alan Morinis, in a session at the Mussar Institute, May 2011.
2. Rabbi Shlomo Wolbe, *Alei Shur*, 2:253–54.
3. Morinis, in a session at the Mussar Institute, May 2011.
4. Adapted from *Orchot Tzadikim*, "The Gate of Zeal," in *The Ways of the Tzaddikim*, ed. Gavriel Zaloshinsky (Jerusalem: Feldheim, 1995).
5. Jacqueline Jules, *The Hardest Word: A Yom Kippur Story* (Minneapolis: Kar-Ben, 2001).

B'HAALOT'CHA—NUMBERS 8:1–12:16
Anavah—Humility in Leadership

RABBI MAX WEISS

"HUMILITY" CAN BE A DIFFICULT WORD in a society like ours, which values individualism over community. It sticks in the throat. To be humble is seen as to be less-than, to be small, to take a step on the road that leads to obscurity. The Mussar definition of "humility" (*anavah*, עֲנָוָה) is different. In Hebrew, the word for self-abasement is *sh'filah*, שְׁפִילָה. Maimonides places *anavah*, "humility," as the center point between self-abasement (*sh'filah*) and arrogance (*gaavah*, גַּאֲוָה). Humility, properly conceived, is a state of being that places individuals into a social structure that allows both them and the society around them to thrive.

In *Parashat B'haalot'cha*, we learn about humility through the example of Moses's life. Think about Moses—adopted into royalty, confidant of God, confronter of Pharaoh, leader of millions—being called "a very humble man, more so than any other human being on earth" (Numbers 12:3). What does humility mean in the context of leadership? How can one be both humble and powerful?

Moses stands at the center of the Torah. He, more than any other person, connects heaven and earth. He is the translator, interpreter, and messenger of God's word. He is judge, builder, arbiter, and community organizer. Moses mediates between God and the people of Israel, even as he stands in the midst of his people, working among them as a connector. With all of his incredible skill, Moses is called "very humble" (Numbers 12:3). Moses's humility is based on his recognition that he lives his life among and with his people, not at the center and not above them. His humility flows from his knowledge of his proper place in the world. This awareness allows him both to lead and to follow, to be in front and to be behind, to know his power and to know his limits. Moses is humble. He possesses *anavah*; he is not self-abasing, nor does his power lead to arrogance.

Moses's clear perception of his own place is evident in several parts of *Parashat B'haalot'cha*. In the *parashah*'s discussion of the *pesach* offering, a group of men—who are unclean because they had been in proximity to a corpse—approach Moses to ask him why they are disqualified from bringing the *pesach* offering. Moses's reply is telling. He essentially says, "I don't know. Let me check": "Moses said to them, 'Stand by, and let me hear what instructions the Eternal gives about you'" (Numbers 9:8).

While the men approach Moses in his role of expert and decision-maker, he acknowledges that he is not in charge. Instead, he embraces his role as mediator between God and the people. Moses acknowledges his limitations. A mark of humility is the ability to recognize and act from the limits of one's knowledge and sphere of control. Humility is the public acknowledgment of one's limited place in the world. Moses claims exactly the space he needs to in order to serve God's will and his community's needs.

In one of the most poignant episodes in the Torah and in Moses's life, he cries out to God. The burden of leadership is too much for him to bear. The Israelites are once again dissatisfied with the food—the food is terrible, and the portions are too small—and complain bitterly to Moses. So once again, Moses, realizing his limitations, takes the issue to God; but the way he does so is telling. He asks:

> Did I conceive all this people, did I bear them, that You should say to me, 'Carry them in your bosom as a nurse carries an infant,' to the land that You have promised on oath to their ancestors? . . . I cannot carry all this people by myself, for it is too much for me. (Numbers 11:12–14)

Moses compares his own role to that of a mother—a person who gives of her body and soul consistently, constantly, and entirely, always attentive to the needs of an infant child. And Moses says, "That's not me!" Moses knows who he is. His humility is not self-abasing, not self-abnegating. In his internal state, as he shows in many conversations with God, he is full of self-doubt. He simply tries to do what needs to be done for the sake of the people, but he knows who he is and what he is both capable and incapable of doing.

God responds to Moses's complaint by helping him to share the burden of leadership. God tells Moses to appoint seventy elders as leaders: "Then, after coming down in a cloud and speaking to him, the Eternal drew upon the spirit that was on him and put it upon the seventy elders. And when the spirit rested upon them, they spoke in ecstasy, but did not continue" (Numbers 11:25).

The *anavah* that Moses possesses enables him to share leadership. He is humble enough not only to recognize his limits, but to accept what is best for his community, even if that diminishes his personal authority. Moses allows himself to be smaller so that others can be larger. Arrogance would have pushed Moses to do it all by himself; self-abasement would have made him think himself incapable of doing anything. Humility helps him recognize a solution that works. Moses understands, despite a moment of despair, that sharing the leadership is ultimately best for his community and for himself.

When two of the elders, Eldad and Medad, begin to have ecstatic visions and prophecies, Joshua tells Moses to restrain them. Moses replies, "Are you wrought up on my account? Would that all the Eternal's people were prophets, that the Eternal put [the divine] spirit upon them!" (Numbers 11:29). Moses understands that sharing the burden of leadership means accepting a new role in the community, publicly and gratefully. This new place and its limits are defined by the needs of his community and his own needs as well.

The leadership that Moses lives, a leadership of humility, balanced between arrogance and self-abasement, is a model sorely needed in our fame-obsessed and self-obsessed modern world, where the scale has tipped too far in favor of arrogance. In a seminal work on Mussar, *M'silat Yesharim*, Moshe Chayim Luzzatto suggests that a curative is needed to bring the arrogant individual back to the center point, the point that Moses occupies. Luzzato argues, "The general matter of humility is for a person not to attribute importance to himself for any reason whatsoever."[1] Luzzatto's suggestion is that we who are too arrogant need to practice self-abasement so that we can occupy the center space, the true space of humility.

Moses's life offers a model of leadership that is worth emulating, a leadership rooted in humility. Utilizing this model, goal-oriented leaders do not place themselves first, but place the goal first and create the space for other leaders to work with them, just as Moses works toward his goal alongside the elders in the wilderness.

Questions to Ask

How do our own gender and our gendered expectations
    impact our individual and societal definitions of humility?
How can one practice *anavah* while executing leadership?

Practice for the *Middah* of *Anavah*

Make a scale on a piece of paper, with "self-abasement" on one side and "arrogance" on the other. Think about the last time you acted as a leader. Where would you place your interactions on this scale? Why?

Another *Middah* to Consider

Several times in this *parashah*, the *middah* of anger (*kaas*, כַּעַס) is evident. The punishments of the Israelites and of Miriam come to mind. When is this *middah* useful?

NOTE
1. Moshe Chayim Luzatto, *M'silat Yesharim*, chap. 22.

SH'LACH L'CHA—NUMBERS 13:1–15:41

Savlanut—To Be Patient
and to Love

RABBI SONJA K. PILZ, PhD

SAVLANUT (סַבְלָנוּת) means "patience," we read in the dictionary. *Savlanut* means "love," I often think. Without *savlanut*, love dies.

In fact, the very root of the word *savlanut*—ס-ב-ל—bears a number of meanings. It means "to carry a burden" and "to be carried," "to lift something up," "to be the one who carries a burden," and most important, it means "to suffer." In essence, the word seems to describe an act of seizing one's own pain without burdening others. In the twentieth century, Rabbi Shlomo Wolbe wrote the following:

> What is patience? The patient person is exactly like someone who is carrying a heavy package. Even though it weighs upon him, he continues to go on his way, and doesn't take a break from carrying it. The same is true in all the relationships that are between people: we see and hear many things that aren't according to our will, and still we continue to be good friends.[1]

Often, to love means to endure and forgive each other, while continuing to celebrate and care for each other. Love requires us to contain our own pain while continuing to care for others. In the framework of Mussar, this is the essence of patience—and to me, this is the essence of love, too.

Some years ago, I began to read the Torah as a love story between God and God's people. My new way of reading is based on Rabbi Akiva's famous allegorical interpretation of the Song of Songs as a love story between God and God's people.[2] Our entire *Tanach* and all

its midrashic expansions may be seen an allegorical story of a people who are seeking and yearning to find their way into an intimate
relationship with God;[3] hoping, dreaming, imagining, and believing
that God does the same; that God is waiting for us to find our way to
love, patience, justice, intimacy, and trust.[4]

The main threat to this biblical love story seems to be a lack of
patience—often from God's side and sometimes from the side of
the people. We have reason to wish for a God who is "compassionate
and gracious, slow to anger, and abounding in steadfast love" (Exodus 34:6 and Psalm 103:8)—and God has reason to tell us that we
shall not "let [our] spirit be quickly vexed, for vexation abides in the
breasts of fools" (Ecclesiastes 7:9). In the course of our love story,
both we, the people, and God have already experienced the results of
a lack of patience—and we have reason to fear them!

Sh'lach L'cha exemplifies the terrible results of God's impatience.

At the beginning of this *parashah*, Moses sends twelve men into the
Promised Land to find out whether the Land will allow them to enter
peacefully and effortlessly or, if efforts should be needed, whether
the Land will be worth the effort after all (Numbers 13:17–20). The
spies spend forty days in the Land,[5] enjoying the fresh grapes, pome-
granates, and figs of the Land (the seasonal fruit leading to the conclusion that the spies entered the Land around the time of the High
Holy Days) before they return to the people. Once they arrive, they
appear to tell their truth:

> [The Land flows] with milk and honey, and this is its fruit.
> However, the people who inhabit the country are powerful,
> and the cities are fortified and very large; moreover, we saw
> the Anakites [very tall people] there. Amalekites dwell in the
> Negeb region; Hittites, Jebusites, and Amorites inhabit the hill
> country; and Canaanites dwell by the Sea and along the Jordan.
> (Numbers 13:27–29)

The Land, to put it clearly, is taken.

One of the spies, Caleb son of Jephunneh, raises an individual
opinion. He encourages the people not to worry and to take the Land

by storm (Numbers 13:30). However, ten of the spies express hesitation and a paralyzing fear (Numbers 13:31–33). Eventually, those feelings overtake the people. Anxious and despondent, they give up on their dreams and turn their eyes back to the desert—yes, even back to Egypt and enslavement. Moses, Aaron, Caleb, and Joshua son of Nun, the twelfth spy, mourn in disappointment and desperation (Numbers 14:5–9).

At this point, God loses it. In raving anger, God first threatens to kill them all and then, tamed by Moses's arbitration, condemns this generation—so lacking in faith, trust, and courage—to a destiny of being homeless wanderers throughout their lives, never able to enter the Land again. The lone exceptions will be the faithful Caleb—and, presumably, Joshua (Numbers 14:11–35). The people as a whole are forgiven, with the words made famous by our High Holy Day liturgy, *Salachti kidvarecha* (סָלַחְתִּי כִּדְבָרֶיךָ), "I pardon, as you have asked" (Numbers 14:20), which turns our story into a High Holy Day story about patience and forgiveness altogether! Nevertheless, the people face the consequences of their lack of trust and courage, consigned by God's anger, impatience, and disappointment—a total lack of control and patience!—to live out their days in desert wanderings. At the end of the *parashah*, God lets the ten unfaithful spies die (Numbers 14:36–38)—an understandable impulse to end a relationship marked by betrayal.

I want to dwell in this moment of God's anger. Read through my allegorical paradigm of the *Tanach* as a love story between God and God's people, God's anger and impatience seem to be the understandable reaction of a disappointed partner: "I wanted you to trust Me, and you didn't! I want you to be brave and go on a journey with Me, and you doubted My ability to take care of you!"

We all want to be trusted and loved. We want our partners to embark with us on our journeys, our kids to trust in our advice, our parents to build on our ability to support them in times of need, our friends to support our decisions, our teachers to see our potential, and our bosses to promote our careers. Yet, as we all know, life often disappoints us. Others' lack of trust in us, their doubts, and their anxieties repeatedly paralyze both them and us. We react with anger, impatience, and disappointment. At other times, our own anxieties are paralyzing us, leading us to lose trust in ourselves and others. We give up—the hopeless opposite of being patient!

In our Torah portion, God expects the people to be both brave and trusting, and when they are not, God reacts with angry disappointment. God punishes the spies and the people for being anxious and hesitant.

However, Mussar defines *savlanut* not only as a character trait, but as a practice of endurance over time. Like love, patience can only become manifest in time—what good would it be if we were patient or loving for exactly a second?

Mussar teaches patience—patience both with ourselves and with others: The patience it takes to forgive ourselves our own anxieties and paralyzing doubts, and the terrible consequences those might unfold in our lives. The patience it takes to postpone and adjust our visions. The patience it takes to perceives ourselves and others clearly. The patience it takes to assess and accept reality, including our fears, and the time we need to become more faithful and trusting.

Had God loved more, had God been patient . . . maybe then, God would fully forgive the fearful Israelites. Maybe then God would understand that the divine desire to conquer the Land—NOW!—and to begin a new era of Torah's laws—NOW!—cannot be fulfilled by this assemblage of anxious former slaves—and that fulfilling God's vision might not even be their wish! Maybe God would learn then that building trust takes time—and so does learning to love. Maybe then God would seize God's pain and disappointment with patience and would begin the slow and loving task of teaching a people how to trust.

Reading the *parashah* through the lens of a love story reveals a story of yearning for intimacy, of a lack of trust on the side of the people and a lack of patience on the side of God.

Mussar asks: Why are you impatient? Mussar asks: Why can't

you take the time? And, finally, once you will have discovered your patience, Mussar asks: Are you waiting with love?

It is not our task to be trusted and loved. It is our task to be patient, and to love.

Questions to Ask

Joshua and Caleb are described as examples of trusting, faithful, and courageous people. They are not described as patient. Imagine the next forty years of their lives. How might they have learned to forgive their partners, families, friends, and people, who trusted neither them nor God enough to embark on the journey? Which insights might have led to growing patience and understanding from their side?

Sometimes we find ourselves impatient, disappointed, and angry over the pacing of others. We want things to happen, and we want them to happen NOW! Visualize and assess a situation of that kind which you have experienced in your own life. What was your interest? What kept the other person from meeting it? Were your expectations fair and appropriate?

The *parashah* teaches a lesson about trust (*bitachon*, בִּטָּחוֹן), anger (*kaas*, כַּעַס), and patience (*savlanut*, סַבְלָנוּת). Find the characters in the story embodying these *middot*. Are there characters who embody more than one of these *middot*? Which *middot* are these?

Practice for the *Middah* of *Savlanut*

Decide to focus on one relationship in your life in which trust in you has yet to be built. Take time to understand what might keep the other person or people from trusting you. Maybe you need to ask them this question. Then, dwell in this understanding. Give and take time. Work on yourself. Have patience with the other person—and be patient with yourself.

Another *Middah* to Consider

Another *middah* to reflect on deeply is *g'vurah* (גְּבוּרָה, "strength"). The Israelites decide to dwell in their anxiety. How might the story have continued if the people decided to work on their courage and strength instead?

NOTES

1. Quoted in Alan Morinis, *Every Day, Holy Day: 365 Days of Teachings and Practices from the Jewish Tradition of Mussar* (Boston: Trumpeter, 2010), 93.
2. Traditionally based on Rabbi Akiva's saying in *Mishnah Yadayim* 3:5.
3. This is the story unfolding according to Rashi's calendar, taught to me by Rabbi Maggie Moers Wenig. For a short summary, see "*Matan Torah* according to Rashi," Ohr Somayach, accessed July 23, 2019, https://ohr.edu/991.
4. This theology developed in conversation with Hans Jonas, *The Concept of God after Auschwitz* (New York: New School for Social Reseach, 1987).
5. Forty days: the same amount of time that Moses spent on the mountain, in close intimacy with God (Exodus 32).

Z'rizut—Zeal:
Every Moment Counts

RABBI MICHAL SHEKEL

IT ALL HAPPENS SO FAST. Seemingly out of nowhere, Korach rises up and challenges the existing leadership. Korach moves quickly and decisively. The Hebrew states, *Vayikach Korach* (וַיִּקַּח קֹרַח), "Korach took" (Numbers 16:1). This is the same verb used in Exodus 2:1, where "a certain man of the house of Levi," Moses's father, "went and married (*vayikach*—וַיִּקַּח) a woman of Levi," Moses's mother. In both instances, the verb suggests a deliberate act that will have far-reaching consequences.

Korach's action has a ripple effect, as a group of 250 leaders quickly fall in line behind him. Almost immediately, they confront Moses and Aaron, challenging their leadership. Reading the text, one senses there is no time to think, only to react. Korach acts zealously, with little regard for the consequences, while his followers are driven by their emotions.

The tenor changes once Moses is involved. In contrast to Korach, Moses acts deliberately, rising to Korach's challenge but postponing any confrontation until the following day. In so doing, Moses creates an opportunity for mindful reflection. Sadly, his attempt to avoid tragedy is futile. Korach, Dathan, and Abiram are carried away by their zeal: their passion hardens into fanaticism, and ultimately they pay the ultimate price for the choice they make.

Both Korach and Moses display characteristics of the *middah* known as z'rizut (זְרִיזוּת), commonly understood as "zeal, alacrity" for completing an action, usually a mitzvah. The negative side of this trait is mere "haste" (*m'hirut*, מְהִירוּת). *Korach* clearly exemplifies the latter.

There are numerous opportunities for change: Moses gives Korach and his followers time to reassess their actions. The rebels are told twice to bring their fire pans on the following day (Numbers 16:6–7, 16:16–17), thus creating an opportunity for them to step back and reconsider. At the very end of the encounter the community is cautioned to move away from rebel leaders Korach, Dathan, and Abiram (Numbers 16:26), a final warning that the rebels willfully ignore.

What causes Korach and his followers to dismiss the opportunities laid before them is *atzlanut* (עַצְלָנוּת, "laziness"), which in Mussar is understood to be the opposite of *z'rizut* ("zeal"). Moses Chayim Luzzatto explains this in the eighteenth-century Mussar text *M'silat Yesharim* (*The Path of the Upright*):

> We often see people who know in their heart what their duty is, who are certain as to the proper means of saving their soul, and who are aware of their duty to their Creator, yet who fail to be governed by this knowledge for no other reason than indolence. . . .
>
> When love of ease overmasters their intellect, they are so inclined to listen to such arguments that they are deaf to the voice of the wise and discerning. . . . Indolence does not allow them even to give heed to the words of those who reprove them. They regard them all as blunderers and fools; they think they alone are wise.[1]

Furthermore, Luzzatto warns that laziness is a part of human nature. *M'silat Yesharim* describes laziness as a weight that drags a person down. If no effort is made to counteract it, the person continues to sink ever lower. What better symbol of this heaviness is there than the ground collapsing under Korach and swallowing him up?

While Korach dramatically represents the negative aspect of the trait of *z'rizut* that can ultimately lead to destruction, the *parashah* also offers insights into the positive facets of this character trait.

In challenging Moses's and Aaron's authority, Korach believes that he is Aaron's equal in the priesthood. However, these two individuals are polar opposites when it comes to *z'rizut*. Aaron, like Moses, embodies the positive aspects of *z'rizut*. In Numbers 17, after the rebels' tragic end, the community rails against Moses and Aaron, accusing the two leaders of being responsible for the death of the rebels. Almost immediately, God sends a plague to destroy the people. Moses and Aaron fall on their faces, and then Moses wastes no time in telling Aaron to make expiation on behalf of the community. "Aaron . . . ran to the midst of the congregation, where the plague had begun among the people. He put on the incense and made expiation for the people; he stood between the dead and the living until the plague was checked" (Numbers 17:12–13).

Falling on their faces was a way of collecting their thoughts, being mindful, and focusing before assuming the task at hand. Once they have completed their emotional preparation, their response is immediate and carried out swiftly. Thus, the matter is fulfilled with proper *z'rizut*, as the trait is described by Rabbi Ira Stone: "See then that the [person] who is an ardent worshiper of God does not act sluggishly in the performance of . . . mitzvot. [This person] moves with the swiftness of fire, and [does not] rest until [the] object is obtained."[2]

Once the plague is checked, the question of leadership is to be settled. God commands Moses to gather the staffs from each of the tribal chieftains; each staff is inscribed with the chief's name. Aaron's name is on the staff for the tribe of Levi. God's choice of the true leader will be indicated by that leader's staff sprouting.

Not only did Aaron's staff sprout, it had "produced blossoms, and borne almonds" (Numbers 17:23). Aaron's staff can be seen as a symbol of *z'rizut*: It is the first to sprout, and it produces almonds. As Rashi reminds us, the almond is the first tree to blossom. One of the biggest challenges with *z'rizut* is finding the balance between thoughtful intention and action. How can we be sure that we are acting positively rather than emotionally, as was the case with Korach's followers? At what point does stepping back to assess the situation become an excuse for inaction? Extreme caution can lead to the excuses that constitute laziness. Overeagerness invites destructive carelessness. In his commentary on *M'silat Yesharim*, Rabbi Ira Stone points out:

> ... our lives are lived along the arc between the *yetzer ha-ra* ("evil inclination") and the *yetzer tov* ("good inclination"); but also the *experience* of being aware of the choice between the two at every moment. . . .
>
> Acting with alacrity or zeal in that space requires a high level of spiritual skill—for in every moment we are confronted by the choice between the *yetzer ha-ra* and the *yetzer tov*.[3]

This awareness of that moment of choice is the key to *z'rizut*. It is the moment when Moses and Aaron fall on their faces when confronted by the rebels. There, they find the balance between focus and action. The critical moment is spent slowing down, deliberating, wrapping oneself in intentionality, in order to be able to be fully engaged in completing the task with constructive zeal.

In the last chapter of the *parashah*, God reiterates the role of the priests, their duties, their share of the tithes, and the fact that they do not own land. This priestly role and relationship with God is described as a *b'rit melach*, a "covenant of salt" (Numbers 18:19). What better symbol can there be for the countermeasure to reckless zealousness than salt, which slows decay? Thus, with Aaron's staff and the covenant of salt, we have metaphors for the two elements that are crucial to successfully achieving the trait of *z'rizut*: eagerness to address the task and deliberation to ensure we can do so.

Without a priesthood in our own day, we are all commanded to be a priestly people. Our lesson, then, is to learn from the failed priest, Korach, and from the model of a laudable priesthood, Aaron. The message of *Parashat Korach* is that while we often act reflexively, our challenge is to respond reflectively.

Questions to Ask

Often our zeal is carried out with the best of intentions—for example, we want our partner or children to succeed; or, if we run interference for the new team member, then we can move on to the next step of the project more quickly. Visualize a situation where you zealously stepped in to help an individual, while in retrospect you should have let them find their own way. What motivated you to be zealous? What factors should be taken into consideration in deciding when to step in and when to stay out?

Faced with a task, you find yourself making excuses for putting it off. What causes you to procrastinate? What are steps you can take that will motivate you to carry out your responsibility?

It is always easier to remain within our comfort zone. How often do we read material that only supports our beliefs or refuse to listen to viewpoints that challenge our own? How often do we deem those we disagree with as flawed individuals, while failing to consider our own faults? Korach was dismissive when he challenged Moses and Aaron. His followers made accusations against the two based solely on their emotional reactions. Think of a situation where you dismissed an individual because you disagreed with what he or she believed. What are steps you can take to engage that person respectfully, even though you may disagree with his or her beliefs?

What would you do in the following situation? Scrolling through your social media, you see an item that resonates with you emotionally. The sender urges you to spread the word and forward it to your contacts. Do you forward it immediately? Do you research the veracity of the item? If it pertains to an individual, do you consider the consequences for that person? If you know the item is already going viral, does that affect your decision in any way?

Suggested Practice for the *Middah* of *Z'rizut*

Are you the type of person who responds quickly to every e-mail? If so, designate a day on which you will not do so. Write out each response, but save it as a draft. Read it again an hour or two later—maybe a day later, if the matter is not urgent—and see if you would have responded differently.

Are you the type of person who is slow to respond? If so, designate a day on which you will immediately respond to every e-mail that requires a response. After responding or deciding that a response is not necessary, delete each e-mail. (If you really need to keep it, print it, just on this one day.)

What did you learn from radically modifying your *z'rizut* in your approach to your e-mail? As a result, after the exercise, consider how you may apply what you learned to other areas of your life.

If you are given to responding too zealously, how might you be more deliberate?

If you're not quick enough to respond, how might you become more responsive?

Other *Middot* to Consider

Kinah (קִנְאָה, "jealousy"): This is Korach's underlying emotion.

Sh'tikah (שְׁתִיקָה, silence): Aaron remains silent in the face of threats to his position and reputation. His actions speak rather than putting up a verbal defense (as Moses does).

NOTES

1. Adapted from Moses Hayyim Luzzatto, *Mesillat Yesharim: The Path of the Upright*, trans. Mordecai M. Kaplan, commentary by Ira F. Stone (Philadelphia: Jewish Publication Society, 2010), 86–87.
2. Ibid., 92.
3. Ibid., 91.

CHUKAT—NUMBERS 19:1–22:1

Chutzpah—Impudence, Unmitigated Gall, Spritual Audacity, and Courage

RABBI JAN KATZEW, PhD

DEATH IS THE DOMINANT THEME in *Parashat Chukat*. The portion is a pivot point, a transition from the generation that experienced negative liberty (freedom from Egyptian slavery) to the generation that would experience positive liberty (freedom to worship God in the land of promise). Miriam the prophet and Aaron the priest die, and Moses learns that he will also die in the wilderness because of his impulsive act of defiance, an act of *chutzpah* (חֻצְפָּה)[1] against God.

Miriam's death is juxtaposed to a complete absence of water (Numbers 20:1–2), and the Sages interpreted this juxtaposition as causation. When Miriam was alive, wherever the Children of Israel made camp in the wilderness, a wellspring supplied abundant water. Since Miriam died, the Children of Israel are without water.[2] The parched people complain to their leaders, Moses and Aaron, and they turn to God, who instructs them to take a rod and assemble the community so they could witness an extraordinary event: "Order the rock to yield its water" (Numbers 20:6–8). Moses takes a rod and, together with Aaron, brings the community together; but then he goes rogue and departs from the divine script: "'Listen, you rebels, shall we get water for you out of this rock?' And Moses raised his hand and struck the rock twice with his rod. Out came copious water, and the community and their beasts drank" (Numbers 20:10–11).

After developing a relationship with God unparalleled in its intimacy, Moses finds himself hoist by his own petard. He has sealed his faith and fate in just one verse, and perhaps in just a single word. Common wisdom may be that Moses's decision to strike the rock twice led to his ultimate demise. However, in this case, common wisdom is not Rabbinic wisdom. The Sages argue that rather than Moses's act of physical anger, his word of *chutzpah*, of impudence, of arrogating human authority to divine action, does him in. His fateful word is "we"—"Shall we get water for you out of this rock?" (Numbers 20:10).[3] Moses, the same person Torah characterizes as the most humble person on earth, takes credit that is not his to take. In this respect at least, Moses is not unique—then or now. Humility and *chutzpah*, which on their surface appear to be on opposite ends of the moral scale, reside within the same person. Indeed, they reside within every person.

Chutzpah at its worst claims power that humans do not possess. By saying "we," Moses commits idolatry. He substitutes himself (and Aaron) for God, and he learns a painful, yet vital lesson that is as timely as it is timeless. We are not God. We are powerful. We can give and take life. We are co-creators of our world. However, when we claim to be responsible for actions that are beyond our control or even our influence, we imitate Moses and exhibit the vice of *chutzpah*.

An example of this behavior inheres in the benign, even generous, act of offering a blessing. A rabbi, cantor, educator, parent, or grandparent may raise her or his hands and say, "I would like to bless you." Not so fast! The most popular of all blessings, the Priestly Benediction recited at life-defining events, does not come from any human being; the verse that follows that blessing in the Torah teaches, *V'samu et sh'mi al b'nei Yisrael vaani avarcheim* (וְשָׂמוּ אֶת-שְׁמִי עַל-בְּנֵי יִשְׂרָאֵל וַאֲנִי אֲבָרֲכֵם), "Thus they shall link My name with the people of Israel, and I will bless them" (Numbers 6:27). A person cannot bless anyone; rather, any person can invoke God's blessing—an enduring and endearing lesson about *chutzpah*. Human beings are powerful, but our power is finite, and our authority is limited. *Chutzpah* reaches and breaches our moral limits.

Leo Rosten, in *The Joys of Yiddish*, recounts a memorable tale of *chutzpah* that mixes macabre wit and ethical wisdom: "*Chutzpah* is that quality enshrined in a man who, having killed his mother and father, throws himself on the mercy of the court because he is an orphan."[4] This extreme example may border on the absurd, but its point is clear and sharp. It is just and right to be held responsible for our actions and to accept the consequences for them.

Nevertheless, *chutzpah* can also be a virtue.

The Rabbis noted that the *yetzer hara*, often translated as "evil inclination," is not always evil—that is, it is actually necessary for acts of procreation, building, and inventions; *chutzpah*, especially in moderation, is good, even redemptive. "According to Rav Nachman, *chutzpah*, even when it is toward God, is worthwhile."[5] Rav Nachman cited the case of Balaam, the pagan diviner, who was told by God not to go with Balak and his entourage (Numbers 22:12). Balaam refused to accept God's command, and due to his resistance, God relented. Balaam ended up accompanying Balak, yet he invoked God's blessing of the Children of Israel. *Chutzpah* is not necessarily wrong in *Parashat Chukat* either. The people's complaint that they have no water is both a *chutzpadik* rebellion and an entirely reasonable plea: after all, they are without water (Numbers 20:2–5)! *Chutzpah* is multifaceted and capable of being a vice and a virtue at the same time.

How are we supposed to know when *chutzpah* is a vice and when *chutzpah* is a virtue? For cogent responses, we need to look within us and between us. Looking within involves examining intention and reflection. What is motivating our *chutzpah*? Are we grandstanding and taking credit for work that is not of our own design? Mussar practice involves looking within and looking around; *chutzpah* is an intrapersonal trait, and it is also an interpersonal trait. We can find *chutzpah* within us and also around us. Looking between us involves considering the impact of our *chutzpah* on other people—our family and our neighbors as well as the strangers among us. Are we taking up a cause that may not benefit us directly, but will give voice to someone who has been silenced? Our moral integrity, that is, our soul, is at stake. When we are *chutzpadik* (when we exhibit *chutzpah*), we should look inside us and ask, "Why am I doing this?" We should look around us and ask, "Who is benefiting from my *chutzpah*?"

Moshe Rabbeinu is indeed our teacher when we learn from his example of *chutzpah* that has gone too far; and yet, we can also learn from Balaam that *chutzpah* has its place, an honorable place, in our moral repertoire. "Any virtue [including *chutzpah*] carried to an extreme can become a vice."[6]

Questions to Ask

When has *chutzpah* served you well? When has *chutzpah* served you ill? How do you understand the distinction and its rationale?

Does *chutzpah* need to be cultivated or curbed in our culture? Why?

Jews in general and Israelis in particular are often stereotyped as *chutzpadik*. When might "Jewish (or Israeli) *chutzpah*" be utilized for good? How might it be a response to our history?

Does God's punishment, causing Moses to die before entering the Land of Israel, fit Moses's crime of *chutzpah*? Explain.

Practice for the *Middah* of *Chutzpah*

Before you do something audacious to challenge authority, ask yourself, "Why am I doing this?" After you have acted to challenge authority, observe the impact on yourself, on the authority figure(s), and on others you care about, and ask yourself, "If I had to do it all over again, would I act similarly?" If your answer is yes, *yishar ko-ach*! More power to you and your *chutzpah*!

Other *Middot* to Consider

Kaas (בַּעַס, "anger"): Moses, in Numbers 20:9–11; God, in Numbers 20:12–13—in both of these instances, the human and divine agents act out of pique and exhibit a loss of patience and empathy.

Yoshrah (יְשָׁרָה, "integrity"): One of the ways our Sages define integrity is "when our inside and our outside are in harmony." When do Moses, God, and the Children of Israel demonstrate integrity in their actions throughout *Parashat Chukat*? See Numbers 21:5; 21:7; 21:8; 21:34–35.

Emunah (אֱמוּנָה, "faith"): In Numbers 20:12 God claims that that Moses and Aaron failed to exhibit trust in divine leadership. What about us?

NOTES

1. חוּצְפָּה (*chutzpah*) is a Hebrew word, although it has entered into many other languages, e.g., Yiddish, German, and English. Its origin is Aramaic, specifically found in the Book of Daniel 2:15, החצפה (*hachtz'fah*), translated frequently as "urgent" or "pressing."
2. See Numbers 20:1 and 20:2. The former verse concludes with the death of Miriam and the latter verse begins with the words "The community was without water." From the hermeneutic principle of סמוכין, i.e., juxtaposition, our Sages inferred causation.
3. See Rashbam, Ramban, Hizkuni, inter alia.
4. Leo Rosten, *The Joys of Yiddish* (New York: Simon and Schuster, 1968), 93. See also Robinson Meyer, "The Amazing Rise of Chutzpah, in 1 Chart (Actually in 2)," *Atlantic*, January 6, 2014.
5. *Babylonian Talmud, Sanhedrin* 105a.
6. This quote is of disputed etiology, but it has been cited in numerous texts for centuries. Colloquially, this aphorism has been attributed to Aristotle, but Stagirite scholars dispute this claim.

Kaas—Reining In Our Anger

RABBI HARVEY J. WINOKUR

"ONE WHO TEARS HIS CLOTHES, smashes property, or scatters money in his anger is as one who worships idols"—to which one might add with respect to this Torah portion: "And one who strikes his donkey."[1]

This *parashah* is known for God giving a donkey the ability to speak, but there is much more to glean from these chapters. Balak, the king of Moab, is so concerned with the column of Israelites approaching his border that he sends messengers to bring Balaam son of Beor, a well-known diviner, to him. God comes to Balaam and instructs him not to go with the messengers, and Balaam obeys. Balak sends his dignitaries a second time, offering great riches to Balaam if he complies. Balaam responds that riches will not persuade him because he must follow the commands of the Eternal. Balaam asks the messengers to remain overnight. During that evening, God comes to Balaam once again. This time God's message is: *Im likro l'cha ba-u haanashim, kum leich itam; v'ach, et hadavar asher adabeir eilecha oto taaseh* (אִם־לִקְרֹא לְךָ בָּאוּ הָאֲנָשִׁים קוּם לֵךְ אִתָּם וְאַךְ אֶת הַדָּבָר אֲשֶׁר אֲדַבֵּר אֵלֶיךָ אֹתוֹ תַעֲשֶׂה), "If these personages have come to invite you, you may go with them. But whatever I command you, that you shall do" (Numbers 22:20).

The next morning, Balaam saddles his donkey and leaves with Balak's messengers. God is, surprisingly, incensed (*vayichar af,* וַיִּחַר־אַף) at his going and sends an angel to block his way. Balaam's donkey is able to see the angel, but Balaam is not. Several times, the donkey swerves to avoid the angel, one time pressing Balaam's foot against a wall. Finally, at a point where the angel is blocking a spot too narrow to proceed, the donkey simply lies down under Balaam. Balaam is furious now, too, and strikes his faithful donkey three times. At this point, God gives the donkey the power of speech and it proceeds to admonish his owner. "Look, I am the donkey that you have been riding all along until this day! Have I been in the habit of doing thus to you? And he answered, No" (Numbers 22:30).

If God gave Balaam permission to go to Balak, why would God then change course and try to stop Balaam on his journey?

In verse 20, God gave Balaam permission to go with the men as long as he only spoke what God told him to speak. The text then says that "when he arose in the morning, Balaam saddled his donkey and departed with the Moabite dignitaries" (Numbers 22:21). The answer lies in the two-letter word "if" in the context, "If these personages have come to invite you, you may go with them" (Numbers 22:20). However, the following morning and without hearing from Balak's men, Balaam sets out on his journey.

Mussar would teach that Balaam shows arrogance and pride instead of humility and sense of mission at exactly the moment at which he saddles his donkey and begins the journey. We are meant to understand that it is Balaam's initial arrogance and lack of sense of mission that are making God angry—and therefore Balaam's anger at his donkey is entirely unjustified—and that, in turn, his donkey is right to get angry at him!

What can we learn about *kaas* (כַּעַס, "anger") by reflecting on God's choice to use a donkey to make Balaam aware of his error in setting forth that morning? What can be learned about anger by looking at Balaam's angry response to the actions of his donkey?

We can identify the *middah* of *kaas* ("anger") in the actions and reactions of Balaam, God, and the donkey. Our Sages equated anger with the cardinal sin of idolatry. When anger flares up in our heart, there is no place for God. If we are required to sacrifice our lives to avoid idol worship, how much more so are we required to rein in our ego and control our tempers to avoid anger? "One who is angry does not even consider the Divine Presence important."[2]

The Mussar masters have identified the *middah* of *kaas* as a key component of human behavior. More often, the word for "anger" in the Torah is *af* (אַף). *Af* is often translated as "wrath" or "fury," which might be considered by-products or precursors to anger.

One of the primary forms of Mussar practice is to model our behavior on what we know of God's ways, that is, "to walk in God's ways" (*v'halachta bidrachav*, וְהָלַכְתָּ בִּדְרָכָיו; Deuteronomy 28:9). It follows that if God is slow to respond angrily to provocation, then we too should strive to delay our reactions. As the verse says, "Though angry, may You remember compassion" (Habakkuk 3:2).[3]

When his donkey repeatedly strays from the path, Balaam responds by angrily striking his donkey three times. Balaam is blinded by his anger and unable to see the angel. He is so full of himself, so lost in ego, that he is dumbfounded by the actions of his donkey. If he were thinking clearly, he would have realized that his faithful donkey was trying to tell him something. Gerhard von Rad, a twentieth-century German theologian, has written, "In anger, God's will is hidden from human eyes."[4]

God is angered, too, but uses the anger to teach Balaam. We read in the Torah that God is "compassionate and gracious" and "slow to anger" (Exodus 34:6). Rather than lashing out at Balaam, God shows mercy by using the donkey to get Balaam's attention. Balaam does not get his anger under control until God gives the donkey the power of speech. Only after the donkey admonishes his master for striking her does he see the angel.

Anger does not allow us to see things clearly or at all. Anger clouds our minds and makes us incapable of rational thought. In many ways, when Balaam is admonished by his donkey, he becomes the donkey. The Talmud instructs that "if someone calls you a donkey, put a saddle on your back."[5]

Through the unique story of Balaam and his donkey, *Parashat Balak* teaches us something about the challenges of being provoked into anger. Building on Mussar teachings, we are able to come to a better understanding of our responsibility to rein in our anger and create a stronger connection to the Eternal. Understanding the ways we become angry is a significant part of our spiritual curriculum.

Therefore, we may pray:

> May my heart be cleansed of useless anger.
> May my eyes see the good in all.
> May I give the other the benefit of the doubt.
> May I be a maker of peace.
> Amen.[6]

A Question to Ask

Is it better to suppress anger or let it be expressed?

Practices for the *Middah* of *Kaas*

First, recall a situation in which you became angry. Identify the triggers of your anger: was it criticism, disobedience, jealousy, or competition, or was it something else you can identify?

Now contemplate the futility of your response: What did you hope to accomplish with your angry response? Did the situation come to a satisfactory resolution?

Consider what you could have done instead of getting angry. Imagine an alternative response, such as admitting your guilt or accepting the criticism. Would speaking softly and calmly have helped diffuse the conflict and brought it to a more satisfactory resolution? Would delaying your response have helped you gain a better perspective of the situation, allowing you to respond calmly and more effectively?

Finally, in your mind's eye, practice this proper response to the exact situation. Put in as many details as you can:

> Rabbi Ilai said, "A person is known by their cup (*kos*)—how they hold their alcohol; their purse (*kis*)—how they deal with money; and their anger (*kaas*). The first two are behaviors. The last one reflects our inner nature."[7]

Other *Middot* to Consider

Yirah (יִרְאָה, "fear, awe"): Balak expresses a fear of the Israelites as they assemble on his territory. He is made afraid by their sheer numbers: "It hides the earth from view" (Numbers 22:5). Balak judges the Israelites based on his knowledge of their actions against the Amorites. He fails to see the gathering as peaceful. Balaam, on the other hand, expresses awe as he accepts God's commands and refuses to go against God's word. When he returns to Balak, he declares, "I can utter only the word that God puts into my mouth" (Numbers 22:38).

Boshet panim (בֹּשֶׁת פָּנִים—"stubbornness"): Balak refuses to listen to Balaam. He sends him from place to place in the hope that he will finally relent and place a curse upon the Israelites.

NOTES

1. *Babylonian Talmud, Shabbat* 105b.
2. *Babylonian Talmud, N'darim* 22b.
3. Alan Morinis, *Yashar: Newsletter of the Mussar Institute*, March 2016.
4. Gerhard Von Rad, quoted in *The Torah: A Modern Commentary*, rev. ed., ed. W. Gunther Plaut (New York: Reform Judaism Publishing, an imprint of CCAR Press, 2005), 1066.
5. *Babylonian Talmud, Bava Kama* 92b.
6. *Babylonian Talmud, Eiruvin* 65b; Mussar Institute, Chaburah program, unit 1.1 on anger.
7. Ibid.

Kaas—An Anger Banquet

RABBI PAMELA WAX

No *middah* is inherently "bad." There are times for anger, particularly as a response to injustice; and there are times when a seemingly virtuous *middah* becomes so imbalanced in one's life that it is a liability rather than an asset. The *middah* of anger serves as a leitmotif throughout this Torah portion, both as a cautionary tale and as a model to follow. A careful reading offers wisdom about how to manage and even to honor it.

In the *parashah*, anger appears in the following ways:

1. The portion is named for a man who took lethal vengeance against two people—an Israelite man and a Midianite woman—for cohabiting.

2. God self-references God's own wrath (*chamati*—חֲמָתִי; Numbers 25:11) and suggests that Pinchas's action was in service of a just cause—that of preventing further death. There are passing references to earlier historical incidents of God's wrath, as well. As the census is taken, we are reminded of the deaths of Korach, Dathan, and Abiram "when they agitated against the Eternal" (Numbers 26:9), as well as the deaths of Nadab and Abihu (Numbers 26:61) "when they offered alien fire before the Eternal." All of those deaths, as well as the twenty-four thousand who died in God's plague against the Israelites' idolatry and liaisons with the Midianites, at the very end of last week's *parashah*, are due to God's unchecked rage.

3. The daughters of Zelophehad bring their anti-discrimination case about current inheritance law under scrutiny, a clear example of anger being used in service to justice.

4. As God tells Moses of his impending death, Moses's anger at the Waters of Meribath-kadesh is obliquely referenced (Numbers 27:14).

5. I will offer a midrashic reading on the fire offerings that appear in this *parashah* as a potential *middah* practice and teaching for anger.

Let us work our way through these five different references, which I offer as a banquet table laden with different offerings concerning anger.

PINCHAS AND GOD

There is, of course, tremendous irony in a tradition that exhorts us to be slow to anger as a means of *imitatio dei* while presenting us with a God who is anything but "slow to anger," requiring the likes of Pinchas to stay God's hand to prevent further death. But from a Mussar standpoint, it is a perfect reminder that we all, even God, "are on the path." A generous reading might be that we do this work best by having friends who will rebuke us when necessary for our bad behavior. Unfortunately, Pinchas was an enabler, not the friend that God needed. Nonetheless, from God's perspective as well as from the thrust of the Rabbinic tradition, we are meant to consider Pinchas's action as passion in the service of a just cause, namely preventing a further disintegration of the covenant, as well as providing an imperative ceasefire to God's destructive wrath. God views Pinchas's deed of zealotry in utilitarian terms: two people died in order to save countless more Israelites from God's own unchecked wrath (Numbers 25:11).

Mussar suggests that there is a time and a place for anger. Avraham ben HaRambam, for instance, writes that "forbearance [*arichut apayim*] is only necessary when our personal concerns and worldly desires are at stake, not when there is a religious issue." He specifically cites Pinchas as an example of passion "for a religious purpose." Nonetheless, he undermines his own argument by saying that "even in religious issues, one must *not* be quick to avenge and punish. There must first be verifications, deliberation, inquiry and ascertainment of the need for punishment"—which, of course, did not take place in our Torah portion.[1]

Rabbi Yehuda Leib Chasman similarly takes note that Pinchas is rewarded with the *b'rit shalom* ("covenant of peace"; Numbers 25:12) because his motives were pure, rather than for any personal reasons that would have been deemed transgressive.[2]

Rabbi Michel Barenbaum further suggests that a base motivation would have necessitated his being liable for murder.[3] One's awareness of motive—an important step toward transformation in Mussar—is a necessary component for discerning the justness of one's own "righteous indignation."

Rabbi Eliyahu Dessler considers Pinchas an exemplar of a praiseworthy zealot, someone "who, if he sees the opportunity to right some terrible wrong, will stride forward and act with zeal for the honor of Hashem. It is not anger that moves him, but an influx of power from Hashem. . . . His anger is 'God's anger,' that is, it is completely for God's sake, with no thought or hint of personal motives."[4]

THE DAUGHTERS OF ZELOPHEHAD

Let's now apply these Mussar teachings to the five sisters who came forward to right a historical wrong. How pure was their motive for speaking up? Did they stride forward and act out of "religious purpose" (for the sake and honor of God)? Did they do so for their deceased father's sake or for "personal concerns and worldly desires"?[5] Does it matter?

The sisters—Mahlah, Noah, Hoglah, Milcah, and Tirzah—make a case for receiving a holding of the land of their deceased father so that his name will not perish. Unlike so many of the fraught sibling relationships in Torah, these sisters unite to confront a patriarchal system that would require sons to inherit land. They rebel against this injustice that would deny their deceased father, and therefore themselves, a stake—and a name—in the tribal lands when they are subdivided among clans and families. Theirs is clearly an angry plea—they demand to know why (*lamah*) their father's name should be lost just because he had no sons (Numbers 27:4); they use imperative language ("give us," *t'nah lanu*), notably without using the magic word *na*, "please" (Numbers 27:4); and they do all this in a very public demonstration before the whole assembly.

It is notable and even breathtaking that these women did not "play nice," in the diffident ways that women stereotypically might, as they made their case. Rabbi Silvina Chemen makes a strong case that "because they consider God's law to be just, or to aim to be just, they show no hesitation in pointing out the unfair nature of the present situation with complete confidence."[6] In other words, their claim was for God, for their father, *and* for themselves with no inherent contradiction between personal and religious motivations.

Mahlah, Noah, Hoglah, Milcah, and Tirzah exemplify "the politics of just protest, claiming rights for themselves and for others disenfranchised by the system."[7] And that *is* an anger worthy of holiness.

MOSES AND MERIBATH-KADESH

In referencing first the incident of Korach, Dathan, and Abiram, and only then that of Nadab and Abihu, our Torah portion revisits potent episodes of God's anger. However, we are also invited to recall Meribath-Kadesh, where we witnessed an instance of Moses's anger and God's punishing response.

There are, at times, dire consequences for our anger, and the reminder of that incident in this particular *parashah* stands in contrast to the reward that Pinchas receives for his.

Here, Moses, contrite and resigned to his punishment of not entering the Land, requests a successor who will lead the people "so that the Eternal's community may not be like sheep that have no shepherd" (Numbers 27:16–17).

From a Mussar perspective, Moses demonstrates a successful *t'shuvah* to a place of wisdom, humility, and compassion from the hubristic anger he demonstrated earlier at Meribath-Kadesh.

FIRE OFFERINGS

Fire has long been a metaphor for anger. Considering the prevalence of the theme in this *parashah*, how could we not take a hard look at these offerings and consider what they might teach us here? I suggest that the "offerings by fire that you are to present to the Eternal as a regular burnt offering" (Numbers 28:3) in the sacrificial section of this Torah portion can be read midrashicly as guidance to a spiritual practice. We should not dismiss our own anger, a.k.a. fire, but rather practice it regularly, just as we would practice the *middah* of patience or the *middah* of generosity. Maimonides speaks about the need, at times, to practice the extremes of a *middah* in order to find the proper place of moderation and balance on the spectrum.[8] Rather than squelching your anger, feel it, dissect it, and let it teach you to channel it for holy purposes.

CONCLUSION

In reading this *parashah* through the lens of the *middah* of anger, we are led to a deep and complicated reality. Rather than pitting the Pinchas story against that of the daughters of Zelophehad, seeing them as opposing approaches toward problem-solving, I conclude that these two major narrative sections offer different but compatible approaches to anger management. *Parashat Pinchas* is, I suggest, a cohesive text aimed toward teaching that a *b'rit shalom* can certainly be achieved through the expression of anger, as long as a measured deliberation and negotiation with an awareness of sacred motive is an underlying imperative. In this *parashah*, we also learn about coming to terms with and growing from the ramifications and consequences of anger, as Moses does when confronted with the fact that he will not be leading the Israelites into the Land. Finally, we learn about *practicing* anger, as the fire offerings may suggest.

I conclude with a prayer that you might use as a *kavanah* for this *middah* of anger:

> *May it be Your will that any anger I feel or express be used only for constructive ends and in service to just causes. May my anger*

lead, ultimately, to greater humility, wisdom, and justice. May I be called to account for any anger that is used for destructive or self-serving ends. May any anger I feel or express be held in balance with love and compassion for all humanity and offered with purity of motive. Amen.

Questions to Ask

If a Pinchas is necessary to save God from God's self, what does this mean for the rest of us and our own capacity for anger?

When is your own anger "for a religious purpose"? How do you discern the purity of your motives?

What are the fire offerings in your own life, and when are they constructive rather than destructive?

What episodes of anger in your own life have had painful consequences? How do those experiences affect the ways in which you express or manage your anger now?

When have you deliberatively channeled your anger for a just cause?

Practice for the *Middah* of *Kaas*[9]

In order to discern whether your anger is being used as a response to injustice and with purity of motive, ask yourself the following questions:

Is your anger habitual?

Does your response come from a place of love, compassion, and honor for the other?

Is your anger in service to God, to others, or to a higher purpose?

Does your anger link to tradition, rather than lead away from it?

Are the outcomes of your anger likely to highlight or lead to other virtuous *middot*?

If, through this discernment process, you determine that your anger may be a function of the *yetzer hara* rather than the *yetzer hatov*, use the *kavanah* above as a regular practice.

Other *Middot* to Consider

Anavah (עֲנָוָה, "humility"): Does Pinchas act out of hubris? Do the daughters of Zelophehad act out of a balanced sense of humility, or are they still a bit too meek? In that episode, we would also wish to consider the humility of Moses, who appropriately brings their case before God, not merely relying on past precedent. Moses again shows humility in Numbers 27:15–17, when he invites God to appoint someone new over the community when it is made clear that he will not enter the Land.

Seder (סֵדֶר, "order"): As we move into a description of the offerings that should be brought to God on different holy days (Numbers 28–29), we are presented with a model for making order in time.

NOTES

1. Avraham ben HaRambam, *The Guide to Serving God* [*HaMaspik L'Ovdei HaShem*] (Jerusalem: Feldheim, 2008), 88–97.
2. Yehuda Leib Chasman, *Or Yahel*, cited in *Growth through Torah* by Zelig Plikskin (Union City, NJ: Gross Bros. Printing 1998), 360.
3. Michel Barenbaum, *Reb Michel's Shmuessen* (Brooklyn: Mesorah Publications Ltd., 1996), 200.
4. Eliyahu E. Dessler, *Strive for Truth!*, trans. Aryeh Carmel, vol. 6 (Jerusalem: Feldheim, 1999), 91.
5. Avraham ben HaRambam, *The Guide to Serving God* [*Sefer HaMaspik*] (Jerusalem: Feldheim, 2008), 97.
6. Silvina Chemen, in *The Torah: A Women's Commentary*, ed. Tamara Cohn Eskenazi and Andrea L. Weiss (New York: Reform Judaism Publishing, an imprint of CCAR Press, and Women of Reform Judaism, 2008), 985–86.
7. Rabbi Sue Levi Elwell, "Pinchas: The Politics of Just Protest," *Ten Minutes of Torah*, Union for Reform Judaism, 5768.
8. Maimonides, *Mishneh Torah, Hilchot Dei-ot* 2:2.
9. A practice by Chasya Uriel-Steinbauer.

Acharayut—Responsibility to the Other

RABBI RACHEL GUREVITZ, PHD

AT FIRST GLANCE, the narrative found in Numbers 32 in *Parashat Matot* seems to offer a straightforward illustration highlighting the *middah* of *acharayut* (אַחֲרָיוּת, "responsibility"). Two of the twelve tribes of Israel, Gad and Reuben, approach Moses requesting permission to settle in the lands on the eastern side of the Jordan River, rather than waiting to receive a portion of Canaan once the Children of Israel finally cross over into the Promised Land:

> Ataroth, Dibon, Jazer, Nimrah, Heshbon, Elealeh, Sebam, Nebo, and Beon—the land that the Eternal has conquered for the community of Israel—is cattle country, and [we,] your servants[,] have cattle. It would be a favor to us . . . if this land were given to your servants as a holding; do not move us across the Jordan. (Numbers 32:3–5)

Moses is perturbed. His first concern is that the Gadites and Reubenites will abandon the other tribes to fight the battles ahead without them. Additionally, he is afraid that their request will be understood by the other tribes as a sign of fear and that the remaining ten tribes might falter from proceeding, just as they had faltered almost forty years earlier (Numbers 13). At that time, after ten of twelve spies had expressed their fears, the Children of Israel did not even try to take over the Land. However, the Gadites and Reubenites reassure Moses. They ask that they first be permitted to build sheepfolds for their flocks and fortified towns for their children to remain safe, but they promise that they will then not only continue to fight, but will be among the leading troops to help the remaining tribes succeed in their conquest of the Land. They promise, "We will not return to our homes until the Israelites—every one of them—are in possession of their portion" (Numbers 32:18). Moses, satisfied with this arrangement, agrees and announces the terms of the agreement to Eleazar the priest, Joshua, and all of the other tribal heads.

Often, narratives that focus on the *middah* of responsibility teach through stories about the consequences of the absence of the trait:

> When God calls upon Adam and Eve after they have eaten the forbidden fruit of the Tree of Knowledge of Good and Evil, they fail to take responsibility (Genesis 3). Adam blames Eve, and Eve blames the serpent.
> When Cain murders his brother, Abel, and God calls him to take responsibility, he responds, "Am I my brother's keeper?" (Genesis 4:9). As the readers of the text, we understand that the answer to Cain should be "Yes!"

However, here, in Numbers, we have a story where, as soon as Moses makes the Gadites and Reubenites aware that they have a responsibility to the greater mission of the Children of Israel, they appear to step up and embrace that responsibility without hesitation. Surely a positive example to inspire us?

However, once we take a closer look at the text, alongside the reflections of earlier generations of commentators, we find a more complex picture. First, Moses has to remind the two tribes of their responsibility for the success of the remaining tribes in creating a home in the Promised Land. Second, he has to correct the very way in which they express their priorities. When they promise Moses that they will function as "shock troops" for the other tribes, they state that before doing that, they will first create sheepfolds for their flocks and then fortified cities for their children. However, a few verses later, when Moses agrees to the arrangement, he says, "Build towns for your children and sheepfolds for your flocks" (Numbers 32:24). A midrash points out that Moses reverses the order of the flocks and the children, prioritizing the safety of the children over the safety of the flocks, not so subtly revealing an imbalance in the tribes' priorities: they should feel more responsible for the safety of their children than for the safety of their sheep and cattle.[1] In fact, the midrash suggests that the whole premise for their request in false. Gad and Reuben do not, in fact, have more livestock than the other tribes and could also live in the Land of Israel. However, they perceive themselves as owning so many more flocks than the other tribes that only the land they have already taken control of will suffice their needs. To their credit, once Moses has indicated the error in their ways, they proclaim they will take care of matters in the order that Moses proposes (Numbers 32:26).

Alan Morinis points out that the Hebrew word for responsibility, *acharayut*, might be understood as related to the Hebrew word *achar* (אַחַר, "after") or *acheir* (אַחֵר, "other").[2] The former suggests that we should always be mindful of the aftereffects, or consequences, of our actions. The latter highlights the ways the needs of others should be part of the calculus when we make choices. Perhaps the most famous parable that illustrates this principle is found in a midrash.[3] One man on a boat full of people begins to drill a hole under his seat. The others exclaim, "What are you doing?!" He retorts, "What do you care? Is it not underneath my seat that I am drilling?" to which they respond, "But the water will rise and flood all of us on this boat!"

We all know, in principle, that we carry responsibility for each other. But when it comes to making choices that benefit our own lives, we are often driven—like the Gadites and the Reubenites—by our material interests, without thinking about the impact of our choices on others or our responsibility to the "other." How we navigate these choices in our lives depends not only on how we balance our innate sense of responsibility for others with our own needs, but on how we define these "others." The Gadites and the Reubenites may have approached Moses thinking about the well-being of all families in their own tribes. Moses, however, reminds them that they are part of something even larger. All the tribes were brought together in a moment of revelation at Mount Sinai. They became one people. Each tribe carries responsibility for the well-being of the eleven others.

How wide is our circle of obligation? Mussar teaches the need for balance. We are not expected to think exclusively of others. We are obliged, in fact, to pursue our own life goals and to marshal enough strength and resources to take care of our own families. However, how do when know that we have the balance right?

When we start to think more deeply about the needs of something larger, might we realize that we are all in the same boat?

Taking responsibility is a constant act of reflection and choosing. But it is also an expression of power. In order to illustrate this point, Rashi points to a small detail in our *parashah*.[4] Chapter 32 begins by stating that "the Reubenites and the Gadites owned cattle in very great numbers." However, Numbers 32:2 continues, "The Gadite and the Reubenite men came to Moses." Why are the Reubenites mentioned first in one instance, and the Gadites in the other? Rashi suggests that the Gadites were mighty warriors, superior to the Reubenites. They pushed forward the idea of settling on the east side of the Jordan and did not fear being separated from the other tribes. However, with that strength, they did not fully consider the potential weakness and vulnerability of the remaining tribes until Moses outlined the likely consequences of their choices.

Are we, when we make our choices from a position of power—perhaps due to our economic status, our access to educational resources, our gender, our race, or our sexuality—aware of our privileges? Do we listen to narratives and voices that explain the impact of our privilege on others and that ask us to address those inequalities? Are we practicing the trait of *acharayut*?

> Whoever has the power to protest wrongdoing by members of his or her family but does not is caught up in their sin; whoever has the power to protest the wrongdoing of his or her city but does not is caught up in their sin; whoever has the power to protest the wrongdoing by the whole world but does not is caught up in its sin.[5]

Questions to Ask

Can you identify issues that you have chosen to speak up about or act upon that have expanded your circle of obligation? Can you identify the emotions or forces that led you there?

When have you wished your choices were guided by a broader sense of responsibility? What has held you back?

Under what circumstances do you find yourself consciously making choices that narrow your circle of responsibility in order to prioritize something or someone closer to home?

Practice for the *Middah* of *Acharayut*

Identify a societal issue that you you share with others with whom you're "in the same boat." Take a step, however small, to assume a piece of that responsibility.

Identify an area of your life in which you have been taking care of others at the expense of taking care of yourself. Make a change, however small, to shift your responsibility toward yourself.

Other *Middot* to Consider

G'vurah (גְּבוּרָה, "strength"), as highlighted in the commentary above in regard to the Gadites, can provide another perspective on the entire exchange in chapter 32.

Bitachon (בִּטָּחוֹן, "trust") is an important *middah* in this narrative. The agreement between the Gadites and Reubenites, the priests, Moses, Joshua, and the leaders of the other ten tribes depends on mutual trust.

NOTES

1. *Tanchuma Matot* 7.
2. Alan Morinis, *Everyday Holiness: The Jewish Spiritual Path of Mussar* (Boston: Trumpeter Press, 2007), 198.
3. *Midrash Rabbah* on *Vayikra* 4:6.
4. Rashi's commentary on Deuteronomy 33:21.
5. *Babylonian Talmud, Shabbat* 54b.

Mas'ei—Numbers 33:1–36:13

Tzedek—Justice: Intentionality in the Pursuit of Justice

Rabbi Samuel L. Spector

It was a Tuesday evening, March 18, 1980, in Howard Beach, New York. John Favara was driving home from work to his wife and two sons, who knew John as a devoted and loving father. All of a sudden, the twelve-year-old boy who lived next door darted out from behind a dumpster and into the street on a motor bike. Not having time to react and with the sun setting right in his line of vision, John struck and killed the child. The police determined that the deadly accident was not John's fault. Still, John, as any good human would be, was devastated over his responsibility for having caused the child's death, however inadvertently. To make matters worse for John, the boy was Frank Gotti, the son of Gambino crime-family godfather John Gotti. In the months that followed, John's car would be spray-painted with the word "Murderer." On another occasion, Frank's mother, Victoria DiGiorgio, attacked Favara with a baseball bat. He realized that for his family's safety, he had to move them out of Howard Beach; but before he could leave, on July 28, 1980, a group of men shoved John Favara into a van and sped off. He was never seen again. Theories abound about what happened to him—none of them good—and it is widely believed that the Gambino crime family killed him out of revenge. When asked by investigators about Favara, John Gotti responded, "I'm not sorry the guy's missing. I wouldn't be sorry if the guy turned up dead," while his wife replied, "I don't know what happened to him, but I'm not disappointed he's missing. He killed my boy."[1] John Favara caused Frank Gotti's death, but what happened to him in response was unjust.

I grew up in Seattle, Washington, an avid sports fan of any Seattle-based team. No matter which game I attended, there was a man whom I, like everybody else in the city, always expected to see. We did not know Edward McMichael's name, but everyone knew him affectionately as "Tuba Man." After each game, Tuba Man stood outside of the stadium wearing some goofy hat while trying to play rock and roll songs on his tuba, his case open for people to drop money into. He was a much beloved local celebrity. On the evening of October 25, 2008, five teenagers beat Tuba Man to death, punching and kicking him repeatedly as he lay in a fetal position. They stole his money. The city went into mourning. News stations even took a break from covering the historic election between Barack Obama and John McCain, just a week away, to cover memorials for Tuba Man. However, grief turned into outrage when one of the murderers was sentenced to thirty-six weeks in prison, two of the murderers were sentenced to seventy-two weeks, and the other two were never caught and therefore evaded justice. After having served his only six months in prison, one of the perpetrators murdered again. Justice was not served.

One of the most famous verses in the Torah is *Tzedek tzedek tirdof* (צֶדֶק צֶדֶק תִּרְדֹּף), "Justice, justice you shall pursue" (Deuteronomy 16:20). Why "justice" twice? Justice for ourselves and justice for others; and we are to pursue justice through just means.[2]

But what constitutes *tzedek*, "justice"? The answer is not as obvious as it may seem.

The Torah teaches, "Life for life, eye for eye, tooth for tooth, hand for hand, foot for foot, burn for burn, wound for wound, bruise for bruise" (Exodus 21:23–25). We read elsewhere, "The shedder of human blood, that person's blood shall be shed by [another] human" (Genesis 9:6); "One who fatally strikes another person shall be put to death" (Exodus 21:12); and "If anyone kills any human being, that person shall be put to death" (Leviticus 24:17). According to these texts, killing John Favara would be a just punishment for his responsibility in the boy's death.

Parashat Mas'ei, though, requires us to delve more deeply into the text in order to find true *tzedek*, "justice." The *parashah* insists that justice requires us to evaluate each homicide on a case-by-case basis. The Torah teaches:

> When you cross the Jordan into the land of Canaan, you shall provide yourselves with places to serve as cities of refuge to which a [male] killer who has slain a person unintentionally may flee. The cities shall serve you as a refuge from the avenger, so that the killer may not die unless he has stood trial before the assembly. . . . These six cities shall serve the Israelites and the resident aliens among them for a refuge, so that any man who slays a person unintentionally may flee there. (Numbers 35:10–12, 35:15)

Torah acknowledges that the pain of losing a loved one may cause a grieving relative to take vengeance by killing the person who took the life of their family member. Yet, the Torah teaches us that the life of the person who committed the killing is also valuable, and it tells us explicitly that that person is entitled to *tzedek*, "justice," in this case in the form of due process (Numbers 35:12). What is key here is that intention matters and that in case there was no intent to kill, a person should not be put to death.

Further along in the chapter, we read, "If [the killer] pushed [the victim] in hate or hurled something at [the victim] on purpose and death resulted, or if one struck another with the hand in enmity and death resulted, the assailant shall be put to death; that person is a murderer" (Numbers 35:20–21). In this case, intention also matters. The Torah identifies this case as a situation in which someone was intentionally harmed by a perpetrator.

To put a person to death when they were neither at fault nor intending to hurt another person is an abuse of justice. However, the one who deliberately killed is not receiving the benefit of justice, because that person is being put on equal footing to a cold-blooded murderer. The murder of John Favara certainly violated the teachings of justice in *Parashat Mas'ei*. Likewise, in the latter case, we see that the murderers of Edward McMichael committed what the Torah describes as a "murder" and should therefore have been punished severely.

Contemplating the cases of John Favara and Edward McMichael, we are sad to see a lack of *tzedek*—that is, a lack of justice—in the recent history of our own society. Judges and avengers alike did not adhere to the principle of *tzedek* as outlined in the Torah, which requires both pursuing justice through just means and looking at intent alongside outcome. The words of Dr. Martin Luther King Jr. ring true, "Injustice anywhere is a threat to justice everywhere. We are caught in an inescapable network of mutuality, tied in a single garment of destiny. Whatever affects one directly, affects all indirectly."[3] Thus, *Parashat Mas'ei* teaches us to pursue justice and to do so by looking at intentionality. The outcome will be a world of greater holiness and greater *tzedek*, "justice."

Questions to Ask

Do cities of refuge provide justice for the family of the victim?
Mahatma Gandhi said, "An eye for an eye leaves the whole world blind." Does "life for life" truly provide justice?
Is this law a violation of Rabbi Hillel's summary of the Torah, "That which is hateful to you, do not do unto another"?
Should additional circumstances be evaluated when it comes to the pursuit of justice? If a person robs a convenience store for money to buy electronics, should sentencing be different than for a person who robbed a convenience store to have money to provide food and shelter for his family? Likewise, should a murder out of passion, like that of John Favara, presumably by a person whose child had been killed, be treated differently from a murder like the one of TubaMan, who was killed in a robbery?

Practice for the *Middah* of *Tzedek*

Imagine that a person cuts you off in traffic, causing an accident. Are they careless? Mean-spirited? Or perhaps rushing to the hospital for a family emergency? Try to write closing remarks for both defense and prosecution in a trial, and consider the merits of both.

Other *Middot* to Consider

Rachamim (רַחֲמִים, "mercy"): The cities of refuge are acts of mercy for the vulnerable. In the twenty-first century, the term "sanctuary cities" has been revived to protect people who are undocumented migrants. Does that act, reminiscent of the cities of refuge, display mercy?

Kavod (כָּבוֹד, "honor"): Family honor is a theme throughout the *parashah*. Does the family pursuing the person who committed manslaughter feel as though their honor has been robbed by not being able to take the life from the person who claimed the life of their loved one? We also see in this *parashah* that the daughters of Zelophehad must marry men from their father's tribe so that their land does not leave his family to go to another tribe. Would permitting the land to pass to another tribe dishonor Zelophehad's memory? Does the marriage restriction dishonor the daughters on the basis of their gender?

Anavah (עֲנָוָה, "humility"): When one retreats to the city of refuge, they must give up their entire way of life from before they committed manslaughter. This person is now labeled by their circumstance and is judged as such. Imagine your life right now; your socioeconomic status, family situation, position, reputation in the community, and so on. Would being forced to run to the city of refuge be a humbling experience, teaching you what you would give up just to preserve your life?

272 RABBI SAMUEL L. SPECTOR

NOTES

1. Josh Getlin, "Thousands Turn Out for the Dapper Don's Last Ride," *Los Angeles Times*, June 16, 2002.
2. See Rashi and Ibn Ezra on Deuteronomy 16:20.
3. Martin Luther King, "Letter from Birmingham Jail," April 16, 1963. Available online at http://www.africa.upenn.edu/Articles_Gen/Letter_Birmingham.html.

DEUTERONOMY

D'VARIM—DEUTERONOMY 1:1–3:22
G'vurah—Strength:
How Did All This Happen?

RABBI JUDY SHANKS

AT AGE NINETY-THREE, my beloved mother-in-law, Estelle, spends most of her day in bed. She reads a bit, watches too much news, dozes, wakes, and greets visitors with her signature smile. At the foot of the bed, an electronic picture frame randomly flashes photos from every era of her life: starting in her childhood and continuing through just yesterday. Here is Estelle at six with her parents at the Statue of Liberty; next up, she is nervously holding her own great-great-grandson on his first birthday. Some photos prompt a memory, a comment: "Look—that's my Uncle Usher—he owned a chicken farm in New Jersey." . . . "That was my place of business in Phoenix the day we signed the mortgage!" . . . "Wait—who is that? It's me with my little sister! Oh my God, I never thought I would still be here. How did all this happen?"

"These are the words that Moses addressed to all Israel on the other side of the Jordan" (Deuteronomy 1:1). What an understated prelude to the powerful rhetoric that will flow from Moses's lips in his final effort to explain "how this all happened" to himself and to the Israelites. As his life draws to a close, Moses summons the *middah* of *g'vurah* (גְּבוּרָה, "heroic strength"), displayed in all its multiple dimensions, to compose and deliver the series of soaring sermons that fill the Book of Deuteronomy. When memories bubble up, Moses paints vivid pictures for his communal audience, selectively teaching the Torah they will need to embody themselves, when, without him, they will enter the Promised Land. Implicit in every word is the self-awareness of his impending mortality. Through Moses's reflections, we travel now (in the Book of Deuteronomy) on a different kind of sacred journey where past and present conflate, and the long and short views of one (extraordinary) man's life are woven seamlessly into a timeless guide for all future generations. Biblically, Moses's final great gift of leadership is to teach us how to live our last days with *g'vurah*. Our final great task is meeting death.

Rabbi Marc Margolius writes, "A *middah* is not an action; it represents a pool of sacred energy we identify within ourselves as a quality available to generate action (mitzvah) fostering greater holiness or wholeness in this world."[1] Moses's final journey with his people requires him to access and explore his internal pool of strength and then make it accessible to *every* Israelite (Deuteronomy 1:1), who will, he prays, use it to bring holiness into the world he is leaving behind. "The word that Moses spoke was addressed to all Israel, to each one according to his or her character and age, his or her understanding and level of perception, each one according to his or her measure."[2] How does Moses craft such a universal, yet personal teaching? What wisdom will bubble up from his twelve-decade-deep reservoir of life?

Our memories do surface like a rotating picture frame untethered to chronology or even a highlight reel. Moses begins his historical review not in Pharaoh's palace, at the Burning Bush, or on the far shores of the Reed Sea. Instead, he speaks first of the times when leading this Israelite nation became an untenable burden to him. Though covenanted to sanctity, the Israelites' behavior has swung repeatedly from goodness to transgression, from obedience to rebellion, from gratitude to relentless complaint. Moses relates how twice he desperately called out to God to relieve him of the full weight of the people's sins, boundless needs, and expectations (Exodus 18:13–27; Numbers 11:11–15). And now, depleted just by the act of remembering, he cries out again, "How can I bear unaided the trouble of you, and the burden, and the bickering!" (Deuteronomy 1:12).

Perhaps it is Moses's fulsome disappointment at being denied entrance to the Land that prompts him to speak of the pain the people inflicted upon him. He begins his exhortation with a revelation of his own vulnerability and a judgment on the people who pushed him past his breaking point. Mussar teaches that the *middah* of *g'vurah* is connected with strict judgment and thus must always be counterbalanced and tempered by *chesed* (חֶסֶד, "loving-kindness").[3] In *Mishnah, Pirkei Avot*, Ben Zoma asks, "Who is strong (*gibor*[4])? Those who subdue their passions [evil inclination], as it is written, 'One who is slow to anger is better than the strong, and one whose temper is controlled than one who captures a city' (Proverbs 16:32)."[5]

As he reaches his final days, Moses both exploits and contains his undiminished *g'vurah*. He implicitly accepts God's decree that Joshua will take the mantle of leadership and lead the Israelites into the Land. It takes internal strength, fearlessness, and a reining in of the ego to offer unvarnished accounts of moments of his own weakness and failures of leadership. With his words and his silence, Moses seems to forgive himself for his mistakes, while simultaneously extending forgiveness and *chesed* to those standing before him who have stumbled before and will surely stumble again. He cautions the Israelites against the potential danger, to the leader and to the community, of endowing a single person with authority. He reminds them to appoint and maintain phalanxes of "wise and discerning" people as impartial judges bringing peaceful resolutions to conflict (Deuteronomy 1:13–18) and to share the burden of governance.

Moses could have begun his great orations with chastisement and heaped scorn upon the children of those who repeatedly provoked his anger and resentment. Such a decision would have come from pure *g'vurah*, fueled solely by Moses's ego-driven desire to exonerate himself of guilt and responsibility. Such an approach would surely have alienated many who listened, whether from familial loyalty to their forebears or simply from resentment at his harsh tone. As he composes in the whole of the Book of Deuteronomy what becomes his ethical will, Moses must again and again consider how each word will be taken—and remembered—collectively and individually by the Israelites and the generations to come. Granted the blessing of time and the opportunity to speak at length, Moses skillfully blends *g'vurah* and *chesed* in necessary proportion—with messages ranging from castigating them about the spies early in *Parashat D'varim* to lofty inspiration in *Parashat Nitzavim*—to impart the emotions he hopes to inspire and the memories important to implant.

And it is with *chesed* alone that Moses concludes the prelude to his greatest sermons. He hearkens back not decades but centuries to family memories, to the divine promises made to the Patriarchs and Matriarchs, blessing his people and calling on God to continue blessing them: "The Eternal your God has multiplied you until you are today as numerous as the stars in the sky. May the Eternal, the God of your ancestors, increase your numbers a thousandfold, and bless you as promised" (Deuteronomy 1:10–11).

As we sit together, I ask Estelle which strengths she draws on now and which help her in this new, and last, phase of life. "Appreciation and gratitude, those are the most important. I don't dwell on the pain and disappointments. I'm lucky I get to say 'thank you' to all of you. I'm not afraid of what is ahead for me and I accept it is soon. But I don't know yet how I will say goodbye. That is the hardest thing to do, the bravest thing I will do. I am gathering strength to say goodbye."

"So am I," I say, "So am I."

Questions to Ask

Ask yourself: Which *g'vurot*, which "strengths," do I possess that allow me to bring goodness into my world or inspire others to do the same? Which *g'vurot* provoke me to demean or alienate others? When do I most often find myself tempering my *g'vurah* with *chesed*, bringing kindness to my judgments? How can I increase my opportunities for connection through strength?

Imagine your final days and the words you would want to share. Write them down as the beginning of your own ethical will, or gather your *g'vurah* and say them now in the way each listener will best be able to hear.

Practice for the *Middah* of *G'vurah*

Our tradition teaches that combining strength with blessing brings *shalom* ("wholeness" and "peace"). In Psalm 29:11, we read: *Adonai oz l'amo yitein; Adonai y'vareich et amo vashalom* (יהוה עֹז לְעַמּוֹ יִתֵּן יהוה יְבָרֵךְ אֶת־עַמּוֹ בַשָּׁלוֹם, "May the Eternal grant strength to God's people; may the Eternal bestow on God's people well-being.") Identify people and situations where your unique strengths will bring others both help and an added measure of wholeness.

Another *Middah* to Consider

In this portion, Moses recounts how God chooses Joshua to succeed him as Israel's leader. He says, "Imbue him [Joshua] with strength, for he shall allot it [i.e., the Land] to Israel" (Deuteronomy 1:38). Moses needs *anavah* (עֲנָוָה, "humility") to pass his strength to Joshua. Consider what emotions and thoughts Moses might grapple with as he follows God's directive to "imbue Joshua with strength."

NOTES

1. From "Seven Weeks Toward Wisdom: An Omer Program of Wisdom and Growth," Institute of Jewish Spirituality online course, April/May 2019.
2. Rabbi Simchah Bunem of Prszysucha, quoted in Lawrence S. Kushner and Kerry M. Olitzky, *Sparks Beneath the Surface: A Spiritual Commentary on the Torah* (Northvale, NJ: Jason Aronson, 1993), 219.
3. "Strong judgment without lovingkindness is harsh and unfeeling. Power… works best and is sustainable when tempered by mercy and love. The ideal lies in the blending" (Alan Morinis, *A Season of Mussar* [curriculum], 2009).
4. The same Hebrew root as *g'vurah*.
5. *Mishnah, Pirkei Avot* 4:1.

VA-ET'CHANAN—DEUTERONOMY 3:23–7:11
Emunah—The Life of Faith

RABBI DAVID ADELSON, DMin

EMUNAH (אֱמוּנָה, "faith") emerges from our lived experience.
Parashat *Va-et'chanan* can read like a guidebook to constructing
a life built on faith. In the *parashah*, the people are reminded again
and again to trust what they see, hear, and feel as a path to knowing
God. Alan Morinis writes that "faith is not something to be understood intellectually but rather to be appreciated from experience."[1]
We have to learn for ourselves, from moments of our own awareness,
that we are a part of something larger. Only then will we be able to
recall that awareness during times when we are not actually feeling
it. A life that acknowledges the possibility of awareness of the Divine,
even when we don't feel it in the moment, is a life of faith.

Early in *Va-et'chanan*, the people are reminded of their experience
at Sinai. Sinai is our paramount moment of living in the immediate
presence of the Divine. "But take utmost care and watch yourselves
scrupulously, so that you do not forget the things that you saw with
your own eyes and so that they do not fade from your mind as long
as you live" (Deuteronomy 4:9). As Ibn Ezra says, "Even if you forget everything else, do not forget the day when you stood at Mount
Sinai."[2] No other experience offers as dramatic a reason for faith. We
are urged to remember it daily.

A few verses later, we are reminded of the form, or lack thereof,
that God took at the moment of that amazing encounter: "The Eternal One spoke to you out of the fire; you heard the sound of words
but perceived no shape—nothing but a voice" (Deuteronomy 4:12).
Even at this moment of clearest divine communication, God cannot
be fully seen or known, but rather is heard and sensed. Often, it is in

moments of blindness, of mere sensing, that we become aware of our embeddedness in something larger than ourselves. When we see the ocean, contemplate the vastness of space, or feel the loving embrace of a friend, we don't get full proof of God's existence. We must trust that that amorphous sense of knowing, knowing with our whole being, is a glimpse of the Divine.

Next, our *parashah* calls on us to remember that awareness and to base our life on the confidence that arises from it: "Take care, then, not to forget the covenant that the Eternal your God concluded with you" (Deuteronomy 4:23). Why do we need to be told not to forget? Because we tend to forget! Over and over, we experience something larger than ourselves; and then, we forget. Building faith is hard; we must work to develop it throughout our entire lives. But life in covenant, whether expressed through adherence to halachah or by commitment to Jewish community and ethics, holds us to faithfulness even at times when we forget.

However, even life in covenantal community must be constantly re-grounded within our own lived experience. *Orchot Tzadikim*, a fifteenth-century ethical treatise, quotes Rabbah bar Rav Huna:[3] "One who has Torah but not fear of heaven is like a treasurer who has been given the inner keys, but not the outer ones. Through which door can he enter?"[4] In the twentieth century, Rav Kook writes, "A person may believe that the Torah is from heaven, but his understanding of heaven may be so skewed that it allows for not a shred of true faith."[5] The life that we build for ourselves, and the life that our Jewish people has built, can only be fulfilled if it is constantly renewed by immediate awareness (Rabbah's "fear") of the Divine. *Va-et'chanan* reminds us of our need for this immediate, personal awareness of God. After a warning of what can befall us should we go astray, we are told, "But if you search there, you will find the Eternal your God, if only you seek with all your heart and soul" (Deuteronomy 4:29). A life of faith, and a life of behavior built on faith, must always return, return, return to the search for immediate awareness of God.

In our *parashah*, we then move to the restatement of the Ten Commandments, the first of which is "I the Eternal am your God" (Deuteronomy 5:6). This essential commandment is the beginning of faith, on which all of spirituality and religion is based. At the very center is "I am God," and we are repeatedly called upon to return to that essential awareness. It is our nature to drift from awareness of God's call to presence. And then experience, or our intention, brings us back to this first commandment, "I am God."

Further in our portion is the verse that is the pinnacle of faithful affirmation in our daily liturgy: "Hear, O Israel! The Eternal is our God, the Eternal alone" (Deuteronomy 6:4). However we translate and understand this verse, whether as "There is only one God," or "God is unification," or any variation thereupon, uttering this verse aloud as a daily practice is a sure declaration of faith. We may be feeling awareness of God's presence at the moment we utter the *Sh'ma* (שְׁמַע), or we may not. Either way, we affirm the search for God's centrality in our lives.

As we move toward the end of *Va-et'chanan*, we are told to remember the Exodus after we inhabit the Promised Land. That is, we are again encouraged to hold close our personal knowledge of God, even as we move farther away from the moment we gained that knowledge. "Take heed that you do not forget the Eternal who freed you from the land of Egypt" (Deuteronomy 6:12).

After finishing reading the *parashah*, we are left with one question: How can we recall moments of awareness on a daily basis? How can we build a practice of seeking awareness of God in our lives?

Our prayer texts repeatedly remind us of the moments of Creation, revelation, and redemption. Those moments in our collective memory, as recounted in Torah, are moments of living in God's presence, of feeling and sensing God in our individual and shared lives. The experiences of Adam and Eve, of the Patriarchs and Matriarchs, of liberation from Egypt, and of standing at Sinai are unique moments. In *Va-et'chanan*, we are instructed to hold fast to those experiences as powerful examples of what is possible at all moments. We return to them as foci in our liturgy, among other reasons, to establish a practice of mindful remembrance. Regular liturgical repetition can inspire a daily habit of seeking awareness of God in our lives.

A life of faith moves back and forth between the opposing states of feeling and not feeling God's presence. Moments of awareness re-ground us. At all other times, our liturgy reminds us of our prior awareness and sparks our search for future awareness.

Questions to Ask

How do you draw faith from reading biblical accounts of the Exodus and of our ancestors' interactions with the Divine? How does reciting the *Sh'ma* express and/or enhance your faith?

Practice for the *Middah* of *Emunah*

Think of a moment in your life when you felt part of something larger. Stop for a moment, close your eyes, and bring yourself back to that moment. How did you feel in your body? What were the emotions? Now do the same while remembering another moment in your life. And perhaps another. Does the reality of all of those moments leave you feeling that another such moment might be possible, even right now?

Once per day, find a moment to stop and be fully present to a physical or social experience. Feel the warm water on your hands as you wash dishes. Feel connected to a stranger on the street. Observe how the light falls on a tree or building you pass by regularly. Notice affection rising in you in the presence of someone you love. Acknowledge God for making those moments possible.

Say the *Sh'ma* every day for a month, either during the day or before going to sleep at night. Stop and become aware of your body, your emotions, your thoughts. Then say the

Sh'ma. Forgive yourself if you forget to follow this practice one day, but try to remember it as often as you can. At the end of a month, notice any change in your sense of God's presence in your life.

Other *Middot* to Consider

Bitachon (בִּטָּחוֹן, "faith"): Trust and faith are closely linked. Trust might be seen as a result of faith. If we can cultivate faith that God exists and is present, even in the absence of evidence, then we can place trust in that present God to care for us even amid danger or doubt.

Yirah (יִרְאָה, "awe, fear"): Faith is awareness and confidence in God's presence. If we can become secure in that reality, we can feel more deeply the awe/fear being in God's presence can inspire in us.

NOTES

1. Alan Morinis, *Everyday Holiness: The Jewish Spiritual Path of Mussar* (Boston: Trumpeter, 2007), 221.
2. Ibn Ezra on Deuteronomy 4:9.
3. *Babylonian Talmud, Shabbat* 31a.
4. *Orchot Tzadikim, Sha'ar Yirat Shamayim* (Jerusalem: Feldheim, 1995), 607.
5. Avraham Isaac Kook, *Orot HaEmunah* (Jerusalem: Mosad Harav Kook, 1985).

EIKEV—DEUTERONOMY 7:12–11:25

N'divut—Generosity: Inseparable from Hakarat HaTov (Gratitude)

RABBI YAIR ROBINSON

I GO VISIT AN OLDER CONGREGANT at the hospital after a difficult surgery. We talk. We pray. As the conversation wraps up, I ask if the synagogue's caring committee may reach out. Without fail, as soon as the words are out of my mouth, the congregant looks at me—with bewilderment, amusement, and a bit of anger—and responds dismissively, "But Rabbi, I'm *on* the caring committee!" as if to say that he somehow *can't* accept the support. But why? Why is it so hard for this congregant to accept the visit—the support, the sense of appreciation and love from a fellow community member? Encounters like this happen all the time. Someone offers help, and we blanch; they give us an unexpected gift, and we turn beet red from embarrassment; or they offer a compliment, and we stammer and stutter. Why can we not just say thank you and move forward with a little spring in our step? Why is the offer of help swatted away so instinctively? Why can't we accept another person's gifts?

Before we can answer that, we have to explore the question: what is a gift? A gift, I would argue, is something freely given by someone else, to our benefit, where we cannot return the favor. That is demonstrated beautifully in *Parashat Eikev*, which presents Moses describing the various blessings that Israel will experience once they enter the Promised Land, as well as how God will allow Israel to conquer it. In describing those blessings—of sustenance, of health, of children, and of victory—Moses also reminds Israel of their forty years of wandering and miracles that God wrought for them during that time—not only large and obvious miracles, like manna, but the otherwise unnoticed fact that their clothes haven't worn out. In all of these descriptions, there is a reminder, both explicit and implicit: these have all been gifts of God, and God's gifts will continue. Before they cross the Jordan River, Moses reminds them further of God's generosity, lest Israel assume their prosperity is the work of their own hands. In one of the following verses, we read: *V'achalta v'savata uveirachta et Adonai Elohecha al-haaretz hatovah asher natan lach* (וְאָכַלְתָּ וְשָׂבָעְתָּ וּבֵרַכְתָּ אֶת־יהוה אֱלֹהֶיךָ עַל־הָאָרֶץ הַטֹּבָה אֲשֶׁר נָתַן־לָךְ), "When you have eaten your fill, give thanks to the Eternal for the good land given to you" (Deuteronomy 8:10). The Rabbis of the Talmud understand this blessing as the positive commandment to recite the Blessing after Meals, *Birkat HaMazon*. At the heart of this blessing lies an acknowledgment of God's generosity; in *Birkat HaMazon,* the Talmud explains, we bless God as the One who sustains all (*hazan et hakol*) and who is good and does good for all (*hatov v'hameitiv*).[1] Sforno emphasizes both God's act of giving and our inability to reciprocate: "The reason why the Eternal blesses you in such a fashion is so that you will remember that only from God could you have been given a land with such an abundance of advantages."[2]

So, back to our question: Why is it so hard to accept a gift? The answer, I believe, is what a friend of mine, the Episcopal priest Father Russ Bohner, calls "being half-generous."

What does Father Bohner mean by "half-generous"? Most of us think of generosity only as the act of giving, not receiving. We're happy to give. Giving fills us with a certain joy. We love the feeling of giving a gift to a friend or of helping someone out. The same hospitalized congregant would describe in detail how they loved driving congregants to appointments or bringing food to shut-ins. Being on the receiving end, on the other hand, fills so many of us with dread.

Some of this feeling is caused by our false assumption that we need to return the favor. We receive a gift, something freely given, and we perceive ourselves obliged to repay the kindness. When we cannot reciprocate—for example, when we are in a vulnerable position like the ill congregant—we recoil from accepting the offer. Our pride, feeling of unworthiness, and fear of obligation toward the other con- strict us. Instead of accepting the generous offer of support, praise, or a gift, we reject it and are poorer for it. We are good at giving; but we are terrible at receiving, because we fear the need to be grateful.

However, Mussar teaches that the *middah* of *n'divut* (נְדִיבוּת, "generosity"), is intimately related to the *hakarat hatov* (הַכָּרַת הַטּוֹב, "gratitude") commanded in *Eikev*. Moshe Chayim Luzzatto, also known as the Ramchal, elaborates on this idea of God's generosity in his work *M'silat Yesharim* (*The Path of the Upright*). He writes, "Every- one, whatever their circumstances, whether they be poor or rich, healthy or sick, has occasion to perceive many a miracle and many an act of mercy by virtue of the very circumstances in which they are placed."[3] We experience God's generosity, then, and must acknowl- edge it. While this acknowledgment is itself an act of gratitude, we must be in a state of *n'divut* in order to express this gratitude in the form of gifts to others—because we cannot repay God.

How can we express our generosity in response to God's? Ramchal continues, "If we appreciated the kindnesses received from God, we would surely be eager to worship God. All the more, if we would realize that our happiness depends upon God, and that whatever we need and whatever is indispensable comes from God and from none other, we would undoubtedly not serve the Holy Blessed One with indolence, nor be remiss in the performance of our duties."[4]

Rabbi Ira Stone, in his commentary on *M'silat Yesharim*, elaborates:

> Ramchal traces the source of gratitude to the fact that we are neither responsible for our own creation nor for the good that accrues to us by virtue of our creation. Another brings us into creation . . . and another provides for whatever is good in our being, from physical nourishment to emotional sustenance. Gratitude for these gifts is an obligating realization; we are in- debted before we are even conscious. This indebtedness is fun- damental to Mussar in particular and to Judaic thought more generally, and the centrality of mitzvot derives from it. Con- trary to the philosophic idea of free will, the Mussar concept of freedom is played out on a field of preexisting obligations.[5]

In other words, to receive in gratitude obligates us to generosity, knowing that we cannot reciprocate. Just as we cannot repay our parents for bringing us into the world, there is no way to recompense God for divine sustenance. Similarly, the gift, the kind word, or the offer of assistance does not necessarily require us to respond *to the giver* with a similar act, but rather with simple thanks.

We should also pass along our generosity to the next person in need. This generosity toward another person is not nourished by our own emotional and spiritual resources; how could it be? Instead, it is nourished by that original source of generosity—namely, God—and passed forward, infinitely. To flail in the face of someone else's generosity, especially when we cannot directly repay the effort, is essentially an act of rejecting God's generosity, and a rejection of our obligations. In doing so, we remain in a state of "half-generosity."

In *Eikev*, Moses reminds us of God's generosity—of protection, of sustenance, of a land flowing with milk and honey—and our need to express our gratitude for God's gifts. When, in response to *Parashat Eikev*'s central commandment, we express our gratitude for God's sustenance, we also place ourselves in the realm of *n'divut*. We are called to ask, "I have sustenance, but what of those who do not? My life is full of miracles and mercy, but what of other people's suffering? My satisfaction is not, at the end of the day, my own, but an expression of God's generosity; so, what can I do to make sure that God's generosity is felt by as many people as possible?" When we receive the gift, the compliment, the offer of support, we must not bat it aside or think ourselves unworthy; we must accept it, acknowledge it, and reflect on how we can pass that generosity on to others, continuing the cycle of *n'divut*.

Questions to Ask

Take a moment to remember a moment when someone offered you a gift, a compliment, or support. What happened in your body? Did you feel open or constricted? Then, remember a moment when you acted out of generosity toward someone else. How did that person respond? How can you help others to accept and enjoy your gifts and support? (Consider journaling your responses/experiences.)

As you receive someone else's generosity, listen to your own sense of obligation to the other. To where is it directed? How can it be directed?

Look at Deuteronomy 8:10 again. *Birkat HaMazon* is intended to be a spiritual practice for every meal, an act that reminds us of the need to express generosity and gratitude. What practice, if any, moves you to do the same in your life? Consider creating a ritual for each moment of *n'divut* (either for moments when you are the recipient of generosity or for moments when you are the one giving). Incorporate into your ritual your sense of obligation toward others.

Practice for the *Middah* of *N'divut*

To experience a sense of *n'divut*, try this daily practice.

Begin each morning (before turning on your phone!) by reflecting on what you have to be grateful for. Keep a journal, or recite the prayer *Modeh/Modah Ani*. As you reflect on all that you are grateful for, think of the people who have been generous with you (teachers, mentors, parents, even the person ahead of you in line at the coffee shop). As you reflect on them, ask yourself: How can I, on this new day, be similarly generous? Of what state of mind must I be in order to act generously?

At the end of the day, reflect on the generosity you have given and the generosity you have received. What do you need in order to do to do better? Had you missed any opportunities to practice *n'divut*?

Other *Middot* to Consider

Anavah (עֲנָוָה, "humility"): Humility is not an easy concept for this era, and yet so deeply essential to our experience of the world. In Deuteronomy 8:1–10 we are reminded of how our experiences in the wilderness serve as an image for our daily practice of humility.

Savlanut (סַבְלָנוּת, "patience"): We live in an impatient world. This impatience is born out of our experience. As the poet T. S. Elliot wrote in "The Love Song of J. Alfred Prufrock," "we measure our lives in coffee spoons." We expect every day to be filled with novelty and place ourselves and our experience at the center. Looking at the text of Deuteronomy 8, we see another idea modeled by God, one that puts the needs of others ahead of our own. What would it mean for us to measure our lives not by novel experiences, but by the slowly unfolding relationships of honesty, trust, care, and support between us and our partners?

NOTES
1. *Babylonian Talmud, B'rachot* 48b.
2. Sforno on Deuteronomy 8:10.
3. Adapted from Moses Hayyim Luzzato, *Mesillat Yesharim: The Path of the Upright*, trans. Mordecai M. Kaplan, commentary by Ira F. Stone (Philadelphia: Jewish Publication Society, 2010), 95.
4. Ibid.
5. Ibid., 97.

R'EIH—DEUTERONOMY 11:26–16:17

Kavod—Honor:
Encounters with the Other

RABBI JEN CLAYMAN

KAVOD, MEANING "HONOR," comes from the same root as the word for "heavy." To hold something in honor is to give it weight, to view it as weighty, to take it seriously. It is to deem something worthwhile or valuable. *Kavod* can also be translated as "respect" or "dignity."

Parashat R'eih offers us some of the clearest examples of this *middah*, both in its presence and in its absence. On the one hand, we are commanded to honor the poor of our own community; on the other hand, we read commandments about profound dishonor to the holy places of our ancestors' neighboring peoples.

Let's begin with the part of the *parashah* that will likely resonate most deeply with modern readers. The latter chapters of *R'eih* instruct us to honor the experiences of the poor: "Do not harden your heart and shut your hand against your needy kin. Rather, you must open your hand and lend whatever is sufficient to meet the need. . . . Give readily and have no regrets when you do so" (Deuteronomy 15:7–8, 15:10).

While the word *kavod* is not used here, the concept is nevertheless present. In order to give people "sufficient to meet the need," we must have some level of understanding of what they are going through. Understanding derives from taking people seriously, from giving weight to their experiences. Conversely, it is easier to close our hearts to others and disregard their needs when we do not regard them as worthwhile, when we take their experiences too lightly.

Our society too often makes light of, or even ignores, the experiences of others. We ascribe genius to the wealthy and blame poverty on the poor. Policymakers and pundits claim that government assistance for poor people is equivalent to unnecessary coddling, while they simultaneously approve tax relief and massive corporate subsidies for the wealthiest among us, thereby honoring the rich and privileged while dishonoring the poor and unprivileged. Such actions reveal that underneath all the rhetoric about helping "ordinary" people, the "haves" are honored, while the "have-nots" are not. A society that values *kavod* would be far fairer and more just; it would require us to honor the experiences of everyone.

To begin his discussion of *kavod*, Alan Morinis focuses on our very human tendency to judge others negatively. He imagines each of us carrying around a mental clipboard on which we write harshly critical notes about everyone around us. These notes may focus on physical appearance, perceived intelligence, alleged character flaws, and so on.[1] Cultivation of *kavod* can be a corrective to this tendency. Morinis urges us, when considering others, to look at the whole person, created in the image of the Divine:

> It is much easier for us to be critical and harshly judgmental, seeing only others' flaws and failings. When our eyes focus only on the soiled garment, ignoring the divinely inspired being within, there really isn't anything much to honor. Honor, respect, and dignity are due to each and every human being not because of the greatness of their achievements or how they have behaved, but because they are home to a soul that is inherently holy.[2]

Note the role of focus in these imagined encounters between ourselves and the other. Do we focus on the "soiled garment," or can we discipline our minds and hearts to focus on the divinity in each person? Can we put down our critical clipboards and focus on the real people in front of us?

In contrast with the directive of our *parashah*, the rhetoric of politicians and pundits today often reveals the underlying assumption that poor people are lazy or profligate and could lift themselves out of poverty if only they worked harder or spent less. They foreground alleged character flaws and disregard the totality of the persons whose lives their words and policies affect.

What we need is to see the whole experience of every person we encounter, regardless of economic status. What we might at first glance dismiss as laziness, carelessness, or unwillingness to pursue educational opportunities might be something else entirely. Pursuit of *kavod* directs us to put our clipboards down.

If we can to do that, we might see more clearly, for example, that residential red-lining has had a devastating impact on the long-term finances of non-white Americans. We might more readily acknowledge that the GI Bill, which helped so many Jewish Americans gain a foot in the middle class, was not effective for African Americans because it did nothing to alleviate discrimination in real estate and banking. The more we can cultivate *kavod*, the more we can bring this knowledge to bear on our encounters with others.

And so, when we read the latter chapters of our *parashah* with *kavod* in mind, we gain important wisdom about how we can be part of creating a better world. Alas, the opening of *R'eih* gives us something else entirely.

Whereas the end of the *parashah* gives us a *kavod*-filled ideal to which we may aspire, the *parashah*'s opening offers the opposite. It is dominated by specific instructions to dishonor even the very memory of the conquered Canaanites, especially regarding their religious practices: "You must destroy all the sites at which the nations you are to dispossess worshiped their gods. . . . Tear down their altars, smash their pillars, put their sacred posts to the fire, and cut down the images of their gods, obliterating their name from that site" (Deuteronomy 12:2–3).

If we are looking for inspiration in Torah, and in this *parashah* in particular, for increasing *kavod* in the world, how do we deal with a text in which God commands our ancient ancestors to perform acts of dishonor? This is the sort of text that makes some people want to throw all of Torah out the window. And yet, just as we can cultivate *kavod* with respect to the other in our own time, we can also bring *kavod* to bear on our relationship with the Torah's writers. They were imperfect human beings, with fears and prejudices that impacted what they wrote. They experienced the world in ways that are difficult for us to understand. Yet, as we have seen, making the effort to understand their perspective is part of the process of developing the capacity for honor. Making the effort to understand is not the same as defending ideas that we find repugnant. How, then, should we read the opening chapters of our *parashah*?

When I encounter Torah texts that I find offensive, like *R'eih*'s directive to destroy Canaanite religious sites, I ask myself if I can nevertheless learn from the writers' perspective. Here, I am struck by the harsh language regarding the religion of the other. Our translation of the beginning of Deuteronomy 12:2, "You must destroy [their religious sites]," doesn't capture the emphatic nature of the Hebrew, which repeats the verb "destroy" in two successive grammatical forms (*abeid t'abdun*). Everett Fox translates this as "You are to demolish, yes, demolish,"[3] which may better convey the stringency of the original. As if we hadn't gotten the point, verse 3 then uses four synonyms for "destroy" with respect to Canaanite altars, sacred posts, pillars, and god-images. Thus, in two verses, we have three forms of the word "destroy," plus four synonyms.

As a reader, I am struck by all of these words and forms. It seems like overkill—which is a clue that points me toward understanding the writers' perspective. In these words, I detect hatred—and, underneath this hatred, fear and anxiety. The text expresses worry that even the slightest curiosity about the other will lead to betrayal of God and the human community alike.

For the writers of Torah, this was life-and-death stuff. Loyalty to God was not just about personal faith; they believed it determined whether the rains came in their season, ensuring either starvation or prosperity.

But we live in a different time and place. For us, existential threats exist, but they don't come from interfaith dialogue. My curiosity about the religious experiences of others enriches, rather than diminishes, my own religious identity and practice, and I feel certain that my openness to others won't negatively impact the weather.

Fear of the other is real in all of us, just as it was in our ancient ancestors who advocated the utter destruction of others' houses of worship. Mussar practice can be a path to transcending that fear so that we can have better relationships and be part of building a more just and compassionate human community.

We can build our capacity for *kavod* in a variety of ways: personal and communal prayer, journaling, visual arts, therapy, meditation, and so forth. As always, we'll probably encounter resistance along the way. Resistance is proof that a particular *middah* requires our focus. Morinis has a valuable insight regarding the resistance we may encounter when working on *kavod*, namely that our propensity to disregard the experiences of others is really an

> externalization of the standards against which we judge our-selves. And because we are anxious about how we ourselves are stacking up, we judge others. When we find them wanting, we appear better and greater to ourselves. Whether we admit it or not, most of us want honor and feel we are not getting it, cer-tainly not in the measure we feel to be our due. So the factor that drives us to be so critical of others is nothing other than our own search for honor, especially in our own eyes.[4]

In other words, we dishonor others when we are unable to honor ourselves. The key to developing our capacity for *kavod* for everyone else is to remember, even in the face of all of our imperfections and misdeeds, that we too are made in the image of God. We, and others, are deserving of honor; this is a simple truth. *Kavod* is ours simply by virtue of being. We do not get it through achievement or lose it through failure. It simply is. Our job is to develop the habit of focus-ing on this simple truth and to avoid the siren song of judgmental thinking regarding others and ourselves.

Questions to Ask

Where in my life can I develop the habit of opening not only my wallet, but also my heart, to the poor?

In what ways does my tendency to judge others get in the way of my capacity for *kavod*?

What are some examples of the ways in which I negatively judge others?

Practices for the *Middah* of *Kavod*

At least once a day for a set period of time (a week, two weeks, a month), look at someone you encounter and say to yourself, "I see divinity within you." Track each day you remember to do so.

Look for, and journal about, stories of other people's lives that surprise you and disprove your initial assumptions about them.

Incorporate the following blessing into your morning routine (or some other routine part of your day): "Blessed are You, Adonai our God, eternal spirit of the universe, who has made me in the divine image." (*Baruch atah, Adonai Eloheinu, ruach ha-olam, she-asani b'tzelem Elohim.*)

Other *Middot* to Consider

Two other *middot* that come into play in *Parashat R'eih* are *lev patuach*, "open-heartedness," and *n'divut*, "generosity." Deuteronomy 15:7–8 commands us not to harden our hearts against the needy or shut our hands to them; rather we should open our hands. In verse 8, the Hebrew for "open" is doubled for emphasis (*ki fato-ach tiftach et yadcha lo*). We saw this grammatical phenomenon above in Deuteronomy 12:2 concerning the destruction of Canaanite worship spaces. Here, Rashi comments that the doubling of the verb "open" means that we must do this multiple times.[5] Abravanel adds that "the purpose of the repetition—both in the language and in what is commanded—is to make the person charitable; such qualities are developed by doing them over and over."[6] In other words, when we repeatedly open our hands and give, we change our character—we become more innately generous and open-hearted.

NOTES

1. Alan Morinis, *Everyday Holiness: The Jewish Spiritual Path of Mussar* (Boston: Trumpeter, 2007), 107–8.
2. Ibid., 109.
3. Everett Fox, *The Five Books of Moses* (New York: Schocken Books, 1995), 907.
4. Morinis, *Everyday Holiness*, 109.
5. Rashi to Deuteronomy 15:8.
6. Abravanel, in *The Commentators' Bible: The Rubin JPS Miqra'ot Gedolot: Deuteronomy*, trans. Michael Carasik (Philadelphia: Jewish Publication Society, 2015), 104.

Tzedek—Justice:
"Justice, Justice Shall You Pursue"

JUSTICE ANNABELLE IMBER TUCK

PARASHAT SHOF'TIM is the quintessential template for the establishment of a society where the guiding principle is justice. At the outset, power is divided between four separate groups: judges, king, priests, and prophets. Each group is assigned specific duties and responsibilities.

We know that absolute power corrupts absolutely. In order to avoid corruption and injustice that necessarily come from the placement of all power in a single institution or individual, *Shof'tim* designates specific powers for each branch of the government: judges, king, priests, and prophet. Each branch is limited in how it operates by proscriptive rules. The goal is to build a firm foundation for a just society, where *every* person is subject to the same rules and entitled to the same justice.

The appointment of judges or magistrates throughout all the settlements is to be done by the people themselves (Deuteronomy 16:18). These officials shall judge fairly and impartially and must not take bribes (Deuteronomy 16:19). In the event that a case is "too baffling" for the local judge to decide, then the case must be "appealed" to the Levitical priests in Jerusalem (Deuteronomy 17:8–10).

The double exhortation of "Justice, justice shall you pursue" (*Tzedek, tzedek tirdof*—צֶדֶק, צֶדֶק תִּרְדֹּף; Deuteronomy 16:20) could not be more forceful. Moreover, this command is addressed to the communal "you." It applies not only to the judges, but also to every member of the community, including succeeding generations. Rules of evidentiary proof are given when it comes to the number of witnesses

302   JUSTICE ANNABELLE IMBER TUCK

it takes to prove any offense. There must be at least two witnesses to validate any capital offense (Deuteronomy 17:6). With regard to imposition of the death penalty, the hands of those witnesses must "be the first to put [the condemned] to death" (Deuteronomy 17:7). Any person who gives false testimony against another is subject to the same penalty as the witness "schemed" to do to the other person (Deuteronomy 19:16–19). If a person unintentionally commits manslaughter, he or she may flee to a sanctuary city for protection from the victim's blood avenger (Deuteronomy 19:3–6). Finally, *Shof'tim* includes the principle of restitution scaled to the degree of the injury—the value of an eye for the loss of an eye, the value of a limb for its loss, and so on (Deuteronomy 19:21). Compared to earlier laws, this represented an enlargement of state interest in what had previously been considered private injuries.[1]

The second power structure acknowledged by God is the designation of a king, as existed in the nations surrounding Israel. Interestingly, the people of Israel are not required to have a monarch; rather, they are "free to set a king" over themselves (Deuteronomy 17:15). This king must not be indifferent to the poor or "act haughtily" (Deuteronomy 17:20). He must not amass wealth, horses, or wives (Deuteronomy 17:16–17). And, above all, the king must "observe faithfully every word of this Teaching as wells as these laws" (Deuteronomy 17:19). This is a constitutional monarchy, where the Torah is the Constitution, not an absolute monarchy.

The descendants of Aaron, the Levitical priests, represent a third leg in the power structure. Their role is "to be in attendance for service in the name of the Eternal for all time" (Deuteronomy 18:5).

One other power structure found in other nations surrounding Israel was that of the sorcerer, augur, soothsayer, or diviner (Deuteronomy 18:9–14). In order to combat these "abhorrent magic practices" (Deuteronomy 18:9), Moses tells the people of Israel that God will raise up a prophet from among the people (Deuteronomy 18:15). This prophet, like Moses, will speak all that God commands, and the people should heed the words the prophet speaks in God's name (Deuteronomy 18:18).

In considering this *parashah* from a Mussar perspective, the *g'vurah* (גְּבוּרָה, "strength") of absolute power is moderated by a separation of powers; and strict *tzedek* (צֶדֶק, "justice") is tempered by *chesed* (חֶסֶד, "compassion"), in the form of proscriptive rules of evidence, sanctuary cities, and monetary restitution for personal injury.

Justice and compassion even extend to the case of an unsolved manslaughter, where the elders, as representatives of the local community, must absolve the community of responsibility for the slaying by a ritual expiation ceremony called *eglah arufah*, the "broken-necked heifer" (Deuteronomy 21:1–9). As stated in the Mishnah, the prescribed declaration to be made by the elders that "[their] hands did not shed blood, nor did [their] eyes see it done" (Deuteronomy 21:7) meant "no one came within [their] jurisdiction whom [they] neglected to bring to justice," and "no one came within [their] jurisdiction for whom [they] failed to provide protection or whom [they] left without a livelihood."[2]

During my tenure as a trial judge and an appellate judge, the delivery of decisions always involved meting out justice with compassion. The parties deserved to know that they had been heard, so my oral and written decisions included a review of the evidence and an explanation of my legal reasoning. In child custody cases, it was particularly important to reiterate that despite a new living arrangement, the child needed the love and affection of both parents. From my own experience, I understood how painful divorce can be for the entire family.

Every member of the community, including succeeding generations, has an obligation to pursue justice in their own interactions with others. Before judging another person, we must be aware of our tendency to stereotype based upon the other's external appearance. Likewise, implicit bias derived from our own life experiences should be acknowledged. In the Mussar tradition, judging others favorably and giving them the benefit of the doubt should be our default.[3] We are all made *b'tzelem Elohim*, "in God's image" (Genesis 1:27). When we view another as a "whole person," we should search for and acknowledge their redeeming qualities. Just as God shows compassion when we fall short of the mark, so should we temper our judgment of another with compassion. For those situations where we find ourselves "baffled," *Shof'tim* teaches us to seek out a trusted friend for advice.

With the advent of the internet and social media, we tend to "hear" only what we want to "hear" and then share that information electronically with "friends." Such reactive judgment without further investigation and deliberation can be, at best, unfair and, at worst, defamatory, causing irreparable damage. This tendency to "rush to judgment" is most apparent in the "cult of the personality" phenomenon. We either sanctify or demonize public personalities using unverified "facts." Our children are especially vulnerable to cyberbullying, which can harm the online reputations of everyone involved. Each of us has the ability to counteract the current trend toward reactive judgment by adopting a "slow to judge" attitude toward others. During my tenure on the bench, this practice helped me become a better judge.

Shof'tim contemplates a community where social justice prevails. No person stands above any other person, even the king. No member of the community should be indifferent to the powerless or the poor. Likewise, each of us exercises some kind of power over others, whether as a public official, an employer, a teacher, a spiritual leader, or even within our own circle of family and friends. *Shof'tim* challenges us to exercise that power with *both* compassion and justice. It provides the human mechanism to achieve God's goal in creating the world on the basis of *tzedek* and *chesed* in balance with one another.

Questions to Ask

When you encounter a person who looks "different," how would you use *tzedek* and *chesed* to overcome automatic "stereotyping"?
How do you apply the *middot* of justice and compassion in your electronic communications?

Practice for the *Middah* of *Tzedek*

Identify a friend or acquaintance whose conduct leaves you with a negative impression; make a commitment to search for at least one positive quality in that person.

Another *Middah* to Consider

In *Shof'tim*, Moses instructs judges to appear before the Levitical priests when they are presented with a case that "is too baffling for you to decide" (Deuteronomy 17:8). Evaluate the inference that humility (*anavah*, עֲנָוָה) is needed in decision-making.

NOTES

1. W. Gunther Plaut, ed., *The Torah: A Modern Commentary*, rev. ed. (New York: Reform Judaism Publishing, an imprint of CCAR Press, 2005), 528.
2. *Mishnah Sotah* 9:6.
3. Alan Morinis, *With Heart in Mind: Mussar Teachings to Transform Your Life* (Boston: Trumpeter, 2014), 207.

KI TEITZEI—DEUTERONOMY 21:10–25:19

Tzedek/Rachamim—Justice/Mercy: A Conflict of Values

Rabbi Bonnie Koppell

"Justice, justice shall you pursue."   —*Deuteronomy 16:20*

"Everyone who is compassionate to others, it is certain that they are of the seed of *Avraham avinu* ("Abraham, our father") [and Sarah, our mother]. Those who are not compassionate toward others, it is certain that they are not of the seed of *Avraham avinu* [and *Sarah imeinu*]."   —*Babylonian Talmud, Beitzah* 32b

So WHICH ONE IS IT? "Justice" (*tzedek*, צֶדֶק)? Or "compassion" (*rachamim*, רַחֲמִים)? Or is the better question perhaps: When is it justice? When is it compassion? The seventy-four mitzvot contained in *Parashat Ki Teitzei* offer some guidance.

The dilemma is real. Compassion for victims requires a fierce commitment to justice. Appreciating the hurt someone has experienced and empathizing with their pain motivate us to right the situation through an appeal to the law. Yet, a refined sense of justice must be tempered by an understanding of situational factors that underlie the choices we make. Sometimes mercy for the perpetrator is appropriate, too.

In the era of the Torah, slavery was an accepted practice. All sorts of regulations softened the treatment of slaves, but none questioned the morality of the institution. In Deuteronomy 23:16–17, however, we read that if slaves escape and find their way to you, you must give them refuge and not return them to their master. You are required to find a place for them in the community and not treat them ill. Justice would seem to call for returning slaves, as one would return any lost "property" to the rightful owner. Yet, in this case, compassion overrides justice. Justice may be blind. Compassion calls on us to see the other with open hearts. "Always remember," we read, "that you were a slave in the land of Egypt" (Deuteronomy 24:22).

The Rabbis depict God's struggle with the tension between justice and mercy in creating the world. With only strict justice, the world could not endure, populated as it is by imperfect human beings. On the other hand, if there were only mercy, no one would be accountable for their actions, and we would descend into chaos. Thus, the midrash pictures the Holy One combining the two qualities in the act of Creation.[1]

Justice is a foundational virtue in Jewish tradition. God, being in covenant with Abraham, reveals God's intention to destroy Sodom and Gomorrah. Abraham immediately challenges God: "Must not the Judge of all the earth do justly?" (Genesis 18:25). Abraham reminds God of the fundamental importance of justice, without which society cannot function. Yet, in this case, justice requires that the innocent not be punished along with the guilty; true justice requires compassion.

We see the same dynamic playing out in Ki Teitzei with regard to the firstborn child of a less loved wife. The Torah stipulates that in a polygamous situation, preference may not be given to the children of the favorite wife. Justice demands that the firstborn must be treated as the firstborn, and compassion extended to the less loved wife and her child (Deuteronomy 21:15–17).

Moving into Deuteronomy 22 and beyond, we encounter many precepts designed to reinforce our merciful impulse. We must return lost items to their rightful owners (Deuteronomy 22:1–3) and let a mother bird go free before we collect the eggs from a nest (Deuteronomy 22:6). Compassion for animals demands that we not plow with an ox and an ass together (Deuteronomy 22:10), nor muzzle an animal as it plows a field. (Deuteronomy 25:4). Concern for the safety of others underlies the mitzvah to build a parapet around the roof of one's home (Deuteronomy 22:8). Provisions are made to feed the hungry by leaving the gleanings in a field (Deuteronomy 24:19-21). Justice and mercy are at the heart of this *parashah*. Yet, there is much that challenges our contemporary understanding of these two *middot*, particularly as they are revealed in male-female relationships. The opening verses address the challenging and disturbing situation regarding women who are captured in war.

Rape is an all-too-common occurrence in the military environment. For much of history, rape was considered to be a right for combatants, an expected reward for participating in battle, and even today, it is still used as a tool of subjugation. The proscriptions in the Torah are an attempt to temper the instinct to treat women as yet another piece of captured property to be used at will and then discarded. If a soldier encounters a woman he desires, he is forbidden to attack her. She must be brought into his home and allowed a month to mourn her loss before he can "possess" her. She must be given the status of a wife, and provisions are included to ensure his ongoing support for her should he cease to desire her (Deuteronomy 21:10–14).

In Mussar practice, we learn that change must be gradual and *middot* must be continually practiced. Making extreme changes, even to the law, is rarely successful in the long term. Acknowledging the existence of the *yetzer hara*, "the evil impulse," is an important focus of Mussar. Had the Torah simply banned rape, the principle would have been ignored as a bridge too far at the time of the Torah. Thus, the text tries to limit the possibility of rape by requiring a one-month period of time for the soldier to reflect on his behavior and, one hopes, to be moved in the direction of mercy as he observes the captive woman in his home mourning for the loss of her freedom and family. *Sefer HaChinuch* suggests that we are to learn "good and precious *middot*" from this teaching.[2]

Deuteronomy 22:23–29 addresses rape in peacetime, and judging according to modern standards of justice and mercy, we may be appalled by what it is teaching. If the rape occurs in the countryside, the man is held responsible and faces the death penalty. If a man attacks a married woman in the city, they are both executed, the assumption being that she did not cry out for help. And in the case of the rape of a single woman? His only punishment is to be forced to marry her, with no possibility of divorce. Her punishment is to be married to her rapist. His punishment is having to take care of her for the rest of her life. In the ancient world, this provision was considered merciful to the woman. After all, she was no longer "marketable," having lost her status of a virgin. But we cannot help but be appalled by the lack of justice and compassion for the female victim. In our time, we wish that the Torah would completely abolish the practice of rape in wartime and in peacetime![3]

As a military chaplain for thirty-eight years, I observed, firsthand, the sense of dehumanization of the enemy that accompanied combat. We are raised to be sensitive human beings who would never think of taking a human life. When soldiers are thrust into war, it is challenging to overcome a lifetime of training not to cause harm to others. Sadly, they steel themselves for battle by seeing enemy combatants as "other" and thereby overcoming a natural and admirable disinclination to kill. Traditionally, soldiers have achieved that emotional and moral distance by dehumanizing the enemy.

However, there is an emerging understanding of "moral injury" as a foundation of post-traumatic stress. Moral injury can occur when there is a disconnect between our fundamental values—thou shalt not kill—and the reality that war entails—kill or be killed. At the earliest stages of their careers, soldiers should be provided a moral context to understand killing as part of warfare. Without a somewhat sophisticated context, the internal conflict often results in moral injury, manifesting as post-traumatic stress.

I recall the profound impact of Passover seders in Iraq, where, as we spilled a drop of wine from our cups, mentioning each plague, we reminded ourselves that we should never rejoice over the suffering of our enemies. The ritual of spilling wine from our cups is a reminder of the ultimate humanity of every individual, understanding the divine image even in enemy combatants. If we deny that reality, we risk moral disconnect.

Justice versus mercy. In our *parashah*, we find examples of each, and each has its place. Imagining ourselves as formed in the image of God, we remember God's self-description in Exodus 34:6, where the first attribute God ascribes to God is compassion. The Rabbis depict God as praying, "May it be My will that My mercy should conquer My anger and prevail over all My other *middot*."[4] God's prayer is a good prayer for us, too.

Questions to Ask

The Hebrew word for compassion is *rachamim*. It shares a root with the word *rechem*, meaning "womb." What does this tell us about the perspective of the ancient Israelites on women?

We read in *Kohelet Rabbah* 7:16 that "those who are kind to the cruel will, in the end, be cruel to the kind." Can you think of an example where this might be true?

There are many Jewish laws intending to avoid causing pain to any living creature. How does our treatment of animals influence our treatment of humanity?

God's self-description (Exodus 34:6–7) includes thirteen attributes, the first of which is compassion. What can we learn from the fact that *rachamim* is the very first attribute mentioned?

Practice for the *Middah* of *Rachamim*

Reflect on a time where your heart was moved by someone who was in pain. Is it possible that in your desire to empathetically connect with them, another person may have been hurt? What would have been different had you reflected on the need for justice for all of the individuals in this scenario?

Practice for the *Middah* of *Tzedek*

You want what is fair and what is right. You know who is the victim and who is the perpetrator, and you desire to see the perpetrator brought to justice. Is it possible that there is some space in your heart to empathize with the individual you have identified as the wrong-doer? Can you imagine yourself in their place and try to understand the choices that they made?

Another *Middah* to Consider

Acharayut (אַחֲרָיוּת, "responsibility"): Everything we do has an impact in the world. We imagine the world as balanced between good and evil. With our next action, we will shift the balance. It is vital that we take responsibility for the impact of our behavior.

Mishnah, Pirkei Avot 2:10 teaches that the path of the righteous includes thinking through the consequences of our behavior.

Parashat Ki Teitzei emphasizes taking responsibility, too. Do we keep our word? Are we sensitive to the needs of the less fortunate? Do we treat everyone equally? The Torah offers many opportunities to consider our actions and know that we are accountable for what results.

NOTES

1. *B'reishit Rabbah* 12:15.
2. *Sefer HaChinuch* (New York: Feldheim, 1989), 158.
3. We are similarly scandalized by the failure to prohibit slavery outright.
4. *Babylonin Talmud, B'rachot* 7a.

Ki Tavo—Deuteronomy 26:1–29:8
Hakarat HaTov—Gratitude: Acknowledging the Good

Rabbi Andrea C. London

"I deserve it!" is the nemesis of gratitude
(*hakarat hatov*—הַכָּרַת הַטּוֹב).

When we think that our good fortune is owed to us because of our hard work, we are less likely to give thanks for what we have. Such thinking is harmful to our souls and detrimental to our impulse toward generosity. Research has found that being grateful makes us happier and more resilient and improves our self-esteem. Physical benefits include better sleep, lower blood pressure, pain reduction, and a greater desire to engage in physical exercise. Interpersonally, gratitude makes us more compassionate, helpful, and kind.[1] Yet because we live in a society in which many of us are blessed with plenty, we often take for granted what we have or take too much credit for acquiring it. It's often easier to notice what we lack instead of what we have.

Recently, I found myself annoyed when my local grocery store stopped carrying a brand of tea that I like. When I stepped back to scan the shelves for my coveted brand, I realized how ridiculous my frustration was. What I saw were shelves upon shelves of tea varieties. "What an abundance of choices I have!" I thought to myself. My annoyance turned into gratitude, and my mood shifted immediately.

How often do we focus on something small that is irking us or pat ourselves on the back for our good fortune, failing to see our good fortune or acknowledge the source of our blessings? *Parashat Ki Tavo* teaches us how to cultivate the *middah* of *hakarat hatov*—"acknowl-edging the good"—so that we might increase our capacity to be grateful.

The opening passage of *Parashat Ki Tavo* states that when the Israel-ites settle in the Land of Israel, they are obligated to bring some of the first fruits of the yearly harvest to the priest and express gratitude for the land. In the initial verses of the *parashah*, the Israelites are told three times that God has given them the land (Deuteronomy 26:1–3), reminding them that the bountiful harvest they worked for would not be possible without the fertile land on which they toil. They say to the priest that they attribute their bounty to God: "I acknowledge this day before the Eternal your God that I have entered the land that the Eternal swore to our fathers to assign us" (Deuteronomy 26:3). The donor then recites this passage, known to many from the Haggadah:

> My father was a fugitive Aramean. He went down to Egypt with meager numbers and sojourned there; but there he became a great and very populous nation. The Egyptians dealt harshly with us and oppressed us; they imposed heavy labor upon us. We cried to the Eternal, the God of our ancestors, and the Eternal heard our plea and saw our plight, our misery, and our oppression. The Eternal freed us from Egypt by a mighty hand, by an outstretched arm and awesome power, and by signs and portents, bringing us to this place and giving us this land, a land flowing with milk and honey. Wherefore I now bring the first fruits of the soil which You, Eternal One, have given me. (Deuteronomy 26:5–10)

Rabbi Ben Hollander taught that this ritual is an annual *aliyah*, lift-ing us out of the mire of our daily tasks and redirecting us to recog-nize the blessings in our lives. "It acknowledged, in Martin Buber's phrase, God's constantly renewing gift of the land."[2] When we are caught up in the daily grind, our focus can be limited, and we might fail to see the goodness all around us or acknowledge the source of that goodness. This ritual is a corrective to our tendency to take for granted, or to take sole credit for, what we have.

The biblical ritual reminds me of the story about the two *shleppers* ("laggards") at the end of the caravan of Israelites walking through the parted Reed Sea. They are so focused on the mud on the seabed that they fail to look up and see the walls of water that have made their safe passage possible. They completely miss the miracle of the parting of the Reed Sea while carping about the mud.[3]

Gaining perspective on our situations is important, but *Ki Tavo* asks even more of us. Not only are we expected to express our appreciation, but we are also instructed to remember our oppression. The recitation of this passage is a *y'ridah l'tzorech aliyah*—a "descent in order to ascend."[4] We recite the history of our hardship and slavery in order to recognize how far we have come from our enslavement. In fact, the whole trajectory of the Passover seder moves us from recalling the low point of our enslavement—our "degradation" (*g'nut*, גְּנוּת)—to "praising" God for our liberation (*shevach*); not just our ancestors' liberation, but also our own. As we recite at the seder, in every generation we are obligated to see ourselves as having personally been enslaved and redeemed. When we recite this passage from *Ki Tavo*, we are saying, "Look how far we have come."

Each of us can recall moments of gratitude and relief when a painful event has moved into our rearview mirror and no longer has the emotional grip on us that it once had. In Jewish tradition, we recite *Birkat HaGomeil* after recovering from an illness or having made it safely through a treacherous situation. The blessing states, "Blessed are You, Adonai our God, Sovereign of the universe, who has bestowed every goodness upon us... May the One who has bestowed goodness upon us continue to bestow every goodness upon us forever."[5] It is then customary to give *tzedakah* in gratitude for having survived a difficult experience. In the same vein, we read that our gratitude for our liberation should induce us to give to others. "And you shall enjoy, together with the [family of the] Levite and the stranger in your midst, all the bounty that the Eternal your God has bestowed upon you and your household" (Deuteronomy 26:11). At the seder, we say, "Let all who are hungry come and eat," acknowledging that when we remember our hunger, our compassion for those who are in need flows freely.

To grow in empathy toward others, it is not enough to acknowledge our previous difficulty or deprivation. We must also recognize the good fortune that has contributed to our progress lest we become smug or self-congratulatory. Reciting the history of our enslaved past and how God brought us out of slavery and into a plentiful land reminds us that our success is not just a result of our hard work, but is also due to the rich soil we've been given to till.

There's a psychological phenomenon in which people attribute their success mainly to their own efforts and talents, discounting salutary effects and advantages from which they have benefited. This phenomenon is based on our inclination to ignore or discount forces or privileges that have contributed to our success, much as a cyclist impelled forward by a tailwind may feel she is benefiting primarily from her many miles of dedication and training rather than by the wind at her back.

The so-called American dream is based on the deeply ingrained notion that people in the United States can pull themselves up by their own bootstraps if they work hard enough. By extension, the inverse is presumably also the case: that failure to succeed is a mark of one's own shortcomings or indolence. What this myth of upward mobility fails to take into account is that many of us benefit from advantages such as wealth, access to good schools, safe neighborhoods, good health care, powerful social connections, or a myriad of other factors that make success far more attainable—in effect, a wind at one's back.

Hakarat hatov is a spiritual practice that opens our minds and hearts to notice the forces that propel us forward. *Hakarat hatov* can help us to perceive in a radically different light those around us who have fared less well and to acknowledge that the tailwinds from which we have benefited may have manifested as headwinds for others. When we acknowledge our blessings and recognize the Source of Blessing, we become more grateful and develop greater kindness and empathy toward others.

Hakarat hatov can also help us to focus more on what we have than on what we lack. Scarcity is not objectively measurable; it is defined by our own perception. Practicing *hakarat hatov* can shift our perspective from one of lack to one of abundance. This feeling of being blessed with plenty and that our bounty is the product of the fertile soil on which we toil can turn our attitude of "I deserve it" to "I'm fortunate. It hasn't always been like this. Look how far I've come with God's help. How can I share my blessings with others?"

Questions to Ask

How can being joyful make us more generous?

How does acknowledging our blessings make us more compassionate and understanding?

My childhood rabbi, Arnold Jacob Wolf, taught that we should ritualize our ethics and ethicize our rituals. We no longer offer animal sacrifices to give thanks for our well-being. What are ways you could ritualize your gratitude today? What are ritual practices that could increase your generosity?

Practice for the *Middah* of *Hakarat HaTov*

When you awake in the morning, take some time to recognize the blessings in your life. The traditional Jewish morning blessings express our gratitude for our body (*Asher Yatzar*), mind (*Laasok B'divrei Torah*), and soul (*Elohai N'shamah*). There are also the blessings of *Nisim B'chol Yom* (daily miracles), which express our wonder at the simple, often overlooked wonders of being alive, such as being able to get out of bed in the morning, get dressed, and start our day. Create a morning ritual for yourself. You could use some of the traditional blessings and then bring to mind specific things for which you are grateful and praise the Source of Blessing. In the evening, journal about what was good about your day. Have those thoughts in your mind as you say thank you to God, recite the bedtime *Sh'ma*, and go to sleep.

Other *Middot* to Consider

Acharayut (אַחֲרָיוּת, "responsibility"): After the first fruits ceremony is the litany of blessings and curses the Israelites will receive if they obey or fail to obey God's laws. The blessings and curses indicate that what happens in the world is not capricious; there is an order to the moral universe. The difficulty is that it can cause us to take too much credit when things go well for us and too much blame when life doesn't seem to go our way. How can we acknowledge that we are responsible for our lives and the world without falling into blaming the victim or giving too much credit to those who are successful?

Rachamim (רַחֲמִים, "mercy"): After the Israelites recite the history of their persecution and enslavement, they leave an offering for the priests. In the following verse (Deuteronomy 26:12), the Israelites are further instructed to offer a tithe for the widow, the orphan, and the stranger—the most vulnerable people in society. As the curses that follow in the *parashah* remind us, if we don't act compassionately toward those most in need in our society, we all will suffer. This law challenges us to be compassionate to everyone, not just those we know or already care about.

NOTES

1. Amy Morin, "Seven Scientifically Proven Benefits of Gratitude," *Psychology Today*, April 3, 2015, https://www.psychologytoday.com/us/blog/what-mentally-strong-people-dont-do/201504/7-scientifically-proven-benefits-gratitude.
2. Ben Hollander, *To Be Continued . . . : Teachings on Parashat HaShavua*, ed. Michael J. Schwartz (Maitland, FL: Mill City Press, 2017), 259.
3. *Sh'mot Rabbah* 24:1: "In what ways did the Israelites rebel at the Sea of Reeds? It was precisely at the moment they went down into the seabed and found it full of mud, because it was still wet from the water. There were two, Reuven and Shimon, who were among the Israelites. As they walked through the sea, all they could talk about was the mud. Reuven said, 'In Egypt we had mud, and now here too in the sea we have mud. In Egypt we had clay for bricks, and here too we have an abundance of clay for bricks.'

They rebelled at the sea even though this was the parting of the Sea of Reeds! They didn't notice the water; instead they saw the mud."

4. Eighteenth-century Chasidic teaching that we experience distance from God in order to feel closeness to God.

5. *Mishkan T'filah: A Reform Siddur*, ed. Elyse D. Frishman (New York: CCAR Press, 2007), 371.

Nitzavim—Deuteronomy 29:9–30:20

Anavah—Humility: Living a Life of Humility

Rabbi Paul F. Cohen, DMin, DD

On what do the virtues [*middot*] depend? All virtues and duties
are dependent on humility.
> —Rabbi Bachya ibn Pakuda, *Duties of the Heart*

An attitude of humility of willingness to make even the smallest
contributions and to accept a life of commitment and dedication must be part of the potentially creative person's way of life.
> —Silvano Arieti, *Creativity*

PARASHAT NITZAVIM puts forth the message that living a life of
meaning, a life that embraces the covenant between God and the
Children of Israel, requires that we balance two opposite inclinations: to avoid telling ourselves that "we are the worthiest" and to
stop telling ourselves that "we are not worthy of standing before God
and entering the covenant between God and the Children of Israel."
Students of Mussar call this balance *anavah* (עֲנָוָה—"humility").

I am struck by the fact that we read from *Parashat Nitzavim* twice
a year within a short period of time. We read *Nitzavim* for the first
time as part of the annual Torah reading cycle at the end of the Jewish
year and then, according to Reform *minhag*, a second time on Yom
Kippur morning.[1]

Yom Kippur morning is liturgically a moment of deep honesty,
reflection, and repentance. We seek to make ourselves most open to
self-reflection and most vulnerable to self-rebuke as we hear these
powerful words:

> You stand this day, all of you, before the Eternal your God—
> you tribal heads, you elders, and you officials, all of the men of
> Israel, you children, you wives, even the stranger within your
> camp, from woodchopper to waterdrawer—to enter into the
> covenant of the Eternal your God. . . . I make this covenant,
> with its sanctions, not with you alone, but both with those who
> are standing here with us this day before the Eternal our God
> and with those who are not with us here this day. (Deuteronomy
> 29:9–11, 29:13–14)

Imagine that moment. In fact, we are called upon to do more than imagine. We are called upon to experience that moment; to be present for it. We, too, stood with Moses on the banks of the Jordan River, each and every one of us, ready to enter into the covenant with God.

Within the Mussar teachings, *anavah* is not defined as "making oneself small." Instead, humility is defined as recognizing the exact extent of our abilities, importance, and status. Each of us—and the text makes clear that this means all of us—was worthy of standing before God and entering into the covenant. The text of *Nitzavim* lays out the entire spectrum of human ages, genders, ethnicities, and occupations—and it recognizes that all of us are worthy of standing before God and entering the covenant: from leader to follower (Deuteronomy 29:9), from elder to child, from tribal members to visitors, men and women alike (Deuteronomy 29:10).

At the same time, a close reading of the text reveals that none of the people listed stands above another. This is a refreshing reminder. We may think that our value is measured by the status of our occupation. We might think our age or our gender makes us more worthy than others. It does not. Alan Morinis defines humility as "limiting oneself to an appropriate space while leaving room for others."[2] However we regard our personal abilities, importance, and status, we are allotted only so much, and we are charged to make space for everybody else.

Martin Buber[3] reflected on the fact that Abraham says, "I am but dust and ashes" (Genesis 18:27), while in the Mishnah, it is written,

"Each person should say: For me the world was created."[4] He draws the conclusion that a person should always wear a garment with two pockets. In one pocket we should place a slip of paper on which is written, "I am dust and ashes." In the other pocket, we should place a slip of paper on which is written, "For me the world was created." We should pull out the appropriate slip when we need it.

When puffed with pride, we should take out and read the slip that says, "I am but dust and ashes," contemplate the meaning of this sentence, and our arrogance will vanish. When we feel depreciated and depressed, we should pull out the other slip of paper, read, "For me the world was created," contemplate the meaning of that sentence, and our depression will vanish. Our sense of self-worth will be replenished. Buber brings forward the necessity of finding the balance between the overwhelming sense that we are not worthy and an exaggerated feeling of self-worth. He understands that this can be a moment-to-moment and day-to-day balancing act. In each moment, we can hear the echo of *Parashat Nitzavim* reminding us of the inherent worth we have represented by our embrace in the covenantal love of our God.

Poet Marianne Williamson expresses the idea that one of the biggest obstacles in experiencing *anavah* is fear, the fear that we are powerful and gifted and do not use our power and our gifts to their fullest extent. This is the parallel message of *Nitzavim*, that what God asks of us is not too distant, nor is it too difficult. In fact, "[the word of God] is very close to you, in your mouth, and in your heart, to observe it" (Deuteronomy 30:14). Williamson writes:

> Our deepest fear is not that we are inadequate. Our deepest fear is that we are powerful beyond measure. It is our light, not our darkness that most frightens us. We ask ourselves, Who am I to be brilliant, gorgeous, talented, fabulous? Actually, who are you *not* to be? You are a child of God. Your playing small does not serve the world. There is nothing enlightened about shrinking so that other people won't feel insecure around you. We are all meant to shine, as children do. We were born to make manifest the glory of God that is within us. It's not just in some

of us; it's in everyone. And as we let our own light shine, we unconsciously give other people permission to do the same. As we are liberated from our own fear, our presence automatically liberates others.[5]

Nitzavim teaches that living a life of humility means to balance two opposite inclinations: to avoid telling ourselves that "we are the worthiest" and to stop telling ourselves that "we are not worthy of standing before God and entering the covenant between God and the Children of Israel."

Questions to Ask

When have you had difficulties balancing your ego and your sense of *anavah*?
In which situation can you practice acting with more *avanah*?

Practice for the *Middah* of *Anavah*

Place yourself in a situation that challenges your self-confidence. Ask yourself which gifts you could bring forward, and apply them. Place yourself in a situation that inspires self-confidence. Then, make space for others.

Another *Middah* to Consider

Given that we were all standing together in the moment the covenant was established, we inherit the responsibility to fulfill the obligations the covenant entails. How does the *middah* of *acharayut* (אַחֲרָיוּת, "responsibility") manifest in your life?

NOTES

1. Traditional congregations read a portion of *Parashat Acharei Mot*.
2. Alan Morinis, *Everyday Holiness: The Jewish Spiritual Path of Mussar* (Boston: Trumpeter, 2007), 49.
3. *Mishnah Sanhedrin* 4:5.
4. After Rabbi Simchah Bunem, in Martin Buber, *Tales of the Hasidim*, vol. 2 (New York: Schocken Books, 1947), 249–50.
5. Marianne Williamson, *A Return to Love: Reflections on the Principles of a Course in Miracles* (New York: HarperCollins, 1992), 190–91.

Vayeilech—Deuteronomy 31:1–30

Bitachon—Moses's Lifelong Journey toward Trust

Rabbi Debra Kassoff

In Victor Hugo's masterwork *Les Misérables*,[1] the bishop known affectionately by his flock as Monseigneur Bienvenu ("Mister Welcome") eschews the princely stipend and luxurious lodgings he receives as the privileges of his post and lives with his sister and their elderly servant in near-poverty. Devoted as he is to giving charity, comforting the afflicted, and welcoming strangers, the bishop arranges for the doors of their abode to stand always open to any passerby.

"The dangerous ex-convict" Jean Valjean is accordingly welcomed into the bishop's home when nobody else would take him, seated beside the bishop at the table, served with silver—the Monseigneur Bienvenu's one remaining indulgence, left over from a prior life of material comfort—and given a bed in a room next to the bishop's. This, immediately upon hearing from his old housekeeper that a frightening ruffian is abroad in the town, and despite her pleas that, if only this once, he lock the doors.

Monseigneur Beinvenu is remarkable not only for his material and spiritual generosity, but also for his lack of distress in the face of discomfort, danger, or insult. He is, if I may say it of a priest of the Catholic Church, the embodiment of the *middah* of *bitachon* (בִּטָחוֹן): "trust," as it is most commonly translated, but also security, an optimistic confidence. *Bitachon* is an attitude toward God, or providence, best summed up in the immortal words of Nachum Ish Gamzu, the second-century sage and teacher of Rabbi Akiva: *Gam zu l'tovah*, "This too is for the best."[2]

In *Parashat Vayeilech*, Moses, a former prince of Egypt and a former shepherd of Midian, has sacrificed first a life of privilege and then a life of tranquility to confront Pharaoh, his adoptive father, and become not a peace-loving priest (that role will go to his brother, Aaron), but rather the greatest prophet Israel would ever know.

Nobody wants to be a prophet. It's a thankless job. Indeed, Moses now stands with his incorrigible tribe on the shore of the Jordan River, having endured decades of rebellion and uprising from this stiff-necked people. He has wandered the wilderness with them for forty years—teaching them, disciplining them, cajoling them. He has sheltered them from God's terrible glory, on the one hand, and, on the other hand, when necessary, from God's terrifying wrath. He has tended this people as tirelessly as he once tended his father-in-law's sheep. But now he knows his time for leading, and for living, has come to an end (Deuteronomy 31:2).

In the course of his service to the Children of Israel, Moses has learned that he will not get to see his life's mission come to fruition. He knows he will die without crossing the Jordan, without setting foot in the Promised Land. He has come as far as he can. It is time to send the people onward without him, with Joshua at their head. What's more, God now tells Moses that the people will break their covenant after they enter the Land: worshiping idols, incurring God's displeasure once more, and without Moses on hand to intercede (Deuteronomy 31:16–18). Under the circumstances, one might easily understand Moses's reluctance to relinquish his burden of prophecy.

Repeatedly throughout our story, the Israelites fail to manifest *bitachon*. Yet *bitachon* is exactly what Moses tried to teach the Israelites throughout his life, only to discover, in his final moments, in these last chapters of Torah, that he has apparently failed. Moses has repeatedly enacted God's miracles for the Israelites at close range. Still, at every challenging turn, the people rebelled. And now, standing on the verge of the long-awaited fulfillment of God's promise to bring them into the Promised Land, Moses learns that—even after the people have settled, miraculously secure in sturdy homes on the bountiful land that God first promised their ancestors generations before—the Children of Israel will fall short once again.

There have been times when Moses has faltered in his own cultivation of *bitachon*. Nearly as often as the people grumble against Moses, we find Moses crying out to God: "What shall I do with this people? Before long they will be stoning me!" (Exodus 17:4); and, "Why have You dealt ill with Your servant . . . that You have laid the burden of all this people upon me?" (Numbers 11:11).

It is precisely this sort of anxiety and frustration that *bitachon* puts to rest; but for Moses, such rest—such confident assurance that *gam zu l'tovah*, "this too is for the best"—remains troublingly elusive for most of his life. We see Moses's insecurity as late as the opening chapters of Deuteronomy, when we witness his pleading with God to allow him into the Promised Land (Deuteronomy 3:23–25), betraying his lack of trust in the goodness of God's plan to keep him out. But by the time we arrive at *Parashat Vayeilech*, that time and that struggle have passed. We see a Moses finally at peace with his lot, a Moses full of *bitachon*.

Moses is no superhero of *bitachon* like Hugo's Monseigneur Bienvenu. In fact Moses, the reluctant protagonist, a mountain of a man on the run from the law (Moses killed an Egyptian slavedriver in his youth, perhaps accidentally, but nonetheless hid the body and fled), a faithful follower of God yet with his moments of weakness and ambivalence, has more in common with Jean Valjean, the deeply flawed yet sublimely transcendent hero of *Les Misérables*. The bishop has a rare gift, an exceptional talent for *bitachon* that places him nearly on a footing with the angels; Moses, like Jean Valjean—like most of us humans—must continually struggle to achieve his full measure of this trait.

Now at the end of his life, Moses seems to have achieved the state of trusting well-being that *bitachon* represents. Three times in *Vayeilech*, a portion of only thirty verses, Moses variously exhorts the Israelites, or Joshua, or the Levites: "Be strong and resolute" (Deuteronomy 31:6, 31:7–8, 31:23). Moses has tried to communicate this message to the Israelites throughout their wanderings together. But until Moses himself has achieved *bitachon*, he cannot internalize his own wisdom. Perhaps that's why, for so long, he failed to impart it to the Israelites.

What has changed? For one thing, Moses has accepted his pressing appointment with death, and with it the knowledge that the end of his life will not correspond to the end of history. He has retold the history of the Israelite people and, with their story, his own. Now, at the end of his life, Moses feels some combination of resignation in the face of what was and what is—the die is cast, it cannot be undone—and reassurance that whatever mistakes he has made, whatever apparent mishaps and injustices he has suffered, he has served his purpose well. There is much of which to feel proud, much for which to feel grateful.

It may be easier at the end of life, and easier in the presence of something larger than ourselves, to trust, to choose *bitachon*—a sense that the answer to our prayers may not be what we ask for, what we wish, but rather what we, or the world around us, need.

Moses's situation in *Vayeilech* brings to mind the teaching of Rabbi Tarfon, in *Mishnah, Pirkei Avot* 2:20–21: "The day is short, and the task is great. . . . It is not ours to complete the task, but neither are we free to desist from it." Like Moses, we wish to complete the task, but like Moses, we will not. *Gam zu l'tovah*, and yet, "this too shall be for the best."

Questions to Ask

Alan Morinis writes of *bitachon* in *Everyday Holiness: The Jewish Spiritual Path of Mussar* (p. 209), that the "soul-trait of 'trust' actually doesn't just mean trust, it means 'trust in God.'" Can faith in any power larger than oneself—the universe, human history—be substituted for "God" in this formula? Why or why not? Or is faith in God a precondition to *bitachon*? Can an agnostic achieve *bitachon*? Why or why not?

What is the difference between *bitachon* ("trust") and

fatalism? How can we know when and whether to accept
the circumstances that surround us and when to work to
change or influence circumstances?

Rabbi Eliezer famously teaches, "Repent one day before
your death," and when his students protest, asking how
one can know the day of one's death, he responds, "One
should repent today, lest one die tomorrow."[4] In addition
to this text, we have Yom Kippur to simulate the reflective
state of one about to die in order to prompt repentance.
What similar tools do Jewish tradition and our own
imagination offer for the cultivation of *bitachon*, so that
we, unlike Moses, don't have to wait until the day of our
death to find it?

Practices for the *Middah* of *Bitachon*

Alan Morinis points to fear as a tool for the cultivation of
bitachon.[5] For the next month, practice noticing what
triggers fear for you. Set aside some time each day to
reflect on these questions: What is the worst thing that
could happen if your fear came to pass? What would that
look like or feel like? If that worst thing happened, what
would you do next? What if you were to trust (or behave as
if you trusted) that this worst thing happening was somehow for the best or, at the very least, in spite of everything,
destined to produce something good and beautiful? How
would this belief change your experience, feelings, and/or
behavior?

Moses has the benefit of talking with God "face-to-face"
(Exodus 33:11). For him, the distinction between trust in
God and moral passivity is clear. For us, the line between
bitachon and fatalism may blur at times, but it is nevertheless distinguishable. Strive to notice the difference
between unproductive worry and opportunities to act.
Likewise, take note of the difference between feelings

of serenity, strength, and well-being generated by true
bitachon and destructive feelings of either helplessness
or self-righteousness that arise when we passively accept
negative circumstances that we can change. Keep a journal
of your practice. Is there a particular kind of decision or
area of your life in which discernment between a trusting
acceptance of immutable circumstances and base inaction
in the face of adversity is most difficult for you? Such
patterns may point to another *middah* for your spiritual
curriculum.

Another *Middah* to Consider

When Moses tells the Israelites, "Joshua is the one who shall cross
[into the Promised Land] before you" (Deuteronomy 31:3), is Moses
setting down his burden of responsibility (*acharayut*, אַחֲרָיוּת) for the
Israelites, or is he taking one up by choosing to step aside and make
way for new leadership? What different layers of responsibility are
present in *Vayeilech*?

NOTES

1. Victor Hugo, *Les Miserables*, trans. Julie Rose (New York: Modern Library,
   2008).
2. *Babylonian Talmud, Taanit* 21a.
3. Alan Morinis, *Everyday Holiness: The Jewish Spiritual Path of Mussar* (Boston:
   Trumpeter, 2007), 209.
4. *Babylonian Talmud, Shabbat* 153a.
5. Morinis, *Everyday Holiness*, 219.

Haazinu—Deuteronomy 32:1–52

Anavah—Humility:
Recognizing Our Place

Cantor Chanin Becker

A STORY IS TOLD about Rabbi Israel Salanter walking home late one evening and passing by the window of a shoemaker. When Rabbi Salanter observed the man working diligently, mending shoes late into the night by only the flickering light of a candle, he rebuked the shoemaker and wondered why he would allow his work to so dominate his life. Realizing the rabbi's misjudgment, the shoemaker explained succinctly, "As long as the candle burns, Rabbi, there is still time to mend."[1]

Often cited as the impetus for a consistent Mussar practice, this parable provides a metaphor for our ethical obligation to savor every moment of our lives as an opportunity to improve our character. Indeed, as long as the candle burns, there is still time to mend. In *Parashat Haazinu*, Moses epitomizes this basic Mussar teaching. Even as the candle of his life burns quite low, he demonstrates why he is rightfully considered to be an exemplar of the trait of *anavah* (עֲנָוָה, "humility"). The Torah calls Moses "a very humble man, more so than any other human being on earth" (Numbers 12:3). We ought not be surprised that his final song offers a glimpse into the various types of humility Moses personifies throughout his life.

At first glance, Moses appears to be anything but humble—an adjective commonly understood to mean "pulling ourselves back" and "shrinking our egos"—when he gathers all of the Israelites around him and calls on no less than heaven and earth to witness his song. In the world of Mussar, however, humility has a particular definition. Alan Morinis writes that humility is about taking up our rightful space in the universe: "Proper humility means having the right relationship to self, giving self neither too big nor too small a role in your life."[2] If we are truly humble, we understand our appropriate role in the situations we encounter and take up space accordingly. Rav Abraham Isaac Kook elaborates: "Humility is associated with spiritual perfection. When humility effects depression it is defective. When it is genuine, it inspires joy, courage, and inner dignity."[3] On the one hand, we learn to worship God and not our own egos. On the other, we do not overlook our strengths nor shirk from decisions that are ours to make.

With this understanding of *anavah*, we look at Moses and *Haazinu* quite differently. The words of this song are no display of hubris. Instead, they are the vehicles by which Moses demonstrates the humility of letting go at the appropriate moment with precisely the right amount of gravitas. Imagine if a leader who figured so prominently in the Israelites' lives—who served as shepherd, orator, judge, and prophet to generations—had simply faded away with no final charge! The very act of leaving a potent message for his followers illustrates Moses's knowledge of his rightful place in the community. Despite his own emotional needs around the prospect of dying, Moses does not seclude himself nor hold back his wisdom. In fact, the tone of his song suggests that the need to take up the appropriate amount of space intensifies for Moses as his candle burns to its end, as the reality sets in that he will no longer be physically present to instruct his flock.

Beyond the content of his words, the method by which Moses delivers his message reaffirms that he knows his place. In contrast to the countless utterances that Moses has spoken until now, here, for the first time since the parting of the Sea of Reeds, Moses breaks into song! With so little time left to offer his guidance, Moses makes a calculated choice. As Rabbi Jonathan Sacks describes:

> [Moses] had to sum up his prophetic message in a way the people would always remember and be inspired by. He knew that the best way of doing so is by music. So the last thing Moses

did before giving the people his deathbed blessing was to teach them a song. . . . When language aspires to the transcendent, and the soul longs to break free of the gravitational pull of the earth, it modulates into song.[4]

Moses chooses song instead of prose because he understands the need for transcendence at this very moment. He knows that the Israelites require a message that will last beyond the days or months they will mourn him. They need words that can be internalized and persist throughout the ages. Given Moses's uniquely significant role in their lives, the enduring nature of a song affords him an opportunity to be appropriately humble, to offer words that begin to accommodate the depth of loss his people will face.

As he begins to sing, Moses exudes *anavah*:

> May my discourse come down as the rain,
> My speech distill as the dew,
> Like showers on young growth,
> Like droplets on the grass. (Deuteronomy 32:2)

Moses admits that he cares deeply about how his message is received. He hopes his statements will reach the listeners' ears not as harsh chastisements, but as gentle drops of dew upon the grass or as cleansing as a rain that feeds a thirsty earth. Though the content of the song will be strongly worded, Moses wants the Israelites to experience his poetry as nourishment, as a melody that sustains them and helps them to thrive. Notably, he does not say that his thoughts should be commandments or even teachings. Instead, he prays that his song be life-giving and thirst-quenching to the listeners.

Immediately thereafter, Moses turns his attention to the only True Sustainer, to God. Here, he engages in the most striking act of humility we see in the portion: "For the name of the Eternal I proclaim; / Give glory to our God!" (Deuteronomy 32:3). Moses could easily have filled this final song with images of what he, Moses, did for the Israelites. Torah readers know that Moses has made immense sacrifices to lead this people from slavery to freedom, and his dying breaths could have been his golden opportunity to glorify all his accomplishments. But Moses, filled with *anavah*, directs his followers to retain perspective and to remember that it is the presence or absence of God that ultimately determines the quality of our lives. By focusing on God's role in their lives at this particular moment in his own life, Moses drives home a point: "Remember that no matter what you accomplish or achieve—even if you achieve as much as I, Moses have, in one lifetime!—God is the true object of praise, not our own egos." In the words of Rabbi Yehuda Leib Chasman, "[A] humble person is one who understands that all his strengths and accomplishments are a gift from heaven. The more a person recognizes this, the more humble he is."[5]

Throughout the song, Moses acknowledges that his God, their God, is genuinely concerned with the Israelites' being humble, even as humility has not always been their strongest attribute. Moses points out that when he is gone, his people will be ruined if they display an excess of their own ego:

> Jeshurun grew fat and kicked—
> You grew fat and gross and coarse—
> They forsook the God who made them
> And spurned the Rock of their support. (Deuteronomy 32:15)

Growing fat surely symbolizes taking up too much space, idolizing the self and the ego. Moses describes a misguided people who misdirect their worship: "They sacrificed to demons, no-gods" (Deuteronomy 32:17). This behavior leads to distance from God and ultimately to "wasting famine, ravaging plague, deadly pestilence, and fanged beasts" (Deuteronomy 32:24), all let loose by God on a people God so treasured throughout its history. Moses, in his own act of *anavah*, uses his final moments to ensure the people know that humility is not a trait to be taken lightly, for the reign of ego leads to the world's most devastating ills.

In our lives, the struggle for humility is as real as it is elusive. As parents, we struggle with how much to steer our children and how much to let them learn from experience. As teachers, we wonder how much we must spoon-feed and how much we can let our students come to understand on their own. As leaders, we are challenged by when to stand out in front and when to shepherd from behind. In friendships or more intimate relationships, how much do we give and how much do we take? How much should we speak out and when must we listen patiently? Moreover, is there one among us who does not wonder about our legacy and how to leave a lasting impact on this world? So many of us concern ourselves with how much space we will take up in the world after we are gone. Who will remember us and how? Can we consistently act in ways that will even be worthy of remembering?

At the end of his song, Moses offers us a clue: "Take to heart all the words with which I have warned you this day. Enjoin them upon your children, that they may observe faithfully all the terms of this Teaching. For this is not a trifling thing for you: it is your very life; through it you shall long endure on the land that you are to possess upon crossing the Jordan" (Deuteronomy 32:46–47). In his last few moments on earth, Moses gives us a powerful tool to preserve our humility. The message is simple: knowing our space is a lifelong pursuit, but the study of Torah is a sure way to begin. The teachings of the Torah have the capacity to bring balance between taking up too much space and not enough.

Questions to Ask

This *parashah* reminds us that humility is not always about pulling ourselves back.

> Where do you shrink from actions that you are well suited to take?
> Are there moments in your life when you take up more than your place?
> In your prayer practice, how has worship of self (ego) and worship of others (envy) been a distraction from worshiping God? How has your worship experience evolved over time?

Practices for the *Middah* of *Anavah*

Consider "humility" on a balance scale as lying between "arrogance" and "self-effacement." To stabilize this delicate balance, follow the instruction of Rabbi Simchah Bunem of Prszysucha, who taught that each of us should carry two slips of paper with us at all times. In one pocket should be a paper that reads: "I am but dust and ashes" (Genesis 18:27); and in the other, a slip that says: "For my sake the world was created" (*Babylonian Talmud, Sanhedrin* 37b). Throughout the day, put your hand in the appropriate pocket when you need a reminder to tip the scale in a given direction.

In addition, consider the wearing of a *kippah* as a practice of humility. Let its presence on your head remind you that you exist as an entity worthy of taking up space in the world—and that the world does not begin and end with you. Put your hand to your head whenever you find yourself needing to embrace either of these realities.

Other *Middot* to Consider

Moses's death is a complicated moment in our people's history; and his song, *Haazinu*, could be read through the lens of any of several other *middot*.

> We might consider *g'vurah* (גְּבוּרָה, "strength") and *tzedek* (צֶדֶק, "justice"): To what degree is Moses setting boundaries for or chastising the Israelites in this song?
>
> The song itself reflects one man's sense of *emunah* (אֱמוּנָה, "faith") and *bitachon* (בִּטָחוֹן, "trust") in both God and humanity.

NOTES

1. Joseph Telushkin, *The Book of Jewish Values: A Day-by-Day Guide to Ethical Living* (New York: Bell Tower, 2000), 39.
2. Alan Morinis, *Everyday Holiness: The Jewish Spiritual Path of Mussar* (Boston: Trumpeter, 2007), 53.
3. Abraham Isaac Kook, *The Moral Principles*, as quoted in Morinis, *Everyday Holiness*.
4. Jonathan Sacks, "The Spirituality of Song (*Ha'azinu* 5777)," *Rabbi Sacks*, September 13, 2018, rabbisacks.org/spirituality-song-haazinu-5776/.
5. Rabbi Yehuda Leib Chasman, *Or Yahel*, quoted in Alan Morinis and Micha Berger, *Every Day, Holy Day: 365 Days of Teachings and Practices from the Jewish Tradition of Mussar* (Boston: Trumpeter, 2010), 245.

V'zot Hab'rachah—Deuteronomy 33:1–34:12
Emunah—Yearning for Faith

Rabbi Judith B. Edelstein, DMin, BCC

"The highest goal of life is a personal, experiential relationship
with God." —*Rabbeinu Avraham ben HaRambam*[1]

IT IS THE THIRD MEETING of Judaism 101 for adults. This session
on theology is when the meeting becomes personal and interesting. I
ask, "What are your feelings/ideas about God?" and receive a myriad
of answers.

After twenty-two years of chaplaincy and teaching, I have observed
that most Jews, young and aged alike, would like to have faith (*emunah*, אֱמוּנָה), but they are also very confused and even fearful of it—
perhaps it's a scam! No one has actually talked to them about God
since Hebrew school, where they were introduced to the Almighty
through a few Torah stories and prayers. Most could not relate to
or were afraid of God in their youth. Once they learned about the
Holocaust and experienced suffering in their lives, God was done
for. Notwithstanding these obstacles, as adults they ask, "How can
I believe in God?"

Rabbi Eliahu Dessler asserts, "The search for truth leads to *emunah*."
Rabbi Yeruham Levovitz of Mir maintained that *emunah* describes a
feeling of absolute certainty, so that there is no room in one's heart
for any doubt whatsoever.[2] Levovitz's notion is precisely what trou-
bles contemporary liberal Jews. We live in a society where absolute
certainty often leads to extremism, and we know how divisive and
destructive this can be. Yet there is a deep human desire to own a
strongly held conviction, with its potential to make life richer.

"Faith is the courage Abraham and Sarah showed when they heard the call of God and left behind all they had known to travel to an unknown destination."³ Yet, the Israelites in Egypt are initially loyal neither to God nor to Moses. We see this lack of faith first as they are escaping Egypt. When they see Pharaoh's army pursuing them, they challenge Moses: "What have you done to us, taking us out of Egypt? Is this not the very thing we told you in Egypt, saying, 'Let us be, and we will serve the Egyptians, for it is better for us to serve the Egyptians than to die in the wilderness'?" (Exodus 14:11–12). The second act of disloyalty occurs once they cross the Reed Sea. After three days of travel, they complain about Moses and evidence a lack of faith in God due to the bitter taste of the water (Exodus 15:22–24). Their most well-known act of disaffection occurs while Moses is on Mount Sinai for forty days and nights. *Emunah* leaves the people entirely. They abandon God and Moses and implore Aaron to make a god for them (Exodus 32:1). We see the people turning away again and again. Nevertheless, their faithlessness does not stop God from demanding constant fidelity from the people.

But Moses is a different story. The complexity of the relationship between God and Moses is firmly planted in the *middah* of *emunah* in the Book of Exodus. They test each other at the Burning Bush: Moses challenges God; God reassures him; Moses runs away; but eventually, God prevails (Exodus 3:1–15), and the seeds of *emunah* are sowed between them. We see God coaching Moses each time God sends him to Pharoah. God and Moses talk to each other frequently and with intensity. Each soon recognizes the other's strengths and weaknesses, and they provide one another with compensatory support, not unlike new lovers. Moses's confidence in himself increases as he realizes that he can rely upon God and visa versa. As their relationship matures, their *emunah* in each other fluctuates, yet it deepens over time, a depth that can only be appreciated fully in this final *parashah* of Deuteronomy.

Our *parashah*, *V'zot Hab'rachah* opens with Moses's poetic blessing of the Israelites. *Emunah* abounds: Moses praises God, the Israelites, and God's commitment to the tribes. Rashi comments on Deuteronomy 33:1–4, "He [Moses] began with the praise of God. . . . He also mentions the merit of the Israelites. . . . He [God] went toward them . . . like a bridegroom going forward to receive his bride."[4]

Emunah is the theme of these verses. It emanates from Moses toward God and from God toward Moses. Moses's devotion is an example of Dessler's theory on *emunah*: "Great men attained their spiritual heights by constantly working on faith. What was 'faith' for them one day became a rational conclusion the next."[5] Moses perceives of God approaching the Israelites as a bridegroom and touchingly articulates God's devotion to the Israelites. The Israelites follow Moses's example vis-à-vis God as they experience God's devotion to them.

In Deuteronomy 33:5, *emunah* among the Israelites, Moses, and God reaches an apex as God's sovereignty becomes indisputable: "Then [God] became King in Jeshurun." The Ramban comments:

> God became King over Israel when our leaders, elders, judges, and all tribes of Israel gathered for all, together accepted God's reign upon ourselves for all generations. . . . They accepted the Torah from the mouth of Moses, for they took upon themselves and upon their seed to believe in him.[6]

What we have just seen here is a lovefest. Drawing upon other texts, the authors of the Torah coronate the "ultimate" God, while the people stand by in awe of Moses and God.

Reveling in his role a leader of the tribes, Moses blesses Jacob's twelve sons in a format similar to Jacob's blessing of his sons in *Parashat Va-y'chi* at the end of Genesis (Genesis 49:2–28). Interestingly enough, Moses is kinder to them than Jacob was, revealing greater *emunah* in Jacob's sons than their own father.[7] Having integrated the trait of *emunah* so firmly within himself as a result of his relationship with God, Moses's capacity for loving-kindness and generosity spills over to his connections to human beings, and he is better able to manifest *emunah* in others.

God points to the land and tells Moses, "This is the land of which I swore to Abraham, Isaac, and Jacob, 'I will assign it to your offspring.'

I have let you see it with your own eyes, but you shall not cross there"
(Deuteronomy 34:4). The Creator's promise reaches the ultimate
fulfillment. *Emunah* based upon their ancestors is transferred to the
Israelites along with the land. Do they deserve it? What about God's
faith in Moses? Why does God bar him from entering the land? Is it a
lack of *emunah* in Moses or recognition that Moses's effectiveness as
a leader had waned and new blood is needed? God, wholly pragmatic
is not blinded by his *emunah* in Moses.

The Book of Deuteronomy comes to an end as "the Israelites
bewailed Moses in the steppes of Moab for thirty days. . . . Joshua
son of Nun was filled with the spirit of wisdom because Moses had
laid his hands upon him; and the Israelites heeded him, doing as
the Eternal had commanded Moses" (Deuteronomy 34:8–9). The
Israelites' faith in Moses is revealed not only in their mourning for
him, but also in their transitioning their *emunah* in toward Joshua,
based on Moses's and God's authority. Are they fickle to transition so
quickly from faith in one leader to faith in another, or is their *emunah*
in God so strong that they are willing to have faith in anyone God
chooses to lead them?

Despite God's apparent rejection of Moses here, we are told,
"Never again did there arise in Israel a prophet like Moses—whom
the Eternal singled out, face to face" (Deuteronomy 34:10). Reading
the *parashah* through a Mussar lens poses another question. Was the
nature of *emunah* between Adonai and Moses so intense that God
was not able to trust another as completely ever again? Rashi tells us,
"Moses had an easy familiarity with God and could speak with him
any time he desired."[8]

In reflecting on Rashi's comment, I wonder if God has not singled
out anyone again because no other person had sufficient *emunah* to
seek God's face with the same intensity as Moses did. Continuing on
the trajectory of our ancestors, we play hide-and-seek with God and
ourselves. Most of us, like my students in Judaism 101, desire, ponder, and then restrain ourselves, just as *emunah* takes a foothold. We
are Moses at the Burning Bush, fascinated, attracted but filled with

fear. While we withdraw, Moses drew closer. As we have seen, there has not been another Moses. Perhaps all we can hope for is "in the end, what is important about faith is that you seek."[9]

Questions to Ask

What obstacle(s) stand in the way of your living a life based on *emunah*?

Can you imagine seeking God with all your heart and soul? What would it take for you to do put this into action?

Practice for the *Middah* of *Emunah*

Begin and punctuate your day with the first few phrases from *Elohai N'shamah*: "My God, the soul You have given me is pure. You created it, You shaped it. . . . As long as the soul is within me, I offer thanks to You, Adonai, my God."[10]

Feel God's hand in yours at moments of stress and/or sadness.

Another *Middah* to Consider

When Moses died at 120 years of age, "his eyes were undimmed and his vigor unabated" (Deuteronomy 34:7). He retained a core of strength until the last moment of his life. This can be attributed to *emunah* but also to "trust" (*bitachon*, בִּטָּחוֹן). Consider the role that each of these *middot* plays in the *parashah*. See where they overlap and how they differ.

NOTES

1. Avraham ben HaRambam, *The Guide to Serving God* [*Sefer HaMaspik*] (Jerusalem: Feldheim, 2008), xxiii–xxiv.
2. Eliyahu E. Dessler, *Strive for Truth!*, pt. 2, *Lectures on Jewish Thought* (Jerusalem and New York: Feldheim, 1988), 224.
3. Rabbi Lord Jonathan Sacks, *The Way of Faith: Love as Loyalty*: Unit 7, rabbisacks.org/tenpaths/students/faith/.
4. Rashi on Deuteronomy 33:1–4.

5. Dessler, *Strive for Truth!*, 223.
6. Ramban on Deuteronomy 33:5.
7. Rabbi Lord Jonathan Sacks, *The Way of Faith: Love as Loyalty*: Unit 7.
8. Rashi on Deuteronomy 34:20.
9. Alan Morinis, *Everyday Holiness: The Jewish Spiritual Path of Mussar* (Boston: Trumpeter, 2007), 231.
10. *Mishkan T'filah: A Reform Siddur*, ed. Elyse D. Frishman (New York: CCAR Press, 2007), 3.

Glossary

acharayut. "Responsibility."

Akeidah. "Binding"; refers to Genesis 22, the story of the Binding of Isaac.

anavah. "Humility."

Aseret HaDibrot. "The Ten Commandments."

atzlanut. "Laziness."

Ayekah. "Where are you?"

Baruch Dayan ha-emet –"Blessed is the Judge of truth"; a phrase commonly repeated after putting on a mourner's ribbon.

beit midrash. "House of study."

binah. "Understanding"; the third of the ten *s'firot.*

bitachon. "Trust."

boshet panim. "Stubbornness."

B'reishit Rabbah. Midrash on the Book of Genesis.

b'tzelem Elohim. "In God's image."

bushah. "Sense of embarrassment or shame."

chesed. "Love, benevolence, kindness, grace"; the fourth of the ten *s'firot.*

cheshbon hanefesh. "Self-assessment."

chevruta. Study system with pairings of study partners.

chochmah. "Wisdom"; the second of the ten *s'firot.*

chutzpah. "Audacity."

daat. "Knowledge."

din. "Judgment."

emet. "Truth."

emunah. "Faith, trust."

gilui arayot. "Sexual transgressions."

g'nut. "Degradation."

g'vurah. "Strength"; "restraint, patience, judgment"; the fifth of the ten *s'firot.*

hakarat hatov. "Recognizing the good"; "Gratitude."

histapkut. "Simplicity."

kaas. "Anger."

kavod. "Honor."

kinah. "Jealousy."

korban. "Sacrifice."

lev patuach. "Open-heartedness."

mancheh (pl. *manchim*). "Discussion leader, moderator, advisor."

m'chilah. "Forgiveness."

m'hirut. "Haste."

middah (pl. *middot*). "Virtue, value, characteristic, attribute."

midrash (pl. midrashim). Rabbinic exegesis on Torah.

Mishkan. The Tabernacle that the Israelites built in order to worship God in the wilderness.

Mishnah. Early Rabbinic compilation of legal material.

m'nuchat hanefesh. "Calmness of the soul"; "equanimity."

Modeh/Modah Ani. Prayer of gratitude.

Mount Moriah. The site of the Binding of Isaac (Genesis 22:2) and the Temple Mount (2 Chronicles 3:1).

Nazir. "Ascetic; Nazirite."

n'divut. "Generosity."

n'divut lev. "Giving from the heart."

netzach. "Eternity"; "action, alacrity"; the seventh of the ten *s'firot.*

nishmat chayim. "Breath of life."

n'shamah. "Spirit, soul."

ometz lev. "Courage."

pachad. "Fear."

parashah (pl. *parashiyot*). Torah portion.

parashat hashavua. Weekly Torah portion.

parshanut haTorah. Torah commentary.

Pirkei Avot. Lit. "chapters of the ancestors"; an early Rabbinic compilation of ethical teachings, part of the Mishnah.

rachamim. "Mercy, compassion."

ratzon. "Desire, favor, will."

savlanut. "Patience."

seder (pl. *s'darim*). "Order."

s'firah (pl. *s'firot*). In Lurianic Kabbalah theology: a divine emanation.

Shabbaton. Immersive learning experience throughout Shabbat.

shalvah. "Serenity."

Shechinah. "Dwelling"; the lowest of the ten *s'firot*, also called *malchut*; the form of God that resides among the people of Israel; the feminine aspect of God.

shevach. "Praise."

sh'filah. "Self-abasement."

sh'tikah. "Silence."

sh'vil hazahav. "The golden path"; "moderation."

sh'virat hakeilim. "Shattering of the vessels"; a kabbalistic Creation myth.

sidra. (Aram.) Torah portion.

Sifra. Midrash on the Book of Leviticus.

Tanach. The Hebrew Bible.

teraphim. Statues of foreign gods.

tiferet. "Beauty, glory"; the sixth of the ten *s'firot.*

tikkun. "Repair, correction."

tikkun middot. "Correction"; "improvement of character."

t'shuvah. "Repentance."

tzadik (fem. *tzadeket*). "Righteous."

tzaraat. "Leprosy."

tzedakah. "Righteous acts of providing for those in need."

tzedek. "Justice."

tziduk hadin. "God's strict justice."

tzimtzum. In Kabbalah, God's "contraction."

yetzer hara. "The evil inclination."

yetzer tov. "The good inclination."

yirah. "Awe, fear."

yishuv hadaat. "Settled mind"; "equanimity."

y'sod. "Foundation, connection"; the ninth of the ten *s'firot.*

yoshrah. "Integrity."

z'rizut. "Alacrity."

Contributors

Rabbi David Adelson, DMin, is dean of the New York campus of Hebrew Union College–Jewish Institute of Religion (HUC-JIR). He served as rabbi of East End Temple in Manhattan and as a hospital chaplain, and he has been a leader in the Reform Movement and IAF community organizing. He serves as a spiritual director and is on the faculty of Bekhol Levavkha, a spiritual direction training program at HUC-JIR. He was ordained in 1999 and earned a doctor of ministry in 2016.

Rabbi Daniel S. Alexander, DMin, DD, ordained by Hebrew Union College–Jewish Institute of Religion in 1979, directed the Hillel Foundation at the University of Virginia for nine years and served Congregation Beth Israel in Charlottesville, Virginia, for twenty-eight years, becoming rabbi emeritus in 2017. An occasional lecturer at the University of Virginia and a spiritual director, he is a husband, father, and grandfather. He currently volunteers as a court-appointed special advocate for foster children in central Virginia.

Rabbi Nicole Auerbach is the director of congregational engagement at Central Synagogue in New York City. She is the author, with Dr. Ron Wolfson and Rabbi Lydia Medwin, of *The Relational Judaism Handbook: How to Create a Relational Engagement Campaign to Build and Deepen Relationships in Your Community* (2018). She was ordained by Hebrew Union College–Jewish Institute of Religion in 2016.

Rabbi Elizabeth Bahar, ordained in 2009, joined Congregation Ahavath Chesed–The Temple in 2018 after serving Temple B'nai Sholom in Huntsville, Alabama. While there, she promoted inclusivity and innovation, earning recognition by the *Forward* as one of "America's 33 Most Inspirational Rabbis" (2015) as well as leadership awards in the interfaith community.

Cantor Chanin Becker graduated from Princeton University with a degree in English literature and drama and was ordained as a cantor by the Hebrew Union College–Jewish Institute of Religion. She has served as the cantor at Temple Isaiah in Lafayette, California, and at Scarsdale Synagogue–Temples Tremont and Emanu-El in Scarsdale, New York. Since completing the Manchim Training Program of the Mussar Institute, she has had a particular passion around facilitating Mussar practice groups and seeing the world through a Mussar lens.

Rabbi Barry H. Block serves Congregation B'nai Israel in Little Rock, Arkansas. A Houston native and graduate of Amherst College, Rabbi Block was ordained by Hebrew Union College–Jewish Institute of Religion in 1991 after studying at its Jerusalem, Los Angeles, and New York campuses, and he received his DD, honoris causa, in 2016. A member of the CCAR Board of Trustees, Block has contributed to several previous CCAR Press publications, including "Unplanned Fatherhood" in *The Sacred Encounter*; "Marriage, Money, and Musar" in *The Sacred Exchange*; and "Welcoming Converts" in *Navigating the Journey*. With Dr. Alan Morinis, he co-authored "Mussar and the Development of Spiritual Practices" in *A Life of Meaning: Embracing Reform Judaism's Sacred Path*, and he is a regular contributor to the *CCAR Journal*. Block currently serves as faculty dean at URJ Henry S. Jacobs Camp, a role he held for twenty-one years at URJ Greene Family Camp. He is a past board chair of Planned Parenthood of South Texas. He is the proud father of Robert and Daniel.

Rabbi Mari Chernow is senior rabbi at Temple Chai in Phoenix, Arizona. She was drawn to Mussar study because of the opportunities it affords for reflection, personal growth, and the pursuit of depth. It is, she believes, an example of the exciting Jewish future that is being built on fresh approaches to classical texts and traditions. She loves hiking, skiing, and above all, spending time with her ridiculous and perfect children.

Rabbi Jen Clayman is an independent rabbi in the San Francisco Bay Area. She was ordained from Hebrew Union College-Jewish Institute of Religion in Los Angeles, in 2003, and has served Jewish organizations in California, Washington, New Jersey and Maryland. She has also trained as a Jewish chant leader with Rabbi Shefa Gold. She specializes in adult Jewish learning and teaches for the Bay Area's HAMAQOM: The Place, as well as the URJ's Introduction to Judaism program.

Rabbi Paul F. Cohen, DMin, DD, is the senior rabbi at Temple Jeremiah in suburban Chicago, where he strives to help his congregants feel deeply connected and inspired to do *tikkun olam*. He has strengthened this philosophy by taking on social, economic, and political causes, offering testimony to state legislative committees, and serving on numerous boards of directors. He received his master of arts and rabbinic ordination from Hebrew Union College–Jewish Institute of Religion and a doctor of ministry from the Bangor Theological Seminary. He is a Senior Rabbinic Fellow of the Shalom Hartman Institute in Jerusalem.

Rabbi Judith Edelstein, DMin, BCC, was ordained by the Academy for Jewish Religion in 1997. She has worked as the spiritual leader at various synagogues, as a chaplain, and as a teacher. Her Mussar studies began in earnest through the Mussar Institute under the direction of Alan Morinis. She has been involved with the institute in many capacities for the past ten years. Mussar has transformed her life.

Rabbi Amy Eilberg was the first woman ordained as a Conservative rabbi by the Jewish Theological Seminary of America. She serves as the coordinator of Jewish engagement for Faith in Action Bay Area, a multi-faith, multiracial social justice organization in the San Francisco Bay Area. She previously served as the director of the Pardes Rodef Shalom (Pursuer of Peace) Communities Program, teaching Jewish civil discourse to rabbis, synagogues, and Jewish organizations. Rabbi Eilberg also serves as a spiritual director and interfaith activist and as senior faculty for the Mussar Institute. She is the author of *From Enemy to Friend: Jewish Wisdom and the Pursuit of Peace* (2014).

Rabbi Avi Fertig is the director of Mussar for the Mussar Institute, where he has been guiding courses and programs since 2010. He is the author of *Bridging the Gap* (2007), a comprehensive guide to important Mussar concepts and lessons from the Talmud and the classical works of the modern Mussar movement, as well as numerous other publications on topics of Mussar. Rabbi Fertig studied at the Ner Israel Yeshiva in Baltimore and has also learned and taught at Yeshivat Neve Zion, Yeshivat Reishit Yerushalayim, and the Mir Yeshiva of Jerusalem. Born in the United States, for the past twenty-two years he has resided in Israel and currently lives in Beit Shemesh with his wife and six children.

Rabbi Carol Glass, BCC, SD, has served in Hillel, congregations, hospitals, hospice and a rabbinical school. A spiritual director and a Mussar student of Rabbi David Jaffe, she has been facilitating Mussar groups since 2012. She has published chapters in two books on addiction and spirituality. She gardens avidly and misses the days when she had more time for biking and bird-watching. Rabbi Glass lives in Newton, Massachusetts, with her husband, Rabbi Michael Swartz. They have two grown sons and one daughter-in-law.

Rabbi Lisa L. Goldstein is the executive director of the Institute for Jewish Spirituality. Educated at Brown University and Hebrew Union College–Jewish Institute of Religion, she previously served as the executive director of Hillel of San Diego, where she was honored for her devotion to the students. She has taught meditation, prayer, and Chasidic texts in a wide variety of contexts and is particularly interested in the intersection between spiritual practice and social justice.

Rabbi Lisa D. Grant, PhD, is the Rabbinical School Program director and professor of Jewish education at Hebrew Union College–Jewish Institute of Religion in New York. Her research, writing, and teaching interests focus on adult Jewish learning, spiritual life and practice, and the place of Israel in American Jewish life. She is happily married to Billy Weitzer and the proud mother of two adult children.

Rabbi Lisa J. Grushcow, DPhil, is the senior rabbi of Temple Emanu-El-Beth Sholom, the Reform synagogue of Montreal. She also served as associate rabbi of Rodeph Sholom in New York City, after being ordained by Hebrew Union College–Jewish Institute of Religion in 2003. She holds degrees from McGill and the University of Oxford, in addition to being a Rhodes Scholar, a Wexner Graduate Fellow, and part of the Hartman Rabbinic Leadership Initiative.

Rabbi Jennifer A. Gubitz serves Temple Israel of Boston as the director of the Riverway Project, whose mission is to connect twenties and thirties to Judaism and each other through Temple Israel. Ordained by Hebrew Union College–Jewish Institute of Religion in New York in 2012, she was an HUC-JIR Tisch Rabbinical Fellow and is a graduate of Indiana University's Borns Jewish Studies Program. Rabbi Gubitz grew up as a songleader and educator at URJ Goldman Union Camp Institute in Zionsville, Indiana. Trained as a Mussar facilitator by the Mussar Institute, she has been facilitating congregational Mussar study groups for many years.

Rabbi Rachel Gurevitz, PhD, serves as rabbi of Congregation B'nai Shalom, Westborough, Massachusetts. Her introduction to Jewish spiritual practice came through Jewish Renewal. She spent a year and several summers on staff at the Jewish retreat center Elat Chayyim.

She integrates chant, meditation, and Mussar into the worship and teaching she offers her community.

Rabbi Eric S. Gurvis was ordained at Hebrew Union College–Jewish Institute of Religion in New York. He has served congregations in New York City; Jackson, Mississippi; Teaneck, New Jersey; and Newton, Massachusetts; and is currently rabbi of Sha'arei Shalom in Ashland, Massachusetts. Rabbi Gurvis works with the Mussar Institute coordinating their new CHAVERIM Initiative. He facilitates Mussar groups throughout the Greater Boston Area and in Western Massachusetts. He is a member of the faculty for the Mussar Institute and the Hebrew College Open Circles Learning program. He is a Senior Rabbinic Fellow of the Hartman Institute. He lives in the Greater Boston Area with his wife, Laura. They have four children and a 2½-year-old grandson, in whom they take great delight.

Rabbi Brett R. Isserow was born and raised in Johannesburg, South Africa. Ordained in 1991 by Hebrew Union College–Jewish Institute of Religion in Cincinnati, he served at The Temple in Atlanta, Georgia, and for the last sixteen years at Beth El Hebrew Congregation in Alexandria, Virginia. He has been a Mussar student and facilitator since 2009. In retirement he continues to teach at Beth El and facilitate Mussar *vaadim*. He is married to Rabbi Jinny Isserow, an artist, and they have two adult children, Anna and Jesse.

Rabbi David Jaffe is the founder and dean of the Kirva Institute and leader of the Inside Out Wisdom and Action Project. His teaching, writing, and consulting integrate Jewish spiritual technologies with leadership and social change. He teaches Mussar and other forms of Jewish spiritual wisdom around the country with the Mussar Institute, the Institute for Jewish Spirituality, the Legacy Heritage Foundation, and others. Rabbi Jaffe is the author of *Changing the World from the Inside Out: A Jewish Approach to Personal and Social Change*, which won a 2016 National Jewish Book Award.

Rabbi Andy Kahn grew up in Tacoma, Washington, received his BA in religion from Kenyon College in Ohio, MAs from Queen's University in religion in modernity and Jewish Theological Seminary in Hebrew Bible, and was ordained by Hebrew Union College–Jewish Institute of Religion in 2018. He is currently the assistant rabbi of Temple Emanu-El of New York.

Rabbi Debra Kassoff first served Hebrew Union Congregation in Greenville, Mississippi, in 2000 and has led the congregation continually since 2010. Upon ordination in 2003, she established the rabbinic department at the Goldring/Woldenberg Institute for Southern Jewish Life, an organization committed to supporting, connecting, and celebrating Jewish life in the South. Rabbi Kassoff lives with her family in Jackson, Mississippi, where she strives to create compassionate communities that bridge racial, religious, and cultural divides.

Rabbi Marc Katz is the rabbi at Temple Ner Tamid in Bloomfield, New Jersey. He is the author of the book *The Heart of Loneliness: How Jewish Wisdom Can Help You Cope and Find Comfort* as well as numerous articles.

Rabbi Jan Katzew, PhD, serves as the Rabbinical Program director at Hebrew Union College–Jewish Institute of Religion in Cincinnati, where he also teaches courses in education and Jewish thought, including Mussar. Jan has been a student, practitioner, and teacher of Mussar for more than twenty years, trying to repair the world from the inside out.

Rabbi Richard M.C. Kellner is proud to serve as the senior rabbi of Congregation Beth Tikvah, in Worthington, Ohio. He has dedicated his rabbinate to building relationships, drawing meaning and purpose from our tradition, and engaging in *tikkun olam*. He serves on the leadership team of the Ohio Religious Action Center of Reform Judaism, working to create a coalition across faith lines to build a better Ohio. He also serves the chair of Continuing Rabbinic Education for the CCAR. Rabbi Kellner lives in Columbus along with his wife, Debra, and daughters, Zoe and Shira.

Rabbi Bonnie Koppell is a native of Brooklyn, New York. A 1981 graduate of the Reconstructionist Rabbinical College (RRC), she was the first female rabbi to serve in the U.S. Army. Chaplain (Colonel) Koppell was deployed numerous times to Iraq, Afghanistan, and Kuwait during her thirty-eight-year career. She received two Legion of Merit medals, in addition to numerous other awards. She holds an MA in religion from Temple University, a master of strategic studies from the U.S. Army War College, and a doctor of divinity from RRC. In 1994 she was named "Outstanding Young Leader" for the City of Mesa, and in 2004 she was the "Woman of the Year." The *Forward* honored her in 2010 as one of the "The Sisterhood 50: America's Influential Women Rabbis." Rabbi Koppell currently serves as the associate rabbi of Temple Chai in Phoenix, Arizona, where she directs the Deutsch Family Shalom Center. She is a frequently requested speaker on military and spiritual themes. Married to Ron Kushner, she is the mother of Jessie Rubenstein and Dr. Sarah Wypiszynski. She adores being a *bubbe* to her growing family, including Helena, Michael, and Leon.

Rabbi Jonathan Kraus has served as the spiritual leader of Beth El Temple Center in Belmont, Massachusetts, since 1994.

Rabbi Leah Lewis, MAJS, is the rabbi at Temple Menorah in Redondo Beach, California. Prior to her arrival there in 2017, she served as rabbi and director of lifelong learning at Congregation Shir HaMa'alot in Irvine, California, and as associate rabbi at Leo Baeck Temple in Los Angeles. She was ordained by the Hebrew Union College–Jewish Institute of Religion in 2002. She is married to David Lewis, and together they have three children: Gabriel, Jonah, and Nomi.

Rabbi Andrea C. London is the senior rabbi at Beth Emet: The Free Synagogue in Evanston, Illinois. She has studied Mussar with Alan Morinis and through the Institute of Jewish Spirituality (IJS). She is also a graduate of IJS's Jewish Mindfulness Meditation Teacher Training program.

Rabbi Marc Margolius is a senior programs director at the Institute for Jewish Spirituality, where he directs the Tikkun Middot Project, an initiative integrating Jewish mindfulness and *middot* practice. He also directs the institute's programs for lay leaders and alumni of its clergy leadership program and teaches weekly on the Torah portion through a mindfulness and *middot* lens. He has served as rabbi at Congregation Beth Am Israel, Penn Valley, Pennsylvania, and West End Synagogue in New York City.

Rabbi Sharon Mars is the senior rabbi at Temple Israel, a Reform synagogue in Columbus, Ohio. She received her rabbinic ordination from Hebrew Union College-Jewish Institute of Religion in New York in 1998 and her master of Hebrew letters in her hometown of Los Angeles in 1994. She has served professionally as a rabbi for over twenty years in various settings, from Hillel and summer camp to hospice and prisons. Her social justice work focuses particularly on the areas of substance use disorder, trauma, and mass incarceration. She is a student of Mussar and seeks spiritual grounding through Torah, community choir, classic rock, college basketball, coffee, and people.

Rabbi Joseph B. Meszler is the spiritual leader of Temple Sinai in Sharon, Massachusetts, an educator, and an activist. Rabbi Meszler has been a Brickner Fellow through the Religious Action Center of Reform Judaism, is a member of the Hevraya of the Institute for Jewish Spirituality, and served as a Global Justice Fellow with American Jewish World Service in 2017–18. His books include *Being Human (and Made in God's Image): Sermons on the Weekly Torah Portion, Jewish Holidays, & Topics of Today* (2018).

Rabbi Joshua Mikutis is the Jewish learning designer at JDC Entwine. He was ordained by the Hebrew Union College–Jewish Institute of Religion; he also graduated with a masters degree in Jewish nonprofit management from the Zelikow School of Jewish Nonprofit Management. Originally from Dayton, Ohio, he graduated from Haverford College with honors in religion and history and with a minor in Russian from Bryn Mawr College. Rabbi Mikutis lives in Brooklyn with his wife Anna.

Rabbi Michelle Pearlman places relationships at the center, helping people connect with Judaism, God, and one another. Currently rabbi of Beth Chaim Reform Congregation in Malvern, Pennsylvania, she has served Monmouth Reform Temple, Temple Shalom of Newton, Massachusetts, the Jewish Federation, and the Union for Reform Judaism. She delights in the power of interfaith connections, having worked with the St. Bernard Project, community partners, teens, and adults to help rebuild one hundred homes after Hurricane Sandy.

Rabbi Sonja K. Pilz, PhD, earned her doctorate from the Department of Rabbinic Literature at Potsdam University, Germany; she holds rabbinic ordination from Abraham Geiger College, Germany. Prior to joining the Central Conference of American Rabbis as the editor of the CCAR Press, she taught worship, liturgy, and ritual at Hebrew Union College–Jewish Institute of Religion in New York, at the School of Jewish Theology at Potsdam University, and in many congregational settings. She has served as a rabbinic intern, adjunct rabbi, and cantorial soloist in congregations in Germany, Switzerland, Israel, and the United States.

Rabbi Marcia R. Plumb has studied and taught Mussar for over twenty-five years, in the United States and the United Kingdom. She teaches several Mussar *vaadim* (groups), founded an annual Mussar conference in Boston, and trained with and worked for the Mussar Institute. She teaches an international online Mussar group and an online group for Jewish clergy. She is embedding Mussar into the life of her synagogue, Congregation Mishkan Tefila, in Brookline, Massachusetts, as a path for cultural transformation.

Rabbi Ted Riter began formally weaving Mussar teachings into the fabric of his synagogue community in 1997. He is proud that since that time, many of his students have become Mussar facilitators and teachers in their own right. Ted continues to draw upon Mussar teachings as he brings "ancient wisdom and modern design" to individuals and organizations facing crises and going through transitions.

Rabbi Yair Robinson is the rabbi of Congregation Beth Emeth in Wilmington, Delaware. He lives in Wilmington with his wife, Marisa, and his son, Elishai.

Rabbi Samuel J. Rose is a native of Norfolk, Virginia. He is the rabbi at Temple of Israel in Greenville, South Carolina. Before moving to South Carolina, Rabbi Rose served as the associate rabbi at Congregation Beth Israel in Austin, Texas for six years. He is a graduate of HUC-JIR (Cincinnati) and Temple University. When Rabbi Rose is not diving down a rabbinic rabbit hole of research, he loves playing with his daughter and watching the Philadelphia Eagles play.

Cheryl Rosenstein, DD, is rabbi emerita and former Mussar guide of Temple Beth El in Bakersfield. California. She now practices her Mussar and yoga in her "happy place," Santa Rosa, California. "Mussar," she writes, "has helped me develop the *g'vurah* ("courage"), the *koach* ("strength"), the *emunah* ("faith") and *bitachon* ("trust") to open myself to change. I am grateful and honored to be included in this anthology. I hope to continue to share the power of Mussar practice with others."

Rabbi Peter B. Schaktman is the rabbi of Temple Emanu-El in Utica, New York, where he has led workshops on Mussar. Ordained by the Hebrew Union College–Jewish Institute of Religion in 1989, Rabbi Schaktman has served congregations in Texas, New York, Louisiana, and Hawai'i. He also worked on the staff of the Union for Reform Judaism as a regional and national consultant in program development, synagogue management, and the special needs of small congregations.

Rabbi Judy Shanks is a native of Phoenix, Arizona, and received her BA in religion from Pomona College. She was ordained from the New York campus of Hebrew Union College–Jewish Institute of Religion in 1984 and served two congregations in the San Francisco Bay Area: Temple Beth Hillel in Richmond, California, and Temple Isaiah in Lafayette, California, retiring from congregational leadership in 2018. Rabbi Shanks is married to James Gracer and has two daughters and three grandchildren—so far.

Rabbi Michal Shekel is the executive director of the Toronto Board of Rabbis and spiritual leader of Congregation Har Tikvah of Brampton, Ontario, Canada. She is the rabbinic director of the Greater Toronto Reform *Beit Din* (Jewish court), oversees the Introduction to Jewish Life program, and is the *m'saderet gittin* (divorce officiant) for the Reform Rabbis of Greater Toronto.

Rabbi Alexandria R. Shuval-Weiner, MEd, RJE, MAJS, was ordained by Hebrew Union College–Jewish Institute of Religion in Los Angeles in 2008. She leads Temple Beth Tikvah, in Roswell, Georgia, as its senior rabbi. An ongoing seeker of spiritual nourishment, Rabbi Shuval-Weiner has received training through Ayeka, the Mussar Institute, the Institute for Jewish Spirituality & Wise Aging.

Rabbi Judith Lazarus Siegal was ordained by Hebrew Union College–Jewish Institute of Religion in New York in 2006. She has served as a rabbi at Temple Judea in Coral Gables, Florida, since her ordination, becoming the senior rabbi in 2015. She has a master's degree in social work from the University of Texas, Austin. She enjoys teaching students of all ages, and Holocaust and Israel are two of her areas of expertise. Rabbi Siegal is married to Brian Siegal, who is the director of the American Jewish Committee of Miami and Broward, and they have three children.

Rabbi Marla Joy Subeck Spanjer, DD, is a native of Chicago. Ordained by Hebrew Union College–Jewish Institute of Religion, she has led congregations in Chicago and its suburbs, in Winston-Salem, North Carolina, and in Fort Wayne, Indiana. She was vice president of the Greater Carolina Association of Rabbis. She is married to Marc Spanjer and has a daughter, Michal Shoshana Spanjer.

Rabbi Samuel L. Spector is the rabbi of Congregation Kol Ami in Salt Lake City, Utah. Previously, he was the associate rabbi of Temple Judea in Tarzana, California. Rabbi Spector attended the University of California, San Diego, where he graduated Phi Beta Kappa and cum laude with a BA in Judaic studies. He received his MA in Hebrew letters and rabbinic ordination from the Hebrew Union College–Jewish Institute of Religion in Los Angeles.

Justice Annabelle Imber Tuck is a retired Arkansas Supreme Court justice. She currently serves as a public service fellow/jurist-in-residence at the UALR William H. Bowen School of Law. In that role, she is an active community advocate for equal access to justice, education, and health care. She is a member of Congregation B'nai Israel in Little Rock, Arkansas, and has been learning the Jewish spiritual path of Mussar since 2015.

Rabbi Pamela Wax is the spiritual care coordinator at Westchester Jewish Community Services in White Plains, New York, where she runs the WJCS Jewish Spiritual Healing Center, offering spiritual journeying opportunities for writers, meditators, and seekers, several Mussar groups, spiritual direction, and pastoral counseling (through a Mussar lens). She was the co-author, with Rabbi Marc Margolius, of *Pitchei haLevavot*, a weekly online Mussar Torah commentary offered by the Institute for Jewish Spirituality in 2015–2016, and is the author of a teen Mussar curriculum through Chai Mitzvah.

Rabbi Nancy Wechsler was ordained by Hebrew Union College-Jewish Institute of Religion, New York campus, in 1990. She has served Congregation Beth Shalom in Carmichael, California, since 2003. "Mussar has been perhaps my most powerful lens into Judaism. Not only has it paved a defined path for my Jewish spirituality, but it has become foundational to my rabbinate. Earliest teachers of *middot* were trailblazers, whose efforts I have been honored to join."

Rabbi Max Weiss serves as the rabbi of Oak Park Temple B'nai Abraham Zion in Oak Park, Illinois, where he has served for the last ten years. Prior to that he served congregations in Hoffman Estates, Illinois, and Wynnewood, Pennsylvania. He currently volunteers on the Rabbinic, Educator, and Cantorial Advisory Committee of Olin Sang Ruby Union Institute (OSRUI), where he has volunteered for the last eighteen years. He serves on the board of the Community of Congregations and of the Leaders Network. He is also on the core team for the Illinois Religious Action Center of Reform Judaism. In the past Rabbi Weiss has served on the board of OSRUI, on various committees for the Central Conference of American Rabbis, and on the Institutional Review Board for a local hospital. His interests include community building, working for justice, and American Jewish history. Rabbi Weiss and his wife, Leslie, have three children and live in Oak Park, Illinois.

Rabbi Harvey J. Winokur received his ordination from the Hebrew Union College–Jewish Institute of Religion. He founded Temple Kehillat Chaim in Roswell, Georgia (a suburb of Atlanta). After thirty-six years on that pulpit, he became rabbi emeritus. Rabbi Winokur is a trainer/facilitator for the Mussar Institute and Prepare/Enrich. He is also a certified Jewish spiritual director.

Rabbi Cantor Alison Wissot's deepest mission as a teacher is to make the beauty and joy of Jewish texts and liturgy accessible to all. One of the first to be doubly ordained as both rabbi and cantor by Hebrew Union College–Jewish Institute of Religion, Rabbi Cantor Wissot has served Temple Judea in Tarzana for the past sixteen years. Prior to her cantorial career, Alison worked as an actress in New York and London, and continues to teach Jewish theater at events worldwide.

Rabbi Dr. Shmuly Yanklowitz is the president and dean of the Valley Beit Midrash (Jewish pluralistic adult learning and leadership), the founder and president of Uri L'Tzedek (Jewish social justice), the founder and CEO of SHAMAYIM (Jewish animal advocacy), the founder and president of YATOM (Jewish foster and adoption network), and the author of sixteen books on Jewish ethics. *Newsweek* named Rabbi Shmuly one of the top fifty rabbis in America and the *Forward* named him one of the fifty most influential Jews. Rabbi Shmuly, his wife, four children, and foster children live in Scottsdale, Arizona.